T0233956

Lecture Notes in Computer Science   11370

Commenced Publication in 1973
Founding and Former Series Editors:
Gerhard Goos, Juris Hartmanis, and Jan van Leeuwen

More information about this series at http://www.springer.com/series/8851

Ngoc Thanh Nguyen · Ryszard Kowalczyk
Marcin Hernes (Eds.)

Transactions on Computational Collective Intelligence XXXII

Springer

Editors-in-Chief
Ngoc Thanh Nguyen
Institute of Informatics
Wrocław University of Technology
Wrocław, Poland

Ryszard Kowalczyk
Swinburne University of Technology
Hawthorn, VIC, Australia

Guest Editor
Marcin Hernes
Wrocław University of Economics
Wrocław, Poland

ISSN 0302-9743   ISSN 1611-3349 (electronic)
Lecture Notes in Computer Science
ISSN 2190-9288   ISSN 2511-6053 (electronic)
Transactions on Computational Collective Intelligence
ISBN 978-3-662-58610-5   ISBN 978-3-662-58611-2 (eBook)
https://doi.org/10.1007/978-3-662-58611-2

Library of Congress Control Number: 2018964613

This Springer imprint is published by the registered company Springer-Verlag GmbH, DE
part of Springer Nature
The registered company address is: Heidelberger Platz 3, 14197 Berlin, Germany

Transactions on Computational Collective Intelligence Vol. XXXII

Preface

It is our pleasure to present Volume 32 of LNCS *Transactions on Computational Collective Intelligence*. This volume includes five interesting and original papers which have been selected by the peer review process.

The first paper "Consensus Theory for Cognitive Agents' Unstructured Knowledge Conflicts Resolving in Management Information Systems" by Marcin Hernes consists of 125 pages and is in monograph style. It is devoted to the problem of developing a formal method to resolve conflicts in unstructured knowledge of cognitive agents in management information systems employing consensus theory. The author analyzes the problems related to management information systems and unstructured knowledge processing in these systems. Cognitive agents are characterized with particular emphasis on unstructured knowledge processing, and the use of consensus theory in unstructured knowledge conflicts resolving is also presented. The main part describes the method developed for cognitive agents' knowledge conflict resolving. The correctness of the method was verified using the prototypes of the agents helping to invest in the Forex market and processing user opinions about products and services. Based on the experimental results, it was concluded that the use of the developed method increases the usability of the management information systems assessed and consequently enables the determination of satisfactory solutions for a given management problem. It allows for, among others, reducing the level of risk, costs, and decisions-making time. This work has an interdisciplinary character related to the field of management, economics, and computer science.

The second paper entitled "The Ins and Outs of Network-Oriented Modeling: From Biological Networks and Mental Networks to Social Networks and Beyond" by Jan Treur describes how the interpretation of a network as a causal network and taking into account dynamics add more depth to the network-oriented modeling perspective, leading to the notion of a temporal–causal network. The results allow us to draw conclusions that the proven wide scope of applicability of the network-oriented modeling approach shows that causality and temporality are very general concepts and the specific added structures such as connection weights, combination functions, and speed factors facilitate a sensitive and unifying way of modeling realistic processes. They also offer more theoretical depth, which was illustrated by presenting some mathematical results on how emerging network behavior relates to specific properties of the network structure.

In the third paper, "Local Termination Criteria for Swarm Intelligence: A Comparison Between Local Stochastic Diffusion Search and Ant Nest-Site Selection," Andrew Martin, John Mark Bishop, Elva J. H. Robinson, and Darren R. Myatt discuss two experiments investigating the robustness and efficiency of the new local termination criteria. Their results demonstrate these to be effectively as robust as the classic SDS termination criteria and almost three times faster. The experiments' results are very interesting.

The fourth paper, "Towards Large-Scale Optimization of Iterated Prisoner Dilemma Strategies," by Grazyna Starzec, Mateusz Starzec, Aleksander Byrski, Marek Kisiel-Dorohinicki, Juan Carlos Burguillo, and Tom Lenaerts, analyzes the results of the optimization of the iterated prisoner's dilemma strategies obtained in highly scalable frameworks. The basics of iterated prisoner's dilemma simulations are recalled, then an asynchronous actor model is presented. The authors also recall selected scalability-related results and present those related to optimization. A discussion on several features observed regarding the scale of the simulation as well as on several obtained strategies in a form of finite state machines is also presented. The results shows that it is hard to develop a unique strategy effective against the rest of the opponents' strategies, and that the easiest way to cumulate high payoffs is by defecting a few cooperating neighbors. On vertices with high degree, however, cooperation becomes more efficient.

The last paper entitled "GuruWS: A Hybrid Platform for Detecting Malicious Web Shells and Web Application Vulnerabilities," by Giap Van LE, Tung Huu Nguyen, Phuc Duy Pham, On Van Phung, and Hoa Ngoc Nguyen, presents an approach to a protective, extensible, and hybrid platform, named GuruWS, for automatically detecting both Web application vulnerabilities and malicious Web shells. The experiments conducted prove the outstanding performance of the platform proposed by the authors in comparison with several existing solutions in detecting either Web application vulnerabilities or malicious Web shells.

November 2018   Marcin Hernes
                                                                Ngoc Thanh Nguyen

Transactions on Computational Collective Intelligence

This Springer journal focuses on research in applications of the computer-based methods of computational collective intelligence (CCI) and their applications in a wide range of fields such as the Semantic Web, social networks, and multi-agent systems. It aims to provide a forum for the presentation of scientific research and technological achievements accomplished by the international community.

The topics addressed by this journal include all solutions to real-life problems for which it is necessary to use CCI technologies to achieve effective results. The emphasis of the papers published is on novel and original research and technological advancements. Special features on specific topics are welcome.

Contents

Consensus Theory for Cognitive Agents' Unstructured Knowledge Conflicts Resolving in Management Information Systems

Marcin Hernes[(✉)]

Wrocław University of Economics, Wrocław, Poland
marcin.hernes@ue.wroc.pl

Abstract. Management information systems of distributed nature, play a vital role in any kind of business organizations' activity. The multi-agent systems, based on cognitive agent architecture, deserve special attention in this class of systems. They allow not only to access to the information and quick search for interesting us information, its analysis and drawing conclusions, but also, in addition to responding to stimuli from the environment, have the cognitive ability to learning through empirical experience gained through direct interaction with the environment. It, in turn, allows for the automatic generation of variants of decisions and, in many cases, even taking and putting into action the decisions. The big problem currently, however, turns out to be the processing of unstructured knowledge in systems of this kind. In contemporary companies, unstructured knowledge is essential, mainly due to the possibility to obtain better flexibility and competitiveness of the organization. Therefore, unstructured knowledge supports structured knowledge to a high degree. Simultaneously, one must note that the most prevailing phenomenon is a conflict in unstructured knowledge. It is extremely difficult to resolve conflicts of this kind properly. However, it is also very important, since it can improve the operation of management information system and, consequently, help the organization that employs the system become more flexible and competitive.

The main aim of this work is to develop a formal method to resolve conflicts in unstructured knowledge of cognitive agents in management information systems employing the consensus theory. The first part of this work presents an analysis problems related to management information systems and unstructured knowledge processing in these systems. Next, the cognitive agents are characterized with particular emphasis on unstructured knowledge processing. The use of consensus theory in unstructured knowledge conflicts resolving have been characterized in the third part of the work. The last part presents the developed method for cognitive agents' knowledge conflicts resolving. The correctness of the method was verified using the prototypes of the agents helping to invest in the Forex market and processing user opinions about products and services.

Keywords: Management information systems · Cognitive agents
Unstructured knowledge · Knowledge conflicts · Consensus theory

© Springer-Verlag GmbH Germany, part of Springer Nature 2019
N. T. Nguyen et al. (Eds.): TCCI XXXII, LNCS 11370, pp. 1–119, 2019.
https://doi.org/10.1007/978-3-662-58611-2_1

1 Introduction

Management information systems (MIS), of distributed nature, play a vital part in any kind of business organization's activity. Analysis of related works indicates that an organization management system is a set of activities connected with planning, organizing, decision making, managing people and controlling. The activities are aimed at achieving a given goal and involve processing large quantities of information. That is why an information system is isolated from the management system, the former being a 'multi-level structure' which allows input information to be processed into output information (which in turn enables decision making) with the use of certain models and procedures [1]. If the information system employs computer hardware, then the system is called management information system. The development of computer networks has resulted in contemporary MIS being distributed, operating within a network, mainly the Internet. The systems allow gathering and processing very large quantities of information, yet they also significantly facilitate knowledge management in an organization.

In this work, it is assumed following meaning of data, information and knowledge (according [2, 3]):

1. Data are alphabetic or numeric signs. They do not have any meaning without context.
2. Information is a set of symbols that represent knowledge. Information is what context creates/gives to data. It is cognitive. Normally it is understood as a new and additional element in collecting data and information for planned action.
3. Knowledge is the appropriation of information in the process of learning, acting, interpreting by humans or computer systems. Knowledge refers to the way of using information during the intellectual process.

A distributed computer system is a set of independent computers linked by networks equipped with distributed system software that enables them to create integrated processing environment. A perfect example of this is the Internet. A distributed system involves both distribution of hardware and distribution of information resources. Distributed systems meet the expectations of contemporary users because of their following characteristics [4]:

- resource sharing – the same resources can be used by many users; resources capable of being shared include hardware (hard drives, operating memory, printers), applications and tools, data stored in databases,
- openness – the system can be expanded freely, new peripherals as well as additional software can be added, without the necessity to interfere with existing resources,
- concurrency – the system allows simultaneous processing because there are many processing units involved,
- scaling – the system may be of any size; the number of computers linked may vary from a few to a few thousand units, and the size can be changed at any moment,
- damage tolerance – if one of the system components malfunctions, the system will detect it and pass instructions to another component so that the whole processing is continued,

- transparency – user sees the system as a whole although physically all the components are apart; for instance, one can open a file stored on a remote computer in the same way as a file stored on a local computer.

All above characteristics are also attributed to management information systems of distributed nature. The multi-agent systems, based on cognitive agent architecture, deserve special attention in this class of systems[1]. Generally speaking the cognitive agent is a smart program that not only concludes on the basis of the data received, take specific actions to achieve the desired objective (this can be, for example, decision support), but also, unlike the reactive agent program, it learn at the same time gaining experience. Multi-agent system is most often defined as [5, 6]:

- environment E, which has certain limits,
- set of objects O belonging to environment E having its location; objects can be tested, created, modified and destroyed by agents,
- set of agents A belonging to O, which are the system's active objects,
- set R of relation, that connect objects with each other by assigning semantics to this connection,
- Op of operations, which allow the agents from set A to test, create, use, modify or destroy objects from the set O,
- environment rights - operators of the representation of operations and the environments' response to these operations.

Multi-agent systems allow not only to access to the information and quick search for interesting us information, its analysis and drawing conclusions, but also, in addition to responding to stimuli from the environment, have the cognitive ability to learning through empirical experience gained through direct interaction with the environment [4, 7], which in turn allows for the automatic generation of variants of decisions and, in many cases, even taking and putting into action of the decisions.

Despite that, distributed systems, including management systems, also have heterogeneous attributes that create problems which result from using those systems. The problems include [7, 8]:

- difficulties with maintaining resource security, the system has many components and creating resource security tools is complicated,
- simultaneous, independent processing on different processing units may lead to different results of the same task (for instance, due to using different algorithms for finding a solution to the same task) when only one solution is really necessary,
- heterogeneity of hardware and data structure, since we assume that user should see everything as a whole, there is a problem of connecting resources and defining conditions for access to shared resources.

The big problem currently, however, turns out to be the processing of unstructured knowledge in systems of this kind. Knowledge is the basis for all decision-making processes; it involves experiences, values assessment, context information and analytical insight into the matter, which provides frames for incorporating and assessing

---

[1] The reflections in this paper concern, in the wide scope, integrated, multi-agent MISs.

new information and experiences [9]. Note that knowledge contained in information management systems is normally structuralized and the systems employ various methods for processing structured knowledge and resolving conflicts of such knowledge. However, in contemporary companies, unstructured knowledge is essential, mainly due to the possibility to obtain better flexibility and competitiveness of the organization. Therefore, this knowledge supports structured knowledge to a high degree. The unstructured knowledge is mainly stored in natural language, so it is processed with symbols (not numbers) e.g., users' opinions on a forum. Generally speaking, there are text databases that contain various types of text files, such as newspaper articles, e-books, e-mail, websites and all sorts of text files. The documents describe certain phenomena that occur in the real world, in the environment where a given organization operates. Text files are not internally structured in any way, the knowledge that they contain is non-structuralized or structuralized to a small degree. For example, the structure of an e-mail message contains information on sender, addressee, size, subject, but the rest of the message is a stream of symbols deprived of internal structure. It is important to say that text files are often a source of significant and useful knowledge.

In this work it is assumed, that text document consist of not only data and information, but also the conclusions and suggestions related to given problem. Therefore they consist of knowledge. Due to this fact, in this work we use a term "unstructured knowledge" instead "unstructured data" or "unstructured information".

Simultaneously, one must note that the most prevailing phenomenon is a conflict in unstructured knowledge. One example of this is users' opinion about a product offered by online shops. Some users may have a good opinion, others may present a negative one, and some of them may have no opinion at all. Besides, various opinions about the same product within the same online shop may differ completely. Another example are documents written by employees that describe actions or effects that occur within the organization. The same actions or effects may be described in different manner by each employee.

It is extremely difficult to resolve conflicts of this kind properly. However, it is also very important, since it can improve the operation of MIS and, consequently, help the organization that employs the system become more flexible and competitive.

The main aim of this work is to develop a formal method to resolve conflicts in unstructured knowledge of cognitive agents in management information systems employing the consensus theory.

The following supplementary and cognitive aims were also included:

1. Identification of problems in the development of information systems management and use the cognitive agents in their construction.
2. Recognizing the potential of consensus theory to solve conflicts of unstructured knowledge of cognitive agents.

The utilitarian aim is to verification of the developed method using prototypes of cognitive agents functioning in management information systems.

The main research hypothesis is formulated as follows: Using consensus theory to resolve conflicts of unstructured knowledge of cognitive agents running in management information systems will increase the usability of these systems, which will have a positive impact on business processes in the organization. The positive impact is considered as reducing risk, decision-making time and costs.
The following supplementary hypotheses are also formulated:

1. A management information system that uses cognitive agents to process unstructured knowledge improves business processes performance in the organization. It is realized by shortening time and increasing effectiveness and efficiency to a greater extent than traditional MIS.
2. Consensus theory enables the development of a method for resolving conflicts of unstructured knowledge, which results in satisfactory benefits to the user of the system. These benefits are measured by ratio-based and risk-based measures.

As author's contributions may be considered among others:

– developing a method for resolving conflicts of unstructured knowledge of cognitive agents, using the consensus theory,
– verification of the developed method,
– developing a methods for assessing usability of cognitive agents running in the MIS,
– developing a prototypes of cognitive agents supporting selected areas of MIS functioning,
– analysis of the knowledge management process by cognitive agent programs.

This work has an interdisciplinary character. In order to achieve the goals, an analysis of literature in the field of management, economics and computer science has been done. This made it possible to identify the essence of the problem of conflicts of unstructured knowledge in MIS and also contributed to the approximation of issues related to the theory of consensus and cognitive agents. On the basis of conclusions from theoretical considerations, scientific cooperation with many research groups[2], and taking into consideration the author's experience in the implementation of various types of information systems, the assumptions and the method of resolving conflicts of unstructured knowledge of cognitive agents using the consensus theory were formulated.

The first part of this work presents an analysis a problems related to management information systems and unstructured knowledge processing in these systems. The main outcomes are to systematize analyzed problems and to determine reasons for the emergence of knowledge conflicts in MIS and their potential effects. Next, the cognitive agents are characterized with particular emphasis on unstructured knowledge processing. The main outcomes are to systematize analyzed problems, to analyze a conflicts of cognitive agents 'knowledge and to determine premises for the development of a new method for resolving conflicts of unstructured knowledge of cognitive

---

[2] Especially with: Department of Information Systems Wrocław University of Science and Technology, Cognitive Computing Research Group The University of Memphis.

agents in the investigated systems. The use of consensus theory in unstructured knowledge conflicts resolving have been characterized in the third part of the work. The main outcomes are to systematize analyzed problems related to process of consensus determining, to indicate and to analyze existing applications of the consensus theory in resolving conflicts of unstructured knowledge and to indicate determinants of using the consensus theory in resolving the analyzed conflicts in management information systems. The last part presents the developed method for cognitive agents' knowledge conflicts resolving, which is main outcome of this section. The correctness of the method was verified using the prototypes of the agents supporting the trading on the Forex market and processing user opinions about products and services.

This work summarizes the author's research conducted over the past few years partially published in research papers and the results of the realization the project titled "Using consensus theory in unstructured knowledge conflicts resolving of cognitive agents in information management support systems", financially supported by the National Science Center (decision No. DEC-2013/11/D/HS4/04096).

2   Unstructured Knowledge Processing in Management Information Systems

2.1   The Nature and the Significance of Management Information Systems in Organizations

Modern management information systems represent a key element in the operation of business entities. They are designed to offer support of each phase and function of the business management cycle, namely: planning, decision-making, organizing, directing (employee management), and controlling [10, 11]. As such, it has capacity to support not only the realization of business processes, but also the processes (or even procedures) of managerial decision-making.

Many authors [e.g. 1, 12, 13] seem to agree on the notion that the present management information systems provide effective reinforcement of all the functional areas of business operation.

According to [14], the list of tasks assigned to management information systems should include the following:

- support for day-to-day business operations,
- improving customer satisfaction through better management of product and service quality, cost reduction, and automated analyses of sales figures and customer behaviors stored in the system's data repository,
- support for making and maintaining business relations with suppliers,
- improving employee satisfaction through system support for human resource management,
- support for decision-making processes,
- controlling the risk of business operation.

The list of benefits arising from the use of management information systems in business settings includes [15]:

- automation of business processes,
- knowledge management,
- elimination or reduction of delays in decision-making processes,
- supporting of new business models and strategies (such as e-business, virtual organizations – MISs allow for flexible adapting for different models and strategies).

Due to the broad range of tasks assigned to MIS in business organizations, professional literature has yet to develop a unified definition of such systems. For example, [11] define a management information system as "a human-machine system that uses systemic thinking and has the modern communication techniques as the basic information disposal means and transfer tools. It can supply the information service to managers". On the other hand, [14] describes MIS as a system which "deals with behavioral issues as well as technical issues surrounding the development, the utilization and the impact of information systems used by managers and employees in the firm". Kisielnicki [1] defines MIS as a "separate part of the organization's information system, which is computerized to fit a particular managerial objective".

In view of such diversity of available definitions, and for the purpose of this study, let us assume that management information systems are considered as IT systems which offer support for management.

MIS can be classified according to various criteria. For example, based on the criterion of roles to be played by them in the realization of business cycles, the following types of MIS can be distinguished [11]:

- information systems for planning and decision-making,
- information systems for normative and parametric standardization,
- information systems for reporting.

Since modern management is dominated by a process approach, the process criterion can also be used as basis for MIS classification, as follows [1]:

- process description systems,
- process monitoring systems,
- process support systems.

However, one of the most widely adopted criteria in this context is the criterion of information requirements for decision-making purposes, allowing for classification of MIS into the following [1, 12, 14]:

1. 1st generation systems (1G), offering managerial support at the operational level. These are typically represented by Transaction Systems (TS) that yield basic reports for accounting, wage calculation, etc. Those systems do not offer direct support for decision-making; they merely allow for facilitated access to basic information required in decision-making processes.
2. 2G systems offering managerial support at tactical level, typically in the form of Management Information Systems based on transaction processing, but with more advanced algorithms to offer synthetic information reports for managerial purposes. Analyses of the practical use of this type of systems suggest that they are particularly vulnerable to the problems of information structuring.

3. 3G systems offering full support at all levels of management, including the strategic level. This class of systems includes the following:

(a) Decision Support Systems (DSS) addressed to middle and top-level decision-makers. Those systems operate on datasets of transaction operations records using pre-programmed models of decision support. The most notable characteristics of DSS include the following [15]:
   - an adequate ease of operation,
   - presentation of information in user-accessible formats and technologies,
   - selectivity of information feeds,
   - supporting (rather than replacing) the mental tasks involved in decision-making scenarios,
   - supporting the processing of weakly structured information for managerial purposes.

(b) Group Decision Support Systems (GDSS), offering support for parallel processing of information, group participation in decisions and opinion exchange, projection of results obtainable from alternate solutions.

(c) Expert systems strongly rooted in the development of artificial intelligence algorithms. This class of systems was designed in response to the need to automate not only the processing of available information, but also the generation of conclusions drawn from it – a task typically associated with intelligence. Expert systems operate on the available knowledge repositories [16] (i.e. databases representing facts and rules to be used in their processing) and automated deduction mechanisms. The earliest applications of this class of systems were in medicine, but now include other sectors, such as banking, insurance, and trade.

(d) Executive Information Systems (EIS). Those allow for rapid generation of standard, cross-sectional, or detailed analyses. Results are produced in a graphical form, offering decision makers the potential to easily update their knowledge of the changing environment. In effect, they eliminate the problems and difficulties faced by decision-making authorities in their effective use of information and knowledge, particularly in scenarios involving highly complex knowledge models and structures [17].

(e) Business Intelligence [18] (BI). This class offers data integration, multi-dimensional analyses, data mining and visualization. Based on the information loss observed in systems incapable of storing, integrating, aggregating and analyzing correlations of historical data, the BI class is designed to combat those faults with the view of improving the quality of information supplied for decision-making purposes.

(f) Distributed Information Systems (DIS). They are defined as a set of information systems physically distributed over multiple sites, which are connected with some kind of communication network [19, 20]. These systems are more often building on the basis of Web Services and Semantic Web technologies.

(g) Mobile Systems (MS). These class of systems is based on using mobile devices and applications for supporting business processes, for example logistics [21], commerce [22], and banking [23].

At present, the most advanced level of development in MIS design is represented in IMIS solutions (integrated management information systems), as a class of systems offering full integration of earlier designs to provide a more comprehensive solution tailored to the needs and requirements of both strategic and operational management [24]. IMIS support the realization of business processes in all areas of company economic involvement. Professional literature provides various definitions of the IMIS class. They are typically regarded as representative of the ERP class systems, but it must be noted that the latter – by definition – must follow the standards of the American Production and Inventory Control Society (APICS) and are typically narrower in scope compared to IMIS class solutions [17], as IMIS may be applied in any area of company operation. Based on conclusions presented in literature studies [such as 16, 25, 27], integrated management information systems can be perceived as systems in support of all areas of management in business organizations and their environments, characterized by shared (in a logical sense) database, computation procedures and info-control solutions designed to optimize the realization of business processes through the use of modern info-communication technologies (IT). The above is an extension to a definition presented in [24]. IMIS class solutions are employed with success in various types of business organizations (production, services, finance). Due to their modular or component-based design structure, systems of this class can be introduced in stages and tailored to the specific requirements of the user segment (module compositions used in production companies will be much different from those employed in trade companies) [24].

Principal features of integrated management information systems are defined as follows [24, 27, 28]:

1. Functional comprehensiveness – they are designed to cover all significant areas of company operation, both technical and economic.
2. Integration of data and processes – this applies to data exchange both within the system (between various modules), and with external environment (such as *electronic data interchange*, EDI).
3. Serving the info-controlling function – this involves real-time data feeds for the realization of business processes (for example, automatic verification of stock availability for every invoice issued).
4. Process orientation – systems are designed to offer comprehensive information support tailored to individual business processes, and not to specific elements of the company organizational structure.
5. Open architecture – with capacity to extend the system's functionality by new modular elements.
6. Scalable architecture (based typically on client-server solutions) with capacity to support links to external systems, e.g. those used by business partners.
7. Advanced scope – with full IT support for information and decision-making processes using unrestrained data extraction and aggregation, process variation, optimization, forecasting, etc., and with support for some advanced management concepts, such as *just-in-time* (JiT), *Manufacturing Resource Planning* – MRP II), *Total Quality Management* (TQM), and ISO 900x standards.

8. Advanced technology – offering full compatibility with modern hardware and software standards, and easily migratable between platforms, operating systems, media formats and communication protocols.
9. Full compliance with legislative regulations.

Any of the above generations of MIS can be utilized in tandem with agent technologies, as evidenced in professional literature. These combinations can also be observed in business practice. For instance [29] presents the use of agent solutions in the practical realization of e-production and supply chain management systems. Similarly, [30] discuss the realization of a virtual organization based on a multi-agent system. Another interesting approach is the use of multi-agent programs in the design of a Global ERP, as presented in [26]. This solution presents a framework for a multi-agent system design capable of integrating multiple IT systems that serve to support various areas of company operation, such as Enterprise Resource Planning (ERP), Customer Relationship Management (CRM), Supply Chain Management (SCM), and e-banking.

One of the main tasks faced by MIS (mostly 3G and IMIS, including multi-agent MIS) is to offer support for the knowledge management (KM) process. Knowledge plays a dominant role in value creation processes and is considered to be the most important factor of development in organizations of all types [1], particularly in business organizations. Knowledge corresponds to those immaterial resources at company disposal which are associated with human activities and which may be utilized as a source of competitive advantage. Proper management of available knowledge is an essential requirement that warrants the effective operation of any organization under the present socio-economic conditions.

Knowledge management in business organization is related to processing of structured and unstructured knowledge (more detailed description of these kinds of knowledge has been done in Sub-sect. 2.3), and performed mainly by integrated information systems. The above is understood in professional literature in different ways, inter alia as [11, 31]:

- knowledge creation process and its utilization for improving the efficiency of the organization,
- management of the organization's information, knowledge and experience,
- encouraging employees to share knowledge.

Knowledge management is defined in [32, 33] as "an integrated system of initiatives, methods and tools designed to create an optimal flow of knowledge within and throughout an extended enterprise to ensure stakeholders success". Stakeholders are partners, distributors, customers, enterprise's employees including managers. Success includes among others leadership, industrial performance, efficiency, quality and safety [34]. The work [35] states that higher levels of KM-maturity were found to correlate positively with long-term sustainable growth.

Knowledge management can be divided into the following sub-processes [36, 37]:

- identification,
- acquiring,
- creation,
- organization,

- modeling,
- storing,
- processing,
- utilization,
- integration,

Parallelly with mentioned sub-processes, also following ones are realized:

- validation,
- transfer,
- triggering creativity in employees.

The **identification** (localization) of external knowledge is made through the description and analysis of the organization's environment in the field of knowledge. On the other hand, the identification of internal knowledge consists mainly determining "who knows what" and "can do" in the organization and where the knowledge sources are placed. Identification of knowledge is the basis for a strategic analysis of the organization's knowledge resources and its environment.

Acquiring of knowledge is the process of knowledge movement from the organization's environment to its interior as well as the process during which employees acquire knowledge from internal sources, i.e. from their co-workers, from documentation and databases, from available books and magazines. Acquiring knowledge can also take place through its extraction from competitors or processes products (e.g. benchmarking method). Acquiring knowledge is also done through participation in training, conferences and symposia, as well as during informal contacts with other people. Media are also an important source of knowledge, especially regarding information about potential opportunities and threats.

Creation. It is the process of creating a new, personalized, innovative knowledge for organization, which is then transformed into a codified and often grounded one. In this process, among others, heuristic methods are used. Product innovations, for example, are created today mainly in research and development centers, but a whole range of innovations (e.g. process ones) are created during everyday practice, work of project teams, quality circles or task teams.

Organization. The collected sets of knowledge must undergo a selection process from the point of view of the usability area. At the basis of the selection should be developed criteria, by means of which the collected knowledge is classified. Areas of usefulness can be divided in different ways, e.g. in the cross-section of functions (marketing, production, finances, personnel, etc.), time (knowledge of the past, present, future), accessibility (knowledge available to the public, limited access, secret protected by competitors), according to opportunities and threats, regarding the organization, closer and further environments.

Modeling. It is a process of creating a computer interpretable model of knowledge or standard specifications about a kind of process and/or about a kind of facility or product. The resulting knowledge model can be computer interpretable when it is expressed in some knowledge representation method that enables the knowledge to be interpreted by software and to be stored in a database or data exchange file. There are different methods/approaches to knowledge modeling, such as:

1. Mining approach. The aim of this approach is to build a virtual expert, i.e., a system which can emulate the problem solving behavior of an expert by relying on the same frame of knowledge. In mining approach it is assumed that expertise does in fact consist of (or can be at least reformulated as) a set of rules. The cognitive basis for such an assumption can be traced back to Newell and Simon [38], who proposed production systems as a general computational paradigm for describing intelligent behavior.

2. Modeling sub-process from symbolic representational considerations and evolved to the paradigm of model-based system development, in which a knowledge system is viewed as an operational model capable of simulating a certain observed problem-solving behavior from an intelligent agent (e.g. a human expert in a certain professional). This view contrasts to the traditional approach where a knowledge system was usually considered as a container with knowledge extracted from an expert. The modelling process considers the existence of an abstract level where the knowledge can be functionally described playing its role in the problem-solving process, independent of a particular representation [38].

3. The KADS methodology [39]. In this approach expertise modelling and design are clearly separated. First, "in an analysis stage, the knowledge engineer develops an abstract model of the expertise from the data …this model is (then) transformed into an architecture for the KBS" [40]. KADS takes into account the contextual knowledge, which is, in many cases, essential in decision making process. In this approach often conceptual knowledge models are used. They are independent of implementation and can also serve for others applications. Ontology is an example of such a knowledge model. The KADS methodology is recently developed as CommonKADS, which views the construction of a KBS as a modelling activity, and so these methods require a number of models to be constructed which represent, different views on problem solving behavior, in its or recommends the construction of six models: a model of the organization's function & structure, a model of the tusks (activities) required to perform a particular operation, a model of the capabilities required of the agents who perform that, operation, a model of the communication required between agents during the operation, a model of the expertise required to perform the operation and a model of the design of a KBS to perform all or part of this operation [40].

4. The KEATS approach [41], in which it is distinguished between modelling "overt behavior" (i.e. understanding problem solving behavior) and "internal representation" which was concerned with the realization of this behavior on a computer system.

The goal of **storing** sub-process is to secure the functioning of the organization in the future. Acquired and created knowledge after is stored, and each type of knowledge corresponds to a different method of storage. Knowledge stored on material carriers should be periodically evaluated and verified to eliminate knowledge that has become unusable. In contrast, personalized knowledge is stored in the heads of people.

Processing aims to convert knowledge for action and to achieve the desired results of increased value in the organization or specific operations. In MISs this sub-process is realized by using different processes such as reasoning, learning. The results of knowledge processing is a new knowledge necessary for decision making.

Utilization the knowledge generated during processing is directed to use. The main areas of application of knowledge are: creating visions and concepts for the operation of organizations, products and services, technologies and its use, solving everyday emerging problems.

Integration is an important element of the process allowing to obtain a better quality of previously selected knowledge and is also at the base of knowledge creation, because in the process of creating new knowledge it is necessary to use the existing knowledge resources. The mere integration of previously unconnected knowledge resources can lead to a diametric increase of knowledge. At the base of combining knowledge is sharing knowledge and its acquisition.

Validation - this process serves to maintain the quality of knowledge required to decision-making process. Validation is performed during realization all remaining sub-processes of knowledge management.

Transfer is an action aimed at creating a generally available knowledge from a given resource.

Triggering Creativity in Employees. Getting to hit, innovative ideas individually or in small groups. Intellectual capital (including human resources) management is very important component of knowledge management process. Because decision making, especially routine, is implemented by the system, employees have more time for development work using the knowledge stored in the system.

The main task of knowledge management is to gather and provide relevant knowledge to all participants [34]. It is called as knowledge flow process and defined as follows: creation (related to identification, acquiring, creation organization sub-processes), collection (modeling, storing sub-processes), processing (processing, utilization, integration and validation sub-processes) and sharing knowledge (transfer, triggering creativity in employees sub-processes) in an organized and optimized way, taking into consideration the different activities of the extended organization as well as needs and individual and collective motivations of all participants [43–45].

Each type of knowledge can be converted [46]. When viewed as a continuous learning process, the model becomes a clockwise spiral; organizational learning depends on initiating and sustaining the learning spiral (the model is a spiral, not a cycle, because as one "learns" around the cycle, understanding moves to deeper and deeper levels). The process that transfers tacit (existing only in the mind of the human or intelligent computer software) knowledge in one person to tacit knowledge in another person is socialization. It is experiential, active and a "living thing" involving capturing knowledge by walking around and through direct interaction with customers and suppliers outside the organization and people inside the organization. The process for making tacit knowledge explicit (expressed in character form and stored on knowledge carriers) is externalization. One case is the articulation of one's own tacit knowledge - ideas or images in words, metaphors, analogies. A second case is eliciting and translating the tacit knowledge of others - customer, experts for example - into a readily understandable form, e.g., explicit knowledge. Dialogue is an important means for both. Externalization is a process among individuals within a group. Once knowledge is explicit, it can be transferred as explicit knowledge through a process Nonaka calls combination. This is the area where information technology is most helpful, because explicit knowledge can be conveyed in documents, email, data bases, as well as through meetings and briefings. The key steps collecting relevant internal and external knowledge, dissemination, and editing/processing to make it more usable. Combination allows knowledge transfer among groups across organization. Internalization is the process of understanding and absorbing explicit knowledge in to tacit knowledge held by the individual. Knowledge in the tacit form is actionable by the owner. Internalization is largely experiential, in order to actualize concepts and methods, either through the actual doing or through simulations. The internalization process transfers organization and group explicit knowledge to the individual [46].

Management Information Systems should be designed to support all sub-processes involved in the knowledge management process. In other words – knowledge flow process must be realized. It must also be emphasized that each of such constituent sub-processes should also be capable of learning, that is: discovering new facts, phenomena, and any links (relations) between them.

However, the knowledge management process in itself presents a number of difficulties. The volatile character of modern economies, the rapid development of IT and telecommunication technologies, the pace of globalization and the unrestrained flow of knowledge – these and other phenomena impose on modern organizations the need to rapidly adapt and respond to changes, both within and outside their organizational structure. To solve the wealth of problems generated in association with this trend, managers of many organizations are required to make and issue complex decisions of not only operational and tactical, but most of all – strategic significance that may seriously affect future company operation. Managers in business organizations typically operate under the conditions of risk and uncertainty, since the results of their decisions cannot be forecasted in advance, or can only be projected with limited degree of probability. In addition, in order to safeguard the company competitive advantage, such decisions have to be made in near real time. Thus, to ensure proper realization of the knowledge management process, modern MIS have to satisfy a number of additional requirements, including:

1. Near real-time data acquisition. To satisfy this postulate, MIS need to incorporate modern technological solutions, such as cloud computing, grid computing, in-memory databases, in-database processing.
2. Acquisition of information of suitable value. Information is used as basis for the evaluation of environments, conditions or situations faced by organizations, the prediction of company condition in the foreseeable future, and for the proper examination of internal and external factors of impact upon the effectiveness of the organization as a whole. But most of all, information is a basis for the process of generating new knowledge to allow for making more accurate decisions in the future. Thus, information acquired by IT systems must be of specific value for the organization. More specifically, information must be accurate, reliable, up-to-date, timely, unambiguous, complete, and credible.

3. Automated monitoring of the environment, both internal (employees, processes, internal databases, procedures, regulations, reports) and external (the press, radio, TV, publications, information leaflets and other written content, suppliers, intermediaries, customers, markets – this group of resources is nowadays mostly accessed and circulated over the Internet).
4. Integration and coordination of various knowledge management subsystems. It is advisable to aim for full integration of MIS at all levels i.e., between systems, applications, and business processes.
5. Analyses of the factual significance attached to phenomena and business processes that occur in the organization's immediate environment.
6. Generation of decision variants (based on various decision-support methods) for user consideration or for the purpose of automated processing, particularly at operational and tactical level. This may ultimately lead to the development of real-time decision-making capabilities.
7. Ability to continuously learn from past observations and occurrences.
8. Capacity to automatically tailor the realization of business processes to specific requirements of the target user.
9. Provision of analytical functions as a set of instruments to be used by business analysts.
10. Providing query responses and analytical evaluations in near real-time, to offer quality support for business analysts and designers,
11. Provision of interactive data analyses, with results that can also be accessed from mobile devices.

The above properties of MIS may help organizations face some of the new challenges in company management, such as [11]:

– securing and maintaining competitive advantage in all operations,
– integrating human and technical resources for improved effectiveness,
– processing and transforming information feeds from various sources,
– limiting the organization's environmental footprint, e.g. through reduction of post-production waste,
– responding rapidly to changes in company environment,
– introducing technological innovations.

However, functional analyses of modern MIS suggest that the available solutions are characterized by a lack of a comprehensive approach to the integration of management information systems. It would be advisable, for example, to assume that the ERP system overlaps in range with other subsystems, such as CRM and SCM, the more so that such an approach is strongly suggested in professional publications on the subject of ERP systems [24]. This type of integration would greatly improve the effectiveness of knowledge management processes. In addition, taking into account the modern generation of multi-agent MIS systems, it may be observed that these systems employ reactive type agents; although this type of agent systems offers good support for decision-making processes, but are devoid of learning functionality. For this reason, it seems necessary to employ specialized agent systems designed for specific purposes. After all, the practical design of information gathering agents follows an approach much different from that used in the design of planning agents or resource management agents. In their present form, MIS systems cannot offer full support for the realization of knowledge management processes, mostly due to the lack of analytical evaluation of the real significance of occurrences and phenomena that take place in the organization's immediate environment and the lack of self-learning functionality.

Analyzing the historical development of MIS, one may observe certain trends in their present evolution, such as: the steady transition into cloud computing, full integration of all business processes within the organization, or the use of modern mobile technologies. Of these, the most important trend is the introduction of intelligent technologies, stimulated mostly by the need for business decisions to be made not only on the basis of the available knowledge (this functionality is already present in IMIS class solutions), but also on the grounds of past experiences (previously perceived as a human domain). One of the possible solutions to this dilemma is to delegate the decision-making authorities (particularly those at operational and tactical level) to the competences of automated systems, for instance those based on cognitive agent systems. In contrast to reactive agents, cognitive agent systems are self-contained, i.e. they not only offer rapid access to information with queries, analyses and conclusion-drawing functionality, but are also capable of 'exploring' the immediate environment, 'learning' from observed occurrences, and – in effect – 'gathering experience' in their field of expertise. In other words, they are equipped with cognitive mechanisms that enable them to learn from empirical evidence gathered through direct interaction with their surrounding [47]. In effect, they may be employed for automated analyses of the real significance of phenomena and occurrences, and – in many cases – for the generation of automated decision variants and even the automated activation of the most optimal variant.

Based on the above observations, the next section of this work will address some of the problems and challenges posed by the use of cognitive agent systems as part of the functional architecture of MIS.

2.2   Cognitive Agents and Their Utilization in Functional Architecture of Management Information Systems

The origin of cognitive agent systems is closely related to the development of artificial intelligence. It is worth noting at this point that many of the motives for the design of artificial intelligence solutions (including the cognitive agent systems), as diagnosed in professional literature, seem to correspond particularly well with the demands of modern MIS applications; these include the following [48]:

1. Knowledge used in the design of traditional non-learning agents is explicit, but knowledge of the immediate surrounding is subject to constant change. In effect, results produced by non-learning agents tend to deteriorate with time. This raises the need to provide continuous agent revisions or updates. In contrast, systems based on artificial intelligence are equipped with capabilities to adapt to changes in knowledge of their immediate surroundings. For instance, commercial applications based on non-learning agents offer only a limited set of adjustments to the specific requirements of target users. The lack of support for certain indispensable functions

may be addressed by the commercial designer by appeal, but the process often proves costly and time-consuming.

2. Knowledge used in the design of non-learning agents is readily available, but also unordered and heterogeneous. While it may be used with success after being transformed to a more ordered structure, the process may prove quite costly. Artificial intelligence solutions are capable of calculating such transformations internally. For instance, cognitive agents may be used to process customer opinions expressed in a natural language (unstructured knowledge) and produce results in the form of forecasts of future sales trends, to the effect of improving the company's competitive advantage.

3. Knowledge used in the design of non-learning agents is not complete at the time of its design. Sufficient knowledge is assumed to form at later stages of its operation. A good example here is the introduction of new processes or innovations. Initially, knowledge of such processes or innovation is incomplete, although the integrated management information system is already in operation.

A cognitive agent is defined in professional literature in various terms. The most widely adopted approach defines it as a computer application that satisfies the following criteria [49, 50]:

- is capable of initiating actions within the environment in which it operates,
- is capable of communicating directly with other agents,
- is directed by a set of customs or inclinations which can be formulated as tangible goals or as guidelines for the realization of benefit optimization function,
- has its own set of resources,
- is capable of registering signals from the environment,
- has knowledge of its environment,
- provides its own set of skills and may be employed to render services,
- is capable of self-reproducing and cloning,
- is designed to achieve the realization of goals through the utilization of available knowledge, resources and skills, based on communication with other agents and on signals registered in the environment,
- is capable of exploring the environment and learning from past experience,
- is capable react, learn from other agents and from user.

Thus, it may be assumed that a cognitive agent is an intelligent software application capable of not only making their own conclusions from the wealth of data received from the environment and using those conclusions as basis for the initiation of appropriate actions (for instance, offering decision-making support), but also – in contrast to purely reactive agents – learning from past experience.

Cognitive agents may be incorporated in structural design of MIS of any generation (cf. Sect. 2.1 above), but they are most effective if used as part of integrated management information systems, as only this approach offers full integration of all business processes, including the knowledge management process. Below there are some of the possible approaches to the design of functional architecture of MIS utilizing cognitive agent solutions:

1. Cognitive agent systems are regarded as additional components to subsystems or modules that constitute a traditional MIS[3].
2. The functional architecture of MIS consists solely of cognitive agents (as they are fully capable of preforming functions associated with traditional MIS).

The latter approach to the functional design of MIS based on cognitive agents offers better standardization of the system's components (as all the modules utilize the same set of software components), which helps achieve proper system integration at all levels.

The next part of this work presents a postulate for a model architectural design of an integrated management information system consisting entirely of cognitive agent applications. For our purposes, let us refer to it as a Cognitive Integrated Management Information System (CIMIS)[4].

The first problem that comes to mind in the analytical evaluation of this type of architecture is the lack of literature support for a comprehensive approach to this task (i.e. the lack of assumption that such a system should also comprise areas covered by other modules, such as CRM and SCM, which are often regarded as separate systems), despite the present trend of emphasizing full integrity of all areas of company involvement [51]. Restrictions in access to certain information or functionalities of the system – if any – should only be associated with corporate security policies, rather than arise from technical limitations (e.g. incompatibility of communication protocols or database management systems).

Despite the apparent lack of a unified approach in the definition of subsystem composition to be used in IMIS class systems, literature studies and empirical obser-vations of practical solutions [26, 55, 56] provide some pointers to allow for a sys-tematization of architectural composition of such systems, assuming after [24, 26] that it comprises of the following subsystems:

– Fixed Assets,
– Logistics,
– Manufacturing Management,
– Human Resource Management,
– Financial and Accounting,
– Controlling,
– CRM,
– Business Intelligence.

The Fixed Assets subsystem supports the realization of all processes associated with financial management of fixed assets and calculation of their depreciation values. The subsystem allows for automated generation of bookkeeping records to be used by the Financial and Accounting subsystem, and the provision of current and historic property valuations; it also offers automated stock-keeping with reports generated in various configurations. Other areas of the subsystem's competence include property investment and property maintenance tasks.

---

[3] Traditional MIS are considered as MIS, which systems that do not contain artificial intelligence tools.
[4] The detail of CIMIS functioning has been described, for example, in [52–54].

The Logistics subsystem supports the realization of tasks associated with material supply planning, product distribution, materials and inventory management, end-product management, modelling of distribution networks, transport management, and route optimization.

The Manufacturing Management subsystem offers support for processes typically assigned to technology, construction, and planning departments. It serves to facilitate the realization of functions associated with: process engineering, production capacity planning, production planning, resource use planning, planning and realization of orders, production control and monitoring, visualization and documentation of production processes, and production-to-warehouse transfer. Other functionalities include documentation management, automated recording of machinery use, and certificates management.

The Human Resources Management subsystem is designed to support the realization of such functions as: evidencing of personal employee records and employment agreements, time registration, wage calculation, automated generation of tax and insurance forms, management of company social funds and employee savings/loans plans, settlement of expenses claims, generation of statistics reports on employment, wages and working times, and support for recruitment, training and employee evaluation processes [24].

The Financial and Accounting subsystem supports the full range of evidencing tasks and recording of the company's economic activities; it also provides essential managerial information in such areas as: liquidity, proceeds, costs, financial result, pricing structure, profit margins or sales opportunities. The subsystem offers also support for creation, updating and evidencing of corporate plans of accounts, settlement of accounts, cash counter management and generation of various reports and analyses, including the obligatory reports required by statutory regulations, such as those defined in the Accounting Act.

The Controlling subsystem is tasked with automated processing of data associated with cost accounting and profit/loss accounting, in close collaboration with the Financial and Accounting subsystem. The Controlling subsystem provides support for both strategic controlling (determination of deviations from strategic objectives in major areas of company development) and operating controlling (keeping track of the current use of factors of production and the value/volume of production against their planned values). In effect, the subsystem is tasked not only with planning functions (those in support of the optimal selection of variants of action), but also with functions of directing, controlling, and analytical evaluation.

The CRM subsystem supports the realization of tasks associated with broadly defined customer relations management and keeping track of customer preferences and requirements for the purpose of increasing sales effectiveness. Information provided by the CRM subsystem allow for proper optimization of strategies in marketing, sales, servicing, and realization of promotional campaigns. Information of this type is obtained from current evidence records and analyses of customer segments and sales results. The subsystem is also tasked with planning and sales forecasting duties [24].

The Business Intelligence subsystem offers support of managerial decision-making procedures through intelligent processing of the available data repositories and resources. The subsystem provides technologies and modules for the acquisition of information that can be helpful in typical decision-making scenarios, both in strategic and operational dimension (such as multi-dimensional analyses, forecasting and planning of business strategies, forecasting the outcomes of planned investments) [57]. The Business Intelligence subsystem is also responsible for ensuring timely and secure access to information stored within the organization, for the management and analytical evaluation of processes, and for distribution of reports between various structural units and corporate business partners.

The postulated model of CIMIS should also offer access to cognitive visualization techniques, i.e. instruments for graphical presentation of multi-dimensional sets of data designed to facilitate the identification of problems and generation of new knowledge [58]. This type of functionality is of particular importance for the effective operation of the Business Intelligence subsystem, but can also be employed to good effect in other subsystems. Cognitive visualization is often perceived as an alternative form of support for decision-making processes [59]. This assumption is based on the fact that it is extremely difficult if at all possible to define the entire range of acceptable solutions (i.e. variants that satisfy the user-defined selection criteria), due to the multi-criteria quality of economic decisions (multi-dimensional data). Cognitive visualization, in this context, allows for sizeable reduction in the number of variants.

Figure 1 presents a logical structure of a postulated CIMIS design, assuming that its construction is based solely on cognitive agents. The main attention has been putted on knowledge flow. Conceptual knowledge modelling (used in CIMIS) may improve the effectiveness of this system in two main areas: improving automatic analysis of phenomena that occur in the organization's environment and to help users in interaction with the system. It may lead to improvement of business processes realization.

It is assumed that, in the initial phase, all agents are in an 'unlearned' state. They may be provisionally segmented into subsystem groups as required, with specific agents assigned to specific tasks, such as logistics, production management, financial and accounting, etc.

Within such preliminary groups, agents may be equipped with 'basic knowledge' by the company responsible for system implementation. Further operation of agents, both grouped and non-grouped (i.e. independent agents employed to provide analyses of all subsystems and decision support) is conducted by employees. A company employee may be involved as 'teacher' for one or many agents, to help them gather knowledge required to provide certain services in a non-supervised manner (such as registration of orders, resource supply servicing, production planning, production order management, servicing of processing lines, warehousing, issue of invoices). It is also assumed that the agents – in their 'learned' state – will replace humans in decision-making scenarios, particularly on strategic and tactical levels. Agents may also learn unassisted, through self-analyses of the effects of their own decisions made in the past.

The design incorporates the use of a supervising agent (Supervisor), tasked with control of the operation of the remaining agents, mostly through early detection and automated resolution of knowledge/experience conflicts. The supervising agent provides near real-time analyses of other agents' knowledge and experience structures. In the face of a conflict, the agent produces an automated response based on a consensus-resolution algorithm, and updates the result to serve as the new representation of current knowledge or experience.

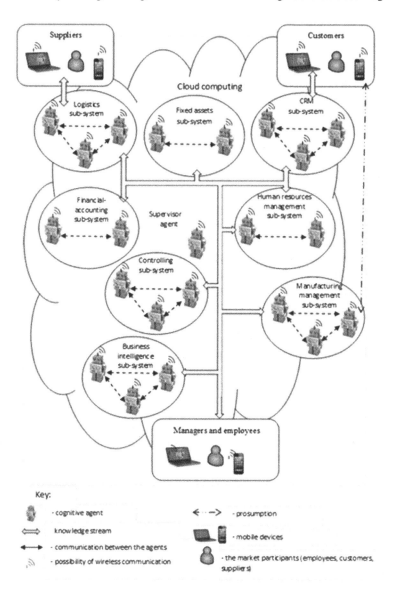

Fig. 1. The logical structure of a CIMIS system (on the basis of [59]).

It must also be noted that all subsystems within the CIMIS are connected to the same cohesive stream of knowledge which can be accessed by management personnel remotely and in real time. This is in response to the often emphasized postulate of functional comprehensiveness i.e. system's capacity to provide services in all areas of company operation, supported by proper flow of knowledge between subsystems, and with potential to produce various types of analyses and managerial reports.

It is assumed that the postulated CIMIS utilizes a broad range of modern telecommunication and information technologies, in particular:

1. Cloud computing defined as freely accessible computing/processing services rendered by external providers, capable of scaling dynamically in response to the changing preferences of the end users [60]. Utilization of cloud computing services in CIMIS design offers a more effective resource allocation and – in effect – may bring sizeable savings, as it allows for a reduction of in-house IT infrastructure expenses, as companies and other users of cloud computing services are only required to pay for the actual use of computing resources.
2. Grid computing, also referred to as parallel computing, involves distribution of computational tasks between multiple processing units arranged in a grid structure, with each fragment computed in parallel.
3. In-Database processing, with computing tasks serviced by internal database engines, designed to make extensive use of Massive Parallel Processing architectures and mechanisms offered by some database engines.
4. In-memory databases – relational data management systems designed to process data and occurrences stored in system's memory (RAM), with the intention of eliminating the need for physical data storage. Database systems of this type are easy to use, but – more importantly – offer unparalleled effectiveness and throughput (compared to traditional database systems), owing to their use of advanced structural solutions and greatly simplified architecture.
5. Software in support of the implementation of cognitive agent systems (see Sect. 3 for detailed characteristics of this class).

In reference to the above technologies, it may also be worth noting that the first four classes of solutions (cloud computing, grid computing, in-database processing and in-memory databases) represent a problem solving approach typical for large scale databases and scalability of infrastructure, whereas the last one (software in support of cognitive agent system implementation) is a representation of intelligent software class of solutions.

Another interesting aspect in the context under study is the use of modern technologies representing the 'big data' class of solutions, which may lead to sizeable effectiveness improvements in decision-making processes, and – in effect – improvements in company overall effectiveness and competitiveness, mainly by processing high amount of structured and unstructured knowledge near real time.

Introduction of a CIMIS solution offers good potential for automation of many business processes through delegation of certain decision-making authorities to cognitive agents, based not only on structured knowledge, but also on heterogeneous and unstructured knowledge.

To sum up, the most important characteristics of the postulated CIMIS approach include:

– Support for the realization of business processes in all areas of company economic involvement, based on the use of modern information and telecommunication technologies;

- Integration of knowledge management processes (both structured and unstructured sets) through facilitated knowledge flow between subsystems and through integration of knowledge; these processes are also important for the improvement of employee qualifications - they have more time for development and creative work;
- Potential for automated issue of decisions and self-learning capabilities (offered by the use of cognitive agent systems);
- Potential for producing various analyses and managerial reports.

It must also be observed that the operation of cognitive agent systems still requires human supervision, at least to a certain degree – particularly with respect to self-learning processes, but also in continuous monitoring of services rendered by already 'learned' agents.

One of the most important services rendered by cognitive agents within MIS systems is the processing of knowledge, particularly that of unstructured type. Problems and challenges associated with unstructured knowledge will be addressed in detail in the next sub-section.

2.3 Characteristics of Unstructured Knowledge in MIS

Knowledge is the fundamental notion for all decision-making processes; it involves experiences, values assessment, context information and analytical insight into the matter, which provides frames for incorporating and assessing new information and experiences [9]. Knowledge is defined in various ways. Three main approaches to the definition of knowledge concentrate on the following aspects [31, 61]:

- structural elements of knowledge, of which the most important is the isolation of certain areas of knowledge, and hence, the treatment of background knowledge as a segment of totality,
- 'mechanics' of knowledge, that is an attempt to put some mechanisms to knowledge acquisition by investigating causes of specific effects,
- "openness" of knowledge, i.e. the assumption that knowledge is never complete, it can always be expanded.

The Oxford dictionaries defines knowledge as: "Facts, information, and skills acquired through experience or education; the theoretical or practical understanding of a subject", also as "The sum of what is known" and "Information held on a computer system" [62]. Some literature studies [63, 64] summarize the definitions of knowledge as related to business organizations noting that knowledge is the basic concept for all decision-making processes, and recognizing that it represents a combination of experience, assessments of values and context of information, as well as an analytical insight into the issue, which provides a framework for incorporating new experiences and information, and their evaluation.

In [65], the authors assumed that knowledge is a subsidiary of contextual information, and that knowledge means understanding (comprehension) of the importance of information. Knowledge is a value added to information by a human or an intelligent computer system, with the experience and ability to comprehend its real potential. Therefore, only by associating information with experience and taking into account the context in which information and experiences are studied, one can produce knowledge, which is the causative factor in the decision-making processes in business organizations.

Taking into account some of the issues related to collective knowledge in business organizations, Dixon [64] notes that the need for leveraging this knowledge arises when organizations have to function under increasingly difficult and complex conditions, such as the turbulent environment and the effects of Big Data.

Hecker [31] distinguishes the following three types of this knowledge:

1. Knowledge shared by a group of individuals, which is acquired from common knowledge and experiences gathered in the course of shared activities.
2. Complementary knowledge, generated as result of interaction, in a complementary way, between individuals. This type of knowledge will not exist on an individual basis.
3. Knowledge not embedded in human mindsets and actions but in collective artefacts, such as organizational rules, processes definitions, products and manufacturing technologies.

In [66, 67], the authors found that all types of knowledge must be considered together. They developed a co-evolution model of individual and collective knowledge.

Knowledge (in its intuitive meaning) can be:

4. Descriptive or procedural. Descriptive knowledge is expressed in declarative sentences or indicative propositions. This is "know-that" knowledge. The procedural is the knowledge of how, and especially how best, to perform some task. This is "know-how" knowledge [68].
5. Explicit or tacit. Explicit knowledge is expressed in character form and stored on knowledge carriers. Tacit knowledge existing only in the mind of the human (or intelligent agent) who owns it. It is created as a result of experience and not fully realized ("I know that I can do it"), manifested only through skilful action [69].
6. Qualitative or quantitative. The qualitative is usually concerned only with qualities such as gross behavior, while the quantitative requires recourse to equations and mathematics [70].
7. Individual or collective. Individual knowledge is possess by individual unit (human, intelligent agent), collective knowledge is possess by group of individuals [66].

In the context of this study, the most important distinction is the classification of knowledge into the following types:

1. Structured knowledge – knowledge stored in machine-processable form (e.g. knowledge warehouses, RDF repositories); in other words, knowledge that can be stored in a structured order of elements and relations between them.
2. Unstructured knowledge – available and distributed through websites, company internal Content Management System (CMS) and repositories, in an unstructured form, for instance as textual document, web pages, multimedia material (e.g., photos, diagrams, videos, voices) and contextual knowledge. This type of knowledge cannot be stored in a structured order. Indeed, as observed in [65], unstructured knowledge accounts for more than 90% of the digital universe.

In management information systems, unstructured knowledge comes mainly in the form of non-formatted text databases which store various types of text documents, such as news reports, e-books, e-mail messages, WWW pages and other written content. Those documents describe or otherwise reference real-world events that occur in the company environment. Hence, the main focus in this section will be placed on the examination of unstructured knowledge stored in text document formats.

The principal characteristics of text documents are that they do not follow any specific structural order – in other words, knowledge stored in those documents is unstructured or poorly structured. For instance, a typical e-mail structure provides certain bits of information in an organized manner, to help identify the sender, the recipient, the volume of message, the subject, and so on. However, the content of the message is represented by a sequence of characters which follow no particular format of internal structure. Nonetheless, and let us emphasize it once again at this point, text documents are often an important source of valuable knowledge.

From the viewpoint of its adaptation to management information purposes, unstructured knowledge can be characterizes by the following attributes:

1. Non-depletable – new knowledge (particularly in virtual space) is generated at a speed that cannot be served by the present processing capabilities of information systems used in business organizations [71].
2. Streaming – unstructured knowledge is no longer a resource; it comes in flow format.
3. Non-linearity – there is no direct correlation between the amount of knowledge held and the benefits resulting from its use in practice. Large knowledge repositories are no longer a factor of impact on the company's market position, but they can obviously be employed in the task of securing that position in the first place. The most decisive factor here is the ability to utilize it to good effect [72].
4. Simultaneity. The same piece of information can be used by multiple organizational units at the same time, regardless of their physical location. Owning knowledge does not give rights to assume the sole ownership of such knowledge or methods of its utilization. To gain and sustain their competitive advantage, companies must be able to utilize available knowledge well ahead of the competition [73].
5. Problem with representation in digital format – the use of any of the available methods of representation (see Sect. 2.5 for detailed characteristics) results invariably in effective loss of some parts of knowledge. It requires AI way of thinking which is different from traditional IT way of thinking and switching between this two mental schemas is sometimes not trivial.
6. Difficult to process in automated manner – despite the current wealth of methods for automated processing of unstructured knowledge (see Sect. 2.6 for detailed characteristics), the quality of results produced by such algorithms are less precise that offered by human processing capabilities.
7. Dominance. This quality describes the prioritized position of knowledge (particularly the unstructured knowledge) in relation to other types of resources at company disposal. Knowledge is of strategic significance for the operation of modern

business organization. It also determines, to a certain extent, their competitive advantage on the market. Often skilful use of the available knowledge can offer major improvements in the management of other resources, and – in effect – help secure the strategic company objectives.

Unstructured knowledge can be utilized in management information systems provided that it satisfies certain requirements. Of these, the most fundamental ones are as follows:

1. Practical utility – knowledge processed by the system must ultimately be usable for managerial purposes to support the realization of business processes (including support for decision-making tasks) [74]. Processing of useless knowledge reduces the effectiveness and efficiency of other processes (not to mention the unwarranted increase of knowledge management expenditures).
2. Value for the organization – it must be noted that value attached to specific knowledge is a highly subjective measure; the same piece of knowledge may be found of great value for some, and be regarded of no value by others.
3. Reliability. Information is considered reliable if it can be verified in several independent sources. With regard to knowledge, reliability assessments are much more complex. Knowledge is generated from conclusions drawn on the basis of information, but the reasoning process (be it human, or based on automated IT services) may be approached from various angles. Thus, based on the same information, different systems will produce different knowledge and will store it in a different format. In effect, knowledge from one source may be considered reliable, although it cannot be verified based on other sources.
4. Timeliness – decisions must be made on the basis of most current knowledge. If a source provides outdated knowledge, the resulting delay in response may reduce the level of satisfaction from such a decision. Therefore, the system should be able to perform automated query of other sources to gather the most current knowledge.

2.4   Coherence Between Structured and Unstructured Knowledge in the Functioning of Management Information Systems

Note that knowledge contained in MISs is normally structuralized and the systems employ various methods for processing structured knowledge. However, in contemporary companies, unstructured knowledge is essential, mainly due to its potential for improving the flexibility and competitiveness of the organization. Therefore, unstructured knowledge supports structured knowledge to a high degree. It is mainly stored in natural language, therefore it must involve processing of symbols (rather than numbers), e.g. users' opinions as posted on the company's forum. Generally speaking, this type of knowledge is stored in text databases that contain various types of text files, such as newspaper articles, e-books, e-mails, websites and all sorts of text files. The documents describe certain phenomena that occur in the real world, in the environment where a given organization operates. Text files are not internally structured in any way, the knowledge that they contain is non-structuralized or structuralized to a small degree. For example, the structure of an e-mail message contains information on sender, addressee, size, subject, but the rest of the message is a stream of symbols deprived of internal structure. It is important to say that text files are often a source of significant and useful knowledge.

Two basic categories of sources of unstructured knowledge can be distinguished in the analyzed context, namely:

1. External sources, including, among other:
   - company internal documents,
   - corporate web portals,
   - Enterprise Content Management systems (ECM),
   - reports from meetings,
   - collaborative spaces,
   - enterprise social networks,
2. External sources (accessed mostly via the Internet), including, among other:
   - websites of external business organizations,
   - portals (news providers, social networks, thematic and specialist portals),
   - online shops,
   - Internet forums,
   - customers' knowledge about competitors,
   - blogs.

Automated processing of unstructured knowledge for business purposes in management information systems is typically employed in the following areas and applications:

1. Monitoring of external environment, including:
   - monitoring of competitors,
   - expert analyses of the current condition of the markets, economies, finance, and politics,
   - Analyses of customer opinions on company operation and on the range of products and services on offer.
2. Monitoring of internal environment, including:
   - analyses of the effectiveness of business processes, formed on the basis of documents that describe such processes,
   - analyses of employee opinions on the realization of business processes,
3. Financial investments, including:
   - expert analyses and evaluations of present condition of listed companies, forecasts of securities ratings and currency exchange rates,
   - analyses of investor moods,
4. Summarizations of text documents.
5. Reducing the risk of business operations.

With respect to the **monitoring of competitors**, it may be observed that knowledge on the pricing and the quality of competitive products or services comes mostly in structured format. However, this knowledge is not sufficient to provide a basis for rational planning of future activities. It must be supplemented by knowledge of development plans and activities undertaken by the competitor (e.g. innovations), which is mostly available in an unstructured form (e.g. expressed as text statements on a company website). Only then rational decisions can be made on the future strategies or actions to be adopted in response.

In the course of their business operation, companies must take stock of current knowledge on **the present condition of markets, economies, finance, and politics**, both in local, national, and global dimension. This sort of knowledge is, to some extent, available in a structured order, in the form of various indices and gauges of economic performance, such as: GDP, inflation rate, unemployment rate, sales turnover (globally and per sector), value of exports and imports, and so on. Those measures may represent current values or expected targets and forecasts. However, managerial decisions should also incorporate knowledge generated from expert opinions or even political announcements, as those messages can be of great impact upon the balance of demand and supply on local, national, or even global markets.

Taking into account **customer opinions on products and services** supplied by the organization, it should be observed that respondents display a broad spectrum of opinions: positive, negative, or non-committing. In addition, opinions may also target specific attributes of such products or services: while the general opinion on the product or service may be positive, some customers may emphasize certain negative attributes. To add to the complexity, public exchanges in online settings may reach hundreds if not millions of individual opinions on the same product or service. Therefore, human capabilities are not adequate to effectively process and analyze this type of content. At the same time, it may prove highly beneficial to keep current track of such exchange (e.g. by means of product/attribute opinions' polarity[5] evaluations) since this knowledge may serve to improve the operation of management support systems and, in effect, improve company flexibility and competitive advantage. Based on opinion analyses, one may predict, to a high degree of probability, the future trends in product/service sale – this type of conclusion cannot be made solely on the basis of structured knowledge stored in transactional systems, as the effects of such knowledge upon the sales figures for specific product or service are often delayed (cf. Fig. 2). And then it is usually too late to come forward with a satisfying decision. Automated analyses of customer opinions can also help determine those attributes of analyzed product or service which are in great demand among customers. In effect, the company may introduce changes in response to their customers' specific requirements. Results of opinion analyses may, for instance, be employed as basis for changes in production plans to increase the supply of products or services that satisfy the demand expressed by the majority of customers. Of course, decision making on the basis of example presented on Fig. 2 may also lead to errors in marketing strategy, especially in mass retail, where purchasing organization decides what client has to buy (for example Amazon).

---

[5] Opinion polarity is used to differentiate between negative and positive opinions; some sources refer to the process as sentiment analysis.

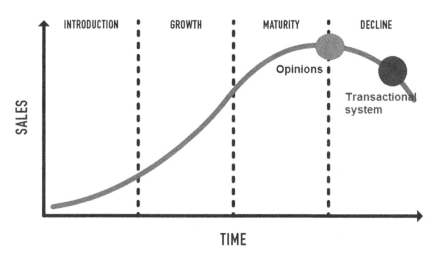

Fig. 2. Sales forecasts based on analyses of structured (transaction systems) and unstructured knowledge (customers' opinions). Source: own work on the basis of [75].

Another important element of effective management is the analysis and monitoring of the current realization of business processes based on documents that describe such processes. This is also another area of coherence between structured and unstructured knowledge. The majority of parameters and gauges of performance used in description of business processes come in structured form. These are typically represented by quantitative measures (technological parameters of production processes, finance and accounting indices). However, to establish the real reasons and effects of certain phenomena, particularly those that represent non-standard solutions, this type of knowledge must be supplemented by detailed analyses (provided in a natural language) to help interpret the causes and effects of changes in quantitative parameters and indices.

Analyses of employee opinions on the practical realization of business processes are also of value for management, as they are often the most reliable source of information on specific problems and shortcomings and – at the same time – a source of competent knowledge on how to improve the practical realization of business processes.

Financial investments represent another area of strong coherence between structured and unstructured knowledge. Management information systems offer support for financial decision-making based on instruments of technical analysis[6] (operating on structured knowledge), but managers can also make good use of observations based on

---

[6] Technical analysis examines current rates and turnover against points of reference and historical data to establish values of assorted indices. This type of analysis can be employed even when without knowledge on the issuer of securities.

fundamental[7] or behavioral analysis[8], based on processing of knowledge held by experts or other investors. This type of information can be obtained from web pages of brokerage offices and banking institutions as well as social networking portals and blogs related to finance. They are typically stored in a natural language and, as such, pose the same problems as other types of processes that operate on unstructured knowledge.

Speaking of the use of expert opinions and opinions of other investors in forecasting future rates and prices of securities, it must be observed that respondents display a broad spectrum of opinions: positive, negative, or non-committing. In addition, expert opinions include detailed evaluations and substantiations. To add to the complexity, public exchanges in online settings may reach hundreds if not millions of individual opinions. To produce knowledge from this type of content, investors must perform analyses and **summarizations** of opinions as basis for their decisions made on financial matters. Human capabilities are not adequate to process and analyze this type of content in an effective and timely fashion, therefore generation of this type of knowledge must be tasked to automated systems that operate on analyses and summarizations of text documents. Summarization, in this context, may apply to contents of individual documents or whole sets of documents. The basic assumption here is that the automated summary should retain all the important information presented in a source document. Summary size is typically employed as one of the process parameters. Automated summaries help users avoid unnecessary commitment required in analyses and detailed readings of source documents and keep their focus on the most important aspects as needed for the purpose of making effective and timely decisions.

Another area to display strong coherence between structured and unstructured knowledge is the **limitation of risk associated with business operation**. Here, application of structured knowledge applies mainly to quantitative measures of risk, such as value at risk, the Sharpe ratio, or various changeability indices. Unstructured knowledge in this context is used mainly in qualitative evaluation of risk. This may involve automated analyses of texts related to business operation of partners and contractors (including, and not limited to: evaluation of financial position, analyses of opinions from employees, customers and suppliers, or analyses of communication and warnings issued by public administration authorities). Having easy access to such information may help limit the risk of potential losses.

This section presented a broad overview of areas that display strong coherence between structured and unstructured knowledge and their use in management information systems. It must be noted, however, that coherence between those two forms of knowledge is observed in all the areas covered and supported by modern management information systems. Therefore, processing of unstructured knowledge should be seen as an important and indispensable element of MIS design. However, to be effectively

---

[7] Fundamental analysis involves the study of a company or other issuer's financial position, their strengths and weaknesses, and perspectives for development. It serves to address the question on the viability of investing in specific type of sectrities (this can also be done across whole economies, as in the case of currency exchange rates.

[8] Behavioural analysis involves the study of behaviours and preferences of financial market participants.

used in business practice, unstructured knowledge used in this process must take a specific form of representation (just like structured knowledge in traditional applications). The next section will present the most fundamental methods used for representation of unstructured knowledge in management information systems.

2.5 Modeling and Representation of Unstructured Knowledge in Management Information Systems

In order to be used effectively, knowledge must be described by some sort of representation that can be stored, processed and transmitted between subsystems. In other words, knowledge must be modeled and registered in the form of a knowledge base. This construct may be produced in a natural language (based on written content). However, to be of any use for management information system's algorithms, representations of such knowledge should be computer-interpretable and, at the same time, they should retain their most essential descriptive properties. Representation of knowledge (result of the modelling sub-process) is defined as 'a specific form of mapping of facts, properties and states of objects in a given area of application used for the purpose of making informed conclusions' [73].

Taking into consideration multi-agent MIS, there are many different methods for agents' structured knowledge representation. The main ones include first-order predicate logic, artificial neural networks multi-attributes and multi-values structures, multi valued logic, fuzzy logic [76–82].

Due to the fact that management information systems are also tasked with automated analyses of the real significance of registered facts and business processes that occur in company environment (cf. Sect. 2.1), formal representations of knowledge (particularly of unstructured type) must also retain any semantic relations that describe such objects.

Management information systems should support the following types of representations of unstructured knowledge:

– text documents,
– graphics,
– video,
– sound.

Since text documents are the most widely used form of recording used for storing unstructured knowledge, this publication places emphasis on textual forms of knowledge representation. Professional literature provides a broad scope of methods that can be used in the representation of text documents, including [9, 83][9]:

– keyword representation,
– vectorial representation – Vector Space Model[10],

---

[9] In this work we consider mainly methods related to third generation of artificial intelligence. There also methods related to previous generations of AI, such as rules, frames, statements.

[10] An algebraic model for representing text documents (and any objects, in general) as vectors of identifiers, such as, for example, index terms [83].

- ontologies,
- semantic Web,
- semantic networks.

Text files are often represented in databases by **keywords** – specific phrases contained in the text (as a symbolical representation of knowledge). However, such representation makes it difficult to make comparisons between documents, especially when it comes to measuring distance between documents – with distance defined as similarity between documents [84].

An alternative approach to representation of text files is an approach based on **vectorial representation** (numerical representation of knowledge). The basic idea of vectorial representation comes down to the fact that any document is represented as a vector of frequency of keyword occurrences. Thus, set N of stored text files can be presented as Term Frequency Matrix (TFM), whose element TFM[d_i, t_i] represents the number of keyword t_i occurrences in document d_i [9]. Any document d_i, $1 < i < N$, is represented as a vector of frequency of keyword occurrences. Element TFM[d_i, t_i] represents word weight of word t_i in document d_i. In the simplest Bool's representation, word weight in a vector of a document can assume only two values: 0 or 1. Word weight of word t_i in document d_i equal 1 means that word t_i occurs in a given document d_i, whereas, if word t_i does not occur in document di then word weight of word t_i in document d_i equals 0. Note that Bool's representation of documents only states whether or not the keyword occurs. Therefore, for instance, a document with a single keyword occurrence is equal to a document where the same keyword occurs many times. Thus, Bool's representation of documents corresponds to their representation based on keywords. In terms of calculating distance, full representation of documents seems far more useful. In this type of representation, word weight corresponds to its occurrence in documents. For instance, if a keyword can be found twice in a document, then word weight of the document is 2, whereas if the keyword occurs fifty times in another document, then word weight of that document is 50.

A set of key words used in TFM-oriented approach to document representation may be very large. The matrix can also be used to represent unstructured knowledge in distributed management systems.

The main advantage of vectorial representation of documents, compared to key-word set-based representation, is the ability to define the measure of distance between documents or user query. If vectorial representation of documents is defined, then documents of similar topics should be characterized by similar occurrence of the same keywords. Having vectorial representation of documents at one's disposal, it is possible to interpret each document as point T in dimensional space, with dimensions corresponding to particular keywords.

Quoting after [85], knowledge representation models used in modern management information systems should satisfy the following requirements:

- presenting output in a format readable for humans,
- processable by IT systems,
- expandable,
- representing knowledge in a form proper for the area or problem at hand.

To ensure the inclusion of the above properties in management information systems, designers may choose to employ some of the available semantic methods of knowledge representation (such as ontologies, semantic web, semantic networks).

There are many definitions of **ontologies** depending on different fields of science. In this work we pay attention mainly on formal definitions. The work [86] defines a formal ontology as a mathematical theory of certain entities, formulated in a formal, artificial language, which in turn is based on some logical system like first order logic, or some form of the lambda calculus, or the like. The work [42], in turn state, that ontology defines a set of representational primitives with which to model a domain of knowledge or discourse. The representational primitives are typically classes (or sets), attributes (or properties), and relationships (or relations among class members). The work [87] defines an ontology as a special kind of information object or computational artifact, a formally model the structure of a system, i.e., the relevant entities and relations that emerge from its observation, and which are useful to given purpose.

Ontology is typically formally defined by the following elements [88]:

Definition 1

$$O = \langle C, I, R \rangle \tag{1}$$

where:

$C-$ set of concepts (classes),
$I -$ set of instances of concepts,
$R -$ set of binary relations defined on C. ◆

It is assumed that ontology refers to the slice of reality $<A, V>$.
Detailed definitions of ontology presented further in the section refer to three levels:

- concepts level,
- instances level,
- relations level.

Definition 2
A concept of an $<A, V>$ - based ontology is defined as triple:

$$C = \langle c, A^v, V^c \rangle, \tag{2}$$

where:

$c -$ the unique name of the concept,
$A^c \in A -$ set of attributes describing the concept,
$V^c \in V -$ the attributes' domain:
$V^c = \cup_{\langle A,v \rangle \in A^c} V_a$. ◆

Pair $\langle A^c, V^c \rangle$ is called the structure of concept c.

Definition 3

An instance of a concept c is described by the attributes from set A^n with values from set V^c and is defined as follows:

$$\text{instance} = \langle i, v \rangle \tag{3}$$

where i is the unique identifier of the instance in world <A, V> and v is the value of the instance, a tuple of type A^n and can be presented as a function: $v : A^c \rightarrow V^c$, such that $v(a) \in V_a$ for all $a \in A^c$. ♦

Value v is also called a description of the instance within a concept. A concept may be interpreted as a set of all instances described by its structure. We can then write $i \in c$ for presenting the fact that i is an instance of concept c.

Definition 4

Let set S of concepts is given. Relation is defined as follows:

$$R = \langle c, c' \rangle. \tag{4}$$

where:

$c, c' \in N$. ♦

Semantic Web allows for searching not only information but also knowledge. Its main purpose is introducing structure and semantic content in the huge amount of unstructured or semi-structured distributed knowledge available on the Web, being the central notion behind the Semantic Web that of ontologies, which describe concepts and their relations in a particular field of knowledge [82].

Semantic networks [89] are knowledge representation schemes involving nodes and links (arcs or arrows) between nodes. Nodes represent objects or concepts and links represent relations between nodes. The links are directed and labelled; thus, a semantic network is a directed graph. In print, nodes are usually represented by circles or boxes and links are drawn as arrows between them.

The use of semantic networks allows for a broad representation of knowledge with focus on correlations between objects. This type of network is typically drafted in graphical form, with nodes representing notions (be it measurable or abstract) and arcs describing relations between individual nodes [89]. Professional literature provides many models of semantic networks. Due to their specificity, semantic networks can be adjusted to serve a broad spectrum of applications. Analyses of semantic networks suggest that their use may improve cooperation and coordination, both in human teams and in automated systems. To satisfy the requirements of end users, those solutions use visualizations of formal structures of the predefined information resources. Another type of ontological knowledge representation, the topic map standard, introduced by International Organization for Standardization (ISO/IEC 13250:2000), is also used. Topic maps are a class of semantic networks which allows for storing information on data ontology and data taxonomy in a semantically ordered manner [90]. A topic map most often consists of "parent-child" relations.

Methods used for representation of other content in management information systems are well documented in professional literature; representations of graphics are discussed in [91, 92], representation of video content is addressed in [93, 94], and sound representation methods are presented in [95, 96].

It must be emphasized at this point that semantic methods may just as well be used for the representation of non-textual content such as graphics, video and sound, after suitable transformations. The use of proper methods for the representation of unstructured knowledge in management information systems offers basis for the automated realization of tasks involved in knowledge acquisition, processing and validation. These sub-processes are the focus of the next sub-section.

2.6 Acquisition, Processing and Validation of Unstructured Knowledge in Management Information Systems

The acquisition and processing of unstructured knowledge stored in text documents can be obtained based on the following methods [97, 98]:

- information (document) retrieval,
- information extraction,
- text exploration,
- natural language processing.

The main purpose of **information retrieval** (IE) is to provide responses to user queries from the content of text files stored in system repositories. To meet this purpose, designers must utilize advanced methods and techniques that offer good evaluation of conformity or semblance between the texts and the essence of the user's query. Information retrieval systems do not inform the user on the subject at hand – they only provide information on the location of documents that correspond with the subject of the query (or report the lack of any such content) [99]. In a typical IR system, users formulate queries composed of one or many words, to be used as patterns for auto-mated search passes.

Information extraction (IE) involves identification of instances in a predefined class of events, their correlations, and their occurrences in documents written in a natural language [100]. IE systems do not produce links to specific documents – they automatically extract information from their content. The type of information to be extracted from documents is defined by users in the form of extraction patterns. Therefore, information extraction should not be mistaken for information retrieval, text mining or complete understanding of the context of texts. IE is typically used in the following areas [101]:

- named entity extraction, aims at finding real-world objects in texts and classifying these objects into predefined categories such as names of persons, organizations, locations, temporal expressions, products, etc.; this angle is covered in [102, 103],
- general entity extraction, aim at finding domain-independent entities with highest possible precision, but acceptable recall; this area is addressed, for example, in [104–106].
- characteristics and attributes of entities extraction, aims at automatically building highly complete profiles for entities; this area is addressed, for example, in [107, 108],

- classes of entities extraction, aims at classifying all extracted entities with respect to suitable concepts; this area is addressed, for example, in [109, 110].
- general relationships between entities aims at finding relationship between entities on the general, mainly semantic level; this area is addressed, for example, in [111, 112].

The purpose of **text exploration** is to mine for information buried in text files using text mass processing methods [113]. One of the main tasks of this technique is to identify text occurrences of objects belonging to a given class or of any relations between them, which are then transformed into a structured form, such as a database. Results of these processes may also be analyzed using further text mining procedures and techniques. The most popular and most common tasks of text exploration are [31, 113]:

- grouping of text files (dividing the initial set of documents into sets that contain most similar documents),
- classifying text files (assigning documents to existing groups),
- document importance ranking,
- analyzing relations between documents (e.g. quote network analysis).
- summarizing (producing a summary that contains the most important information from the source document). A summary can express the content of a single document or a set of documents. One of the parameters of this process is the text volume. A good document summary frees the system user (investor, manager) from the need to read and analyze all of the text documents, and give them opportunity to focus their attention on those aspects which are of essence for making a timely and effective decision.

Natural language processing involves the use of mechanisms for automated "understanding' of the context of text under study. Methods of this category are not involved with term semblance; they operate on broader categories of text analysis, such as [114, 115]:

1. Shallow text analysis, offering a limited set of results compared to deep text analysis. Typical limitations include the restricted identification of non-recurrent or limited-recurrence structures. Structures that require complex analyses of possible scenarios are disregarded or subject to partial analyses. Shallow text analysis is typically employed in the recognition of names, noun phrases and verb groups, without analytical evaluation of their internal structure and function in a sentence. They can also identify basic sentence groups, such as predicate clauses. In addition, they may support the realization of such processes as:
   - tokenization,
   - sentence boundary detection,
   - morphological analysis,
   - elimination of disambiguation,
   - replacement of pronouns,
   - detection of proper nouns,
   - transformation of compound sentences into simple sentences,
   - sentence parsing.

2. Deep text analysis involves computer-aided linguistic analyses of all possible interpretations and grammatical relations found in texts written in a natural language. This type of analysis may prove quite complex; in addition, the resulting information may just as well prove unnecessary. Deep text analyses are typically conducted using Head-Driven Phrase Structure Grammar (HPSG). HPSG is a linguistic framework with substantial wealth of support documentation. As such, it can easily be adopted for typical applications that involve an established set of grammatical analyses, as the method is linguistically grounded and has been confirmed for use by scientific scrutiny. It also has a positive impact in reusability and extendibility, because more people can understand it immediately. HPSGs associate grammatical representations with natural language expressions, including the formal representation of their meaning [116, 117].

Machine learning [118] is an example of shallow text analysis based on frequency analyses of term occurrences within a document set. For example, [119] presents a method for determination of references to product attributes in text documents based on support vector machines, while [120–122] describe approaches to examination of opinion polarity in texts, but only with respect to general opinions rather than those related to specific attributes. In [123–125] authors present an opinion recognition method based on statistically measured comparisons against previously annotated word lexicons. The work [126] presents, in turn, a multi-strategy machine learning, where different learning strategies are used. They depends on actual situation in the environment.

Another useful instrument for both shallow and deep text analyses is the use of rules for annotation (identification) of text fragments that refer to specific subjects. Such rules may be introduced on the basis of templates describing relations between words and semantic classes of words; rules can be generated on the grounds of automated decisions or human analyses of annotated corpuses [100]. Rule-based text analysis involves attribution of meanings to identified fragments of text based on attributes expressed in rules, to be used, for instance, as basis for document categorization. A well-documented approach to rule-based analysis is presented, among others, in [116] in the context of a Semantic Cyberspace Monitoring project for the automated identification of illicit drug trade offers on the Internet.

Modern applications of both shallow and deep text analysis may also include instruments for ontological representation of text in the form of semantic networks, e.g. topic maps. As suggested in [85], topic maps offers potential for storing semantically ordered information on ontology and taxonomy of data and – at the same time – enables good representation of knowledge (both structured and unstructured) on various hierarchical and semantic relations between economic notions (used in text documents related to management and economics). Ontology can also be employed for the recognition of opinion polarity, as described, among others, in [97]. This sort of textual content representation can be obtained, for instance, through the use of cognitive agent systems cooperating within a multi-agent structure. This solution not only helps analyze the polarity of user opinions, but may also trigger automated decisions and actions (responses) based on the result of such analyses. Very important issue in this context is automated concepts extraction. The work [127], for example, presents an approach for building a lexical ontology in Polish (as a WorldNet) called PolNet. Also [128]. Ontological approach for natural language processing, by using TextHunter tool, is, in turn, presented in [128]. The authors develop a suite of language models to capture key symptoms of severe mental illness from clinical text, to facilitate the secondary use of mental healthcare data in research.

With respect to acquisition and processing of graphics and video, it may be observed that computer vision methods (diagnostic digital image, video analysis) are already present in MIS. Vision systems are used, among others, to control various processes and to identify characteristics of objects. The last decade saw a large increase in the number of research studies on assessment of quality of food and agricultural products on the basis of objective instrumental measurements, especially techniques based on image recognition. This technique allows for automated analyses, evaluations and classifications based on specific attributes, such as color, texture, shape, size, and on any relations between these parameters [129]. Computer image analysis as a non-destructive method offering fast, reproducible and objective evaluation of visual properties, is often used for measuring and predicting the quality of agricultural and food commodities and proves quite effective in overcoming the limitations of traditional methods used so far.

With respect to sound processing, speech recognition is the most widely used method. It represents a set of methodologies and technologies that enable recognition and translation of spoken language into text by computers [130]. The main areas of business operation to benefit from speech recognition services include the following [131]:

- consumer communication (voice dialing, unified messaging, voice portals, and access to services for people with disabilities),
- e-commerce (business-to-business and business-to-consumer),
- call center automation (helplines and customer care),
- enterprise communication (unified messaging and enterprise sales).

Processing of knowledge is strictly related to knowledge validation. This process serves to maintain the required quality of knowledge and can be considered as a determined composition of two kinds of tasks [132, 133]:

1. Verification - activities that intend to reach the structural correctness of the knowledge base (KB). It is identified by following criteria:
   (a) completeness (the share of implemented knowledge in the entire hypothetical knowledge on the subject). A knowledge base is complete if all possible conclusions can be reached by the system.
   (b) consistency (relations between individual components of knowledge). A knowledge base is consistent if it lacks contradictive and redundant knowledge.
2. Evaluation - activities that intend to demonstrate the KB ability to reach correct conclusions. It is identified by following criteria:
   (a) adequacy (relation between KB purpose and KB content). Knowledge adequacy refers basically to domain knowledge. Therefore, evaluating adequacy of

knowledge can be performed in relation to domain knowledge in the context of the system's assumed goals,

(b) reliability (evaluation of results of applied knowledge). If results of reasoning are correct then it may come to the conclusion about satisfying reliability of knowledge. In this case it treat the whole system with knowledge base of its own, as a black-box.

(c) economics (relation between effects and outlays). Knowledge is economic when its economic effects are higher than the associated economic outlays. This criterion is very difficult to evaluate since economic effects and outlays are also influenced by many other factors. Economic effects can be evaluated using simulators and right key performance indicators (KPI).

Each of the criteria presented above may be evaluated using different measures. Selected measures will be described in detail in Sect. 4.

It is only natural that such a broad selection of sources and methods of unstructured knowledge processing, coupled with wide assortment of decision-support methods and criteria of evaluation may result in conflicts between distinct sets of knowledge generated by individual subsystems of MIS. Reasons for emergence of such conflicts and their most important effects will be the subject of the last sub-section.

2.7 Reasons for the Emergence of Knowledge Conflicts in MIS and Their Potential Effects

Practical operation of management information systems will naturally lead to generation of conflicting sets of knowledge (both structured and unstructured) produced by individual cognitive agents. The main reasons for the emergence of knowledge conflicts in MIS include the following [7, 134, 135]:

1. System dispersion, in particular:
   - dispersion of goals and tasks; any given task may be solved by numerous agents and each agent utilizes their own method of support; in addition, individual agents are tasked with realization of largely independent goals which in themselves may be seen as conflicting or mutually exclusive,
   - dispersion of information and knowledge; information as basis for knowledge generation or automated decision making by cognitive agents is accumulated from heterogeneous sources and agents may have access to only partial information or knowledge required for processing – this may lead to knowledge conflicts between agents, particularly when the task at hand involves collective transformation of information into knowledge by many agents; also real experts and those who want to be considered as expert (social network/youtube activity) may be a source of conflict; it can be discovered by crossing links and text mining.
2. The lack of centralized agent control and coordination mechanisms – agents do not follow any predetermined course of action – they continuously negotiate their own goals and actions, which may result in knowledge conflicts,

3. Autonomy of cognitive agents – agents are capable of determining their own goals and methods for their realization, they are designed to prioritize actions that maximize their own profits,
4. Scarcity of resources or limited access to resources – such as bandwidth or system memory limitations.

Thus, it may be assumed that knowledge conflicts in multi-agent MISs are the result of incoherence or contradiction between sets of knowledge generated by individual cognitive agents. Incoherence represents a scenario when one agent confirms or negates the occurrence of a given object's property or attribute in a given timeframe while another agent has no information on the matter at hand or chooses to withhold it [136]. Contradiction, on the other hand, refers to a scenario when one agent confirms the occurrence of such attribute in a given timeframe while another agent reports its absence [136]. Therefore, knowledge conflicts are generated when the same real world object is assigned with different attributes or when different values are assigned to the same attribute by two or more agents.

According to [138, 139], the most important sources of knowledge conflicts (also with respect to unstructured knowledge) include the following:

1. Strife for control over a particular resource. Knowledge conflicts arise when one agent believes that the other has no right to access information on a particular resource, while the other agent believes to be in the right to demand it.
2. Ideological conflict. This represents a scenario with two or more agents displaying conflicting beliefs in the matter at hand. These may come as a result of differences in operating environments or different assumptions on the viable course of action.
3. Required level of integration between elements. If a system is designed to integrate several elements, conflicts will naturally occur (e.g. differences in knowledge structure or methods of knowledge representation).
4. Control over the knowledge management system. Conflicts may arise when each agent assumes the right of control over knowledge management processes.

Detailed analyses of reasons for the incidence of conflicts related to unstructured knowledge suggest that their complexity runs much deeper than that observed with respect to structured knowledge. This can be attributed to the following phenomena:

– heterogeneity of meanings attached to textual content written in a natural language; two fragments of text composed of the same set of words can bear two different meanings; similarly, two texts of different composition may express the same meaning,
– heterogeneity of results produced by unstructured knowledge processing algorithms; if two or more agents use different methods for the processing of unstructured knowledge, the results of such processing will be different even though the textual content remains unchanged,
– heterogeneity of methods used for representation of unstructured knowledge[11]; the same fragment of text may be represented through various methods.

---

[11] See Sect. 2 for a detailed review of unstructured knowledge representation methods and techniques.

The above phenomena may also apply, to some extent, to structured knowledge, but their manifestations are decidedly more profound with respect to knowledge of unstructured type.

As a result of knowledge conflicts, agents in management information systems may produce dissimilar sets of decisions or solutions. In other words, the emergence of knowledge conflicts prevents the system from reaching a satisfying conclusion (i.e. producing a decision that satisfies certain user-defined criteria expressed in parameters, e.g. a specific margin of return on investment at a given risk level). Consequently, decision makers will not receive adequate support from the system and will have to manually perform analytical evaluations of solutions fed by different agents. Naturally, this may prove arduous and lengthy, and the resulting decision may be outdated. Under the present turbulent environment of economic operation, decisions need to be made in near real time, and decisions made on the grounds of incomplete information are burdened with excessive risk. Therefore, the emergence of knowledge conflicts may seriously affect the operation of the organization as a whole.

It should be emphasized at this point that knowledge conflicts in management information systems should never be ignored nor rooted out; they need to be properly identified, classified and resolved. Only then the system will be able to provide quality support for managerial applications by producing viable variants of decisions for managerial consideration (or perform them in an automated manner). Identification, classification and resolution of knowledge conflicts in management information systems based on cognitive agents helps ascertain system validity, i.e. ensure that solutions and decisions suggested by the system satisfy the requirements of decision makers.

Next section of this paper presents problems related to knowledge processing by cognitive agents.

3   Cognitive Agents in Knowledge Processing

3.1   Architectures and Functional Solutions of Cognitive Agents

The cognitive agents are more often used in multi-agent systems. For example a work [140] presents cognitive multi-agent systems for resolving real-time processing problem. Authors use 4D/RCS hybrid architecture in this purpose. In [141] the ECABA cognitive architecture is used for supporting automatization of building process. A cognitive agent-based medical diagnosis system is presented in [142]. The work [143] presents use cognitive computing to define actions' patterns able to maximize environmental parameters as, for instance, user's comfort or energy saving.

At the core of the creation of agent technologies lies the development of artificial intelligence, combination of automation principle (black box) and distributed knowledge-based systems. In addition, the development of object-oriented programming languages, distributed systems, and human-computer interface has also contributed to this [5, 144, 145].

The basic task of researching artificial intelligence and, in particular, agent technologies, as stated by Duch [146] is to create systems that reach levels of competence that exceed human capacities in various areas. It should be emphasized that while artificial intelligence systems are becoming more proficient at counting, possess better memory, conduct more complex real-time or near real-time analyses (which is a task impossible for a human being) or are even capable of winning games against humans, e.g. chess, cognitive functions related to perception, recognition and the analysis of relationships between objects are beyond the capabilities of this type of systems. Of course, simple perception functions such as image or sound recognition are already realized in artificial intelligence systems, but the use of recognized objects for reasoning, text analysis, natural language dialogue, problem planning and problem solving, as well as creating and using representations of complex knowledge forms is currently very difficult to implement [146].

Such simple applications do not simply require basic biological inspirations for the operation of single neurons or their small groups. It is necessary to take into account the large-scale architecture of the brain, the models of specialized areas, which we are becoming more and more acquainted with.

Such an approach can be described as neurocognitive computer science. Cognitive functions are supported by different types of memory [147]:

- recognition memory, allowing identification of known objects or discerning deviations from expectations;
- association memory, automatically leading to simple conclusions and the implementation of classical conditioning processes;
- procedural memory, i.e. memory of manual skills and sequences of activities;
- semantic memory, allowing interpretation of meaning and access to complex knowledge structures;
- working memory that allows combining the different pieces of information into a larger whole.

All these types of memory are supported by neural networks with a specific architecture, adapted to the required functions [148]. The organization of storing and accessing information through the brain and computers is completely different at a very basic level. Mathematical proof of the universality of computers (Turing machines, neural networks) to some extent have "blind-sided" the researchers in the sense that commonly used computational architectures in many ways limit the processing of information. In some applications, computers are more successful than the brain (e.g. fast data processing and analyzing in algorithmically way), but in many important applications, the brain is unmatched.

It is important to investigate whether cognitive architectures implemented on conventional computers can achieve similar possibilities for both lower and higher cognitive functions [146].

During the work on software agents, various architectures were created for their construction. Architecture is a set of means of implementation, which is used to build agents and functions according to the formal model that it utilizes.

The first architecture was the architecture using planning, i.e. conscious choice of further action. By using symbol representation and reasoning (expert systems), planning was related to systems such as Newell and Simon's GPS and Strips – a linear planning system. These systems consisted of [149]:

– a modelled environment created by symbols using first-order predicate logic,
– a symbolic description of the actions that the agent could perform, with the specific circumstances surrounding these actions and their effects,
– a planning algorithm whose input data is a representation of the environment, a set of action details and a target representation, and as a result an action plan is returned.

However, the first failures associated with the use of planning have led some researchers to challenge traditional symbol-processing AIs as agents used in agent technologies. As a result, there was proposed the so-called behavioral [150] approach to agent creation (behavioral architecture). It was characterized by the fact that their intelligence was the result of interactions between agents and the real environment in which they operate.

In subsequent studies of agents, there was an attempt to create hybrid architecture, a combination of planning and behavioral approach. Hybrid architecture consisted of several layers arranged vertically (only one layer had access to receptors and effectors) or horizontally (each layer had access to sensors and effectors) [149]. Usually, at the lowest level there was a reactive layer based on behavioral architecture, while the upper layers were knowledge layers which dealt with symbolic representation. The highest layer – sociological knowledge – pertained to the sociological aspects of the environment.

Then, there was developed an architecture based on human practical reasoning [149]. In that approach, psychology played a major part. Behavior is understood as attributing attitudes such as beliefs, desires or intentions.

It should be emphasized that the above-mentioned architectures concerned the construction of so-called reactive agents, i.e. those who could draw conclusions and respond appropriately to environmental stimuli; however, they had no cognitive skills and learning process is very simple. In order to take these problems into account, the researchers began work on developing cognitive agents, described in the further part of this paper.

The two most important features of all cognitive architectures are the way they organize their memory and their learning mechanisms. Memory is a repository of knowledge about the world and about oneself, one's goals and current activities. The role of memory is understood in different ways by different authors [151, 152]. Learning is a process that transforms one's stored knowledge and the manner of its use. Memory and learning are the two prerequisites for building the foundations of cognitive systems in which more complex cognitive functions can arise. Organization of memory depends on the representation of knowledge. Taking into account the taxonomy of cognitive architectures based on the above two pillars [146], three main groups of cognitive architectures were identified:

- symbolic,
- emergent,
- hybrid.

In the further part of this subsection, there will be presented an analysis of sample architectures within these three groups.

Symbolic architectures of cognitive agents use declarative knowledge contained in relationships written at the symbolic level, focusing on the use of this knowledge to solve problems. The most common architectures of this type include:

1. State, Operator And Result (SOAR), a classic cognitive agent developed for over 30 years to model general intelligence using a rule-based system as an approximation to knowledge-based systems [152]. This situation is considered in the problem space, i.e. within the set of permissible states of problem description. Production rules "If conditions are met then action is required" (IF … THEN …) are sorted according to the type of operators defining actions in that space. The main learning mechanism is based on the idea of chunking, i.e. the analytical technique of formulating new rules and macro-operations on the basis of repetitive combinations of simple operations that have been previously found useful before [152]. New "chunks of knowledge" lead to shortcut solutions.

2. Executive Process Interactive Control (EPIC) is an architecture that is designed to model numerous aspects of human interaction in the process of interaction with the machine [153]. Several interconnected processors serve for realistic (from the point of view of reaction times) processing of information through the senses of sight, hearing and touch, and the effectors move the cameras, press the keys and produce verbal statements. Processors operate on signals processed into symbolic form, used by a knowledge-based cognitive processor in the form of production rules.

3. CopyCat is an architecture of creating analogies based on the cognitive idea of segmental knowledge described in the work [154] and Center for Research on Concepts and Cognition, Indiana University Bloomington. Initially, the Copycat architecture was written in Lisp, but currently there are also implementations in Java. The functionality of the Copycat architecture is to answer questions like: "A" is related to "B" in the same way "C" is related to what?" [154], taking into account the creation of analogies as the basis of high level cognitive behavior as well as high level perception. High level perception is the result of numerous independent processes called codelets that operate in parallel, compete or cooperate with one another. Codelets form or remove a temporary structure of perceptual memory, attempting to approximate existing possibilities for solving a given problem. Codelets function as a "slipnet" network built on concepts and relationships between them. Changing the activation level of concepts allows one to create links with other concepts.

4. Non-Axiomatic Reasoning System (NARS) is the architecture presented in the paper [155]. This is an attempt at the approximation of the cognitive architecture with the use of non-standard logic. The NARS system is designed for inference based on a knowledge representation language that uses experience-grounded semantics. Non-axiomatic logic means that the validity of logical statements is evaluated on the basis of the system's past experiences with similar situations. It can be used for adaptation in situations where there is no accurate knowledge to allow for unambiguous decisions. The representation language, together with a set of inference rules, memory structures, and a control mechanism, treats the tasks performed as different aspects of the same process. Conclusions also have degrees of truth, estimated on the basis of their suitability.

5. Integrated Cognitive-Neuroscience Architectures for Understanding Sensemaking (ICARUS) is a new architecture [156] designed to control agents (robots and avatars). It uses knowledge representation in the form of reactive skills, each of which defines a sequence of actions in the context of specific objectives. The architecture includes a perception subsystem, as well as planning and executive subsystem and several memory subsystems. Perceptions are low in the hierarchy (they correspond to the initial phases of sensory information processing) while concepts are high (they correspond to recognized objects, the final phase). Having the perceptions, the next step is to look for matching concepts, whereas having goals, the next step is to seek reactive skills that will be useful in their fulfilment. Concept memory includes knowledge of various object classes, the relationships between them, the manipulation capabilities, and the applicability of various procedures.

The **emergent architectures** of the cognitive agents, in turn, use the flow of signals through a network of numerous mutually interacting elements, in which emergent states appear to be interpreted symbolically. The most common types of such architectures include:

1. Neurally Organized Mobile Adaptive Device (NOMAD) is an agent control architecture based on Gerald Edelman's "neural theory of Darwinism" [157]. Agents show how emergent rules work in real-time control and pattern recognition. Information about the world is provided by cameras, distance meters, artificial vibras (as in rats), sense of touch and taste (conductivity) sensors, and proprioceptive sensation, useful for determining position of the head and direction of movement. In the simulator, several subdivisions of the brain are involved, processing the sensory information and controlling the robot. It is taught in a pseudonatural way, i.e. it develops from "birth", knowing nothing at first, in an artificial but diverse environment.

2. Numenta Platform for Intelligent Computing (NuPIC) is a relatively new proposal for an emergent architecture based on Hierarchical Temporal Memory (HTM), which resulted from general considerations over the brain's information processing algorithm [150]. Network nodes are organized in a hierarchical fashion, motivated by the growing size of cortical reception areas in regions that range from primary sensory cortex through secondary and higher cognitive areas.

3. Cortronics, or architecture of confabulation, is a new emergent architecture, inspired by the horn-cortical loop in the brain [151]. Memory is organized in the form of modular attractor networks called lexicons. Each of them consists of a piece of neocortex and a fragment of the hill of cerebral cortex connected to it. Stable states of lexicons are called symbols, each represented by a group of specific neurons. Few of them are common to different pairs of symbols, so there is some common ground between the lexicons. Elementary knowledge is written in the form of connections between neurons of different lexicons. All pieces of bark add up to the whole cerebral cortex, whereas pieces of the hill of cerebral cortex add up to the part that connects to the neocortex. The mechanism of competitive activation of symbols contained in lexicons, called confabulation, serves to anticipate successive states, movements or words. Its action leaves only a few neurons in an active state, creating a symbol that has won in competition with others, or a zero symbol, meaning "I do not know".
4. Brain-Emulating Cognition and Control Architecture (BECCA). In this architecture, perceptual feelings are represented by features and combinations of qualities. Knowledge of the world is represented as the connection between feelings. The architecture consists of two modules: the creator of the features of the learning module, which function in an iterative way [158]. Architecture is designed to build agents operating in the environment.

Hybrid architectures of agent programs, in turn, are a combination of symbolic and emergent approaches combined in various ways. The most common hybrid architectures include:

1. Adaptive Components of Thought-Rational (ACT-R) is a multi-decade cognitive architecture based on the theoretical foundations of cognitive mechanisms developed by Anderson [159]. The purpose of this project is to build a system that will be able to perform all cognitive tasks at a similar level and with similar errors as people, and to understand the mechanisms underlying perception, thinking and action. The central part of the ACT-R architecture is a collection of modules for perception analysis, motion control, memory modules, and pattern matching. The perceptual movement provides symbolic representations that serve as an interface between the cognitive part and the environment of the system. Two types of memory, declarative and procedural, are used to store facts and procedures. Memory is encoded in symbolic-connectionist structures, using process-level rules as well as chunks at the declarative level in the form of vector representations of a set of properties, linking to a sub-symbolic level in the form of a connectionist network. Symbolic constructions (production rules and memory chunks) have additional parameters that evaluate their usefulness and allow for control of how they are used. These parameters are taught by Bayesian probabilistic rules, which make it possible to determine their suitability on the basis of past experience. The ACT-R memory buffers correspond to the working memory that matches the rules to the current situation.

2. The Connectionist Learning Adaptive Rule Induction ON-line (CLARION) is a hybrid architecture designed to develop cognitive agents for a variety of tasks, as well as to understand brain processes during learning and problem solving [160]. It consists of four main subsystems:
   - motivational subsystem (MS),
   - action-centered subsystem (ACS),
   - non-action subsystem (NCS),
   - meta-cognitive subsystem (MCS).

   Within each of them, two distinctions can be distinguished – explicit (symbolic) and implicit (sub-symbolic). The motivational system provides goals for perception and control analysis, ACS controls the agent's actions, NCS is responsible for the system's overall knowledge, and MCS controls the whole system. The localized memory is responsible for the symbolic knowledge, while scattered memory is responsible for implicit knowledge. A different learning strategy (with or without supervision) is used for each type of knowledge.

3. CogPrime is a multi-representation architecture [161]. The core of the representation consists of hypergraphics connected by relationships based on uncertain logic and associative relationships. Procedures are stored as a function program; episodes are mainly stored as "movies" in the memory of the simulation; as well as other methods. Knowledge is stored in the so-called "AtomSpace" as an emergent-symbolic "weighted, marked hyper-graphic" using cognitive processes. Cognitive processes include features of the uncertainty interface (PLN), learning functions using probabilistic evolutionary programming (MOSES), algorithms for allocating attention (ECAN), algorithms for forming heuristic concepts, and others.

4. DUAL [162] is a fairly new architecture based on Marvin Minsky's "Mind Society". This is a multi-agent hybrid architecture with uniform mental representations, memory structures and information processing mechanisms controlled by interoperable microagents. DUAL does not have a central controller, resulting in constantly changing information flow, adjusting to the situation, and supporting the emergence of new features. Collaborating agents create larger complexes, coalitions and formations, and more useful ones can be reified. The operation of the system can be viewed at different levels of detail, at the lowest level of these microagents, at the meso-level of emergent, dynamic coalitions of these microagents, or at the macro-level of the whole system where psychological interpretation of its properties is possible. Micro-frameworks are used to represent facts, and the importance of these facts in a given context is represented in the connections and interactions between the network elements in which the spreading activation changes the availability of information contained in its nodes.

5. Cortical Capacity-Constrained Concurrent Activation-Based Production System (4CAPS), [163] is a unique architecture designed to perform complex tasks such as understanding natural language, problem solving and spatial reasoning. Its unique property is the ability to compare the activity of 4CAPS modules with brain activity observations as measured by fMRI. At the heart of the project is the belief that

thinking is the result of the simultaneous activity of multiple areas of the brain working together, which can be modeled using modular neural networks. This leads to an architecture where the subsystems (modules) correspond to the different brain regions that process information in different ways. Each module can be part of a larger system with multiple cognitive functions, but has limited computational capabilities that affect its availability to perform tasks. Functions are assigned to different modules depending on the availability of resources, so the topology of the whole network solving a problem is not fixed and the same task can be solved in different ways.

6. The Novamente AI Engine [164] is based on the ideas of complex systems, mental dynamics and emergent patterns, derived from the philosophy of mind emphasizing the role of patterns and the concept of the mind, originally outlined in the psynet model [164]. As in Minsky's "mind society" and Baars' global work space, mental states emerge as a result of self-organisation and interactions related to the realization of goals that affect the patterns of agitation that create mental states. Emergent network activation properties should lead to hierarchical and relational (hierarchical) organization of mental patterns. The inference is based on the probabilistic term logic (PTL) and the Bayesian optimization algorithm (BOA). Actions, perceptions and internal states are represented by tree structures. It is still an experimental architecture, but it is being dynamically developed by a commercial company. There have already been first attempts to use it to control virtual pets, capable of learning based on natural interaction in the virtual world [164].

7. Cognitive Agents Architecture (Cougaar) – develops multi-agent systems using the Java programming language developed by the ALPINE consortium for DARPA (Defense Advanced Research Projects Agency). It consists of numerous layers of interactive applications – systems within systems [165].

8. The Learning Intelligent Distribution Agent (LIDA) is an architecture based on the theoretical foundations of creating "conscious" software agents using the Baars global work space theory [50].

The most functionally developed architectures are hybrid ones. The advantage of these architectures is their emergent-symbolic nature, which makes it possible to process both structured (numerical and symbolic) knowledge as well as unstructured knowledge (written in natural language). In further considerations in this work, there has been uses the LIDA architecture. It is being continuously developed, both theoretically and practically. Created by Franklin, the Cognitive Computing Research Group [166] has developed a framework (in Java) to facilitate the implementation of a cognitive agent. It should also be emphasized that the entire code of the framework is open, i.e. the programmer has access to the definition of all methods, unlike for example the software framework of the Cougaar architecture, where the program code of the agent is the so-called "black box". Details of the cognitive architecture of the LIDA agent program are presented in Fig. 3.

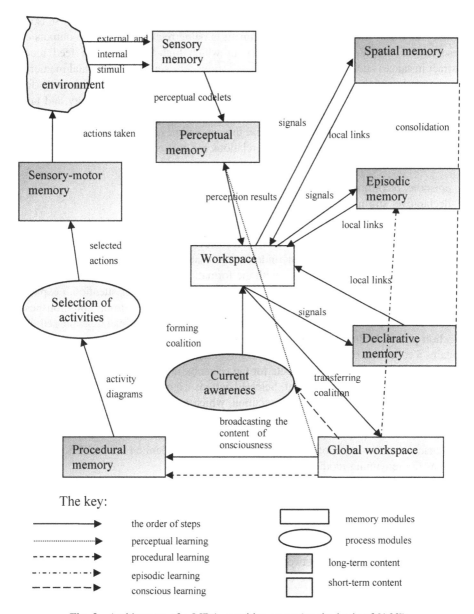

Fig. 3. Architecture of a LIDA cognitive agent (on the basis of [166]).

Most of the basic operations are performed by the so-called codelets that is specialized, mobile information processing programs in the global working memory model. The functioning of the cognitive agent is within the framework of the cognitive cycle and it is divided into three phases: the understanding phase, the consciousness phase, and the selection of actions and learning phase. At the beginning of the understanding phase, stimuli received from the outside environment or generated by internal processes (proprioception) activate the low-level codelets in the sensory memory in which the state of the environment is being recorded [50]. The outputs of these codecs activate perceptual memory in which high-level codelets feed more abstract instances such as objects, categories, actions, or events. In perceptual memory, the knowledge of the environment is represented in the form of a semantic web (for example, concept maps that allow semantically structured data on ontology and taxonomy). Perceptual memory acts as a filter, retrieving the most relevant information from sensory memory at any moment, and the perception results are transferred to the working memory. In this memory, local relations are created using the contents of the following memory:

- episodic, recording phenomena in chronological order,
- declarative, storing the rules,
- spatial, containing spatial maps – multidimensional images.

Then, with the use of perceptual memory instances, the current situational model is generated; in other words, the agent understands what is happening in the organization.

The consciousness phase begins with the formation of coalitions between the most essential elements of the situational model, which then compete for attention, i.e. place in the module of the current consciousness. The content of the current consciousness module is then passed to the global working memory while initializing the activity selection phase. At this stage, action plans are drawn from procedural memory, which contains a collection of all actions that a cognitive agent can take, and sent to the action selection module, where they compete for the selection in this cycle, which is based on the current state of the environment. Selected actions trigger sensory-motor memory to create a suitable algorithm for their execution, which is the final stage of the cognitive cycle [53]. The cognitive cycle is repeated with the frequency of 5 to 10 times per second.

Sensory and sensory-motor memory of LIDA is dependent on the problem domain, whereas the remaining modules are independent of it.

It is worth emphasizing that every cognitive decision support facilitator must possess the ability to grounding symbols, i.e. assign specific symbols of the natural language to relevant objects in the real world. This is necessary to correctly process unstructured knowledge, mainly written in natural language. Grounding is understood as the operation of these cognitive processes, which are responsible for establishing and maintaining the relationship between the signs of the language and the corresponding objects of the world [167]. One of the most common grounding definitions assumes that it is implemented by three specialized sub-processes: ionization – converting analogue signals from external objects into their internal analog equivalents; distinguishing – determining whether the two inputs received by the agent's sensors come from identical or different objects; identification – assigning unique names to the analogue class or in some respect non-distinguishable entries [167].

The learning (done in parallel with the previous actions) of the agent is realized as perceptual, episodic, procedural and conscious learning, and it is controlled from the bottom up, i.e. it starts at the moment of receiving stimuli from the environment.

Perceptual learning involves recognizing new objects, categories, relationships, and is based either on changing synaptic connections between nodes, or on creating new nodes and connections in perceptual memory. Episodic learning means remembering specific events: what, where, when, appearing in working memory, and thus available in consciousness. Procedural learning, i.e. learning new activities and the sequences of actions needed to solve the problems, is realized in two ways. The first is the selection of activities from the known repertoire, and the second is the construction of new representations for the sequence of actions by learning with the teacher[12]. Conscious learning refers to learning new conscious behaviors or reinforcing existing conscious behaviors that occur when a particular element of a situational model is frequently found in the current consciousness module [146].

The type of architecture is highly dependent on the type of problem that is being solved.

3.2   Semantic Method for Representing Knowledge of Cognitive Agents

The main ideas for using semantic network as knowledge representation for the agents are as follows [148]:

– the meaning of a symbol or concept stems from relationships with other symbols and concepts; the human memory is a network of associations,
– information is contained in the nodes and arcs (links) connecting the nodes (node = concept; in the brain, it is a pattern of beats activity of many neurons),
– every concept is a network node,
– the links between nodes are clearly presented,
– the links can be of different types,
– the semantic network is a model of episodic memory, but also semantic memory,
– the nodes represent, among other things: objects, types or classes, events, activities, episodes, places, times,
– links represent, among other things: subclass, the "is-a" relationship, parts of something, logical conjunctions and, or, actions, instruments.

In the hybrid architectures often a combination of different methods of knowledge representation is used (e.g. neural networks and semantic nets or combinations of other methods of knowledge representation) depending on a task, which is to be executed. However, the disadvantages of this approach are the need to implement two (or more) different types of modules for knowledge storing and the complexity of the procedures for conversion of knowledge represented using neural network with the knowledge represented by a semantic network. Therefore, a better approach is to use methods that allow representation of both symbolic and numerical knowledge in an integrated, uniform manner. The first suggestion to use such a method, called "slipnet", is presented in the "Copycat" project. This method is developed in the LIDA cognitive agent [31]. This hybrid architecture allows for symbolic and emergent knowledge processing and it uses the semantic net with node and links activation level (the "slipnet") to represent knowledge. This type of representation enables processing knowledge

---

[12] A teacher can be a human or a computer program that confirms the correctness of learning of the cognitive agent.

represented in a symbolic way, as well as knowledge represented in a numerical way. Thus, it is possible to determine a certainty level of semantic relations between nodes (concepts).

The need for agents' knowledge representation by semantic net with node and links activation level results mainly from the following presumptions:

- in a human brain, from phonology and graphemes of the word to its meaning and model of the situation, we have different patterns of distribution (levels) of stimulation (activation), and associations between them [148],
- Pulvermuller [168] states that because semantic activation followed by 90 ms the phonological activation, then a brain stimulation is a natural base of semantic representation;
- the probability distribution (activation level) is an important issue; concepts related to the same topic better fit together and create a coherent concept graph of an active part of semantic memory, including the inhibition of the activation and propagation processes;
- together with nodes and links and their activation level, the instances and axioms have to be included in the semantic network; they facilitate an automatic storing of an agent's knowledgebase in the physical database.

However, LIDA does not contain the mechanism for automatically storing the agent's knowledgebase in a physical database. After the power is turned off, the agents' knowledgebase is lost. Initially the storing of an agents' knowledgebase in database has been launched after realizing by given codelet its task. However, this method proved to be insufficient in case more complex tasks. Therefore the need appears for developing a method for permanent, automatically storing the agent's knowledgebase in a physical database.

Such method, called "slipnetplus", has been developed in [169], and it is defined as follows:

Definition 5
The "slipnetplus" is called a quadruple:

$$SN = \langle N, I, L, Z \rangle \tag{5}$$

where:

N – set of nodes,
I – set of instances of nodes,
L – set of links i.e. set of fuzzy relations defined on N,
Z – set of axioms. ◆

This definition extends the "slipnet" presented by [154, 170] about the set of instances and the set of axioms.

Let us define the particular elements of "slipnetplus".

We assume the real world $<O, V>$ where O is a finite set of objects and V is the domain of O; that is, V is a set of objects' values, and

$$V = \bigcup_{o \in O} V_o, \tag{6}$$

where V_o is the domain of object o.

We consider the "slipnetplus" referring to the real world (O, V) - such "slipnetplus" is called $<O, V>$-based. The "slipnetplus" detailed definitions must be considered on the four levels:

- the node level
- the instance level
- the link level
- the axiom level.

These definitions are developed in the next part of this sub-section.

The Node Level

Definition 6

A node of an $<O, V>$-based "slipnetplus" is defined as a triple:

$$Node = \langle n, o^n, V^n, al^n \rangle, \tag{7}$$

where n is the unique name of the node, $o^n \in O$ is an object represented by node, and $V^n = \bigcup_{o \in O^n} V_o$ is the objects' domain and al^n is an activation level of node function:

$$al : o^n \rightarrow [0, 1] \blacklozenge \tag{8}$$

Nested triple $\langle o^n, V^n, al^n \rangle$ is called the structure of node n. It is obvious that all nodes belonging to the same "slipnetplus" are different from one another. However, notice that within a "slipnetplus" there may be two or more nodes with the same structure. Such a situation may take place, for example, for nodes "person" and "body". For expressing the relationship between them the links from set L will be very useful.

Set N in the "slipnetplus" definition is a set of nodes' structures.

The Instance Level

Definition 7

An instance of a node n is described by the objects from set O^n with values from set V^n and is defined as a pair:

$$\text{instance} = \langle i, v \rangle \tag{9}$$

where i is the unique identifier of the instance in world $<O, V>$ and v is the value of the instance a tuple of type O^n, and can be presented as a function:

$$v : O^n \times [0, 1] \rightarrow V^n \times [0, 1] \tag{10}$$

such that $v(o, p) \in V_o$ for all $\langle o, p \rangle \in O^n$. $\blacklozenge$

Value v is also called a description of the instance within an object. A node may be interpreted as a set of all instances described by its structure.

We can then write $i \in n$ for presenting the fact that i is an instance of node n.

All instances of the same nodes within a "slipnetplus" should be different from each other. The same instance may belong to different nodes and may have different values.

The Link Level

In a "slipnetplus" within a pair of nodes there may be defined one or more links. Links between nodes describe the relationships between them. For example, between two nodes there may be defined such relations as a Synonym relation or an Antonym relation. Links between the nodes are included in set L of the "slipnetplus" definition.

Definition 8

A set N of nodes is given. The link is the following relation:

$$L : N \times N \rightarrow [0, 1] \tag{11}$$

in a space $N \times N$. ◆

The Axiom Level

The set Z of axioms are formulae of fuzzy logic and can be interpreted as integrity constraints or relationships between instances and nodes, and which cannot be expressed by the relations in set L.

Definition 9

The set N of nodes and set I of instances are given. The axiom is called the following relation:

$$Z : N \times I \rightarrow [0, 1] \tag{12}$$

in a space $N \times I$. ◆

The developed definition of "slipnetplus" can be visualized in a graphical form. The Fig. 4 presents an example of a graphical representation of the "slipnetplus".

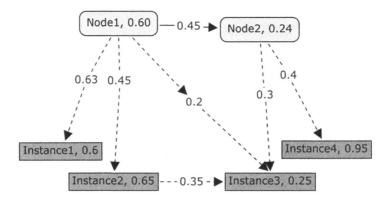

Fig. 4. The example of a graphical representation of the "slipnetplus".

The arrows drawn with a continuous line represent links, while the arrows drawn with dotted lines denote axioms. The presented "slipnetplus" consists of three nodes with their activation levels. The interpretation of the Node1 is as follows: Node1 exists in the real world with an activation level of 0.6. The interpretation of other nodes is similar. Node1 is connected with Node2 by links with the activation level respectively 0.45.

The interpretation of the Instance1 is as follows: Istance1 exists in the real world with an activation level of 0.6. Interpretation of other instances is similar. Node1 is connected with Instance1 by an axiom with the activation level 0.63. Node1 is connected with Instance2 by an axiom with the activation level 0.45. Node1 is connected with Instance3 by an axiom with the activation level 0.2. Node2 is also connected with Instance3, but with the activation level 0.3. Node2 is connected with Instance4, with the activation level 0.94.

Taking into consideration the implementation issues, "slipnetplus" has been implemented in CIMIS. The code of LIDA framework classes related to the "slipnet" implementation has been extended to the "slipnetplus" implementation. The LIDA agents' knowledgebase is automatically stored in database by using instances. The object-oriented noSQL database model is suitable for storing nodes, links, instances, and axioms together with their activation levels.

3.3   The Processing of Unstructured Knowledge by Cognitive Agents

Cognitive agents can be used to implement all knowledge management sub-processes (Fig. 5). Identification and acquisition sub-processes mainly deal with data and information – they are realized by recording in the memory of the agent the significant phenomena taking place in the organization's environment.

The sub-process of knowledge creation begins when the perceptual memory is activated and it is about recognizing the phenomena, distinguishing their characteristics (attributes, qualities) and determining the relationships between the phenomena or attributes, as well as the rules describing them. In this way creation, organization and storing sub-processes are realized. Also knowledge modelling sub-process is realized by using sensory and perceptual memory (for instance knowledge stored in natural language is modeled as semantic network with nodes' and links' activation levels). The knowledge processing sub-process is realized by using all modules excluding sensory memory. The storage sub-process continues and the use sub-process begins when the agent generates the current situational model of the environment that is stored in the global working memory and in the current consciousness module, i.e. the agent's understanding of the current phenomena occurring in the business environment. The use of knowledge can be realized through the selection of possible patterns from the procedural memory, i.e. via making a decision. Selected actions (decisions) activate sensory-motor memory to create an appropriate algorithm for their execution (decision-making).

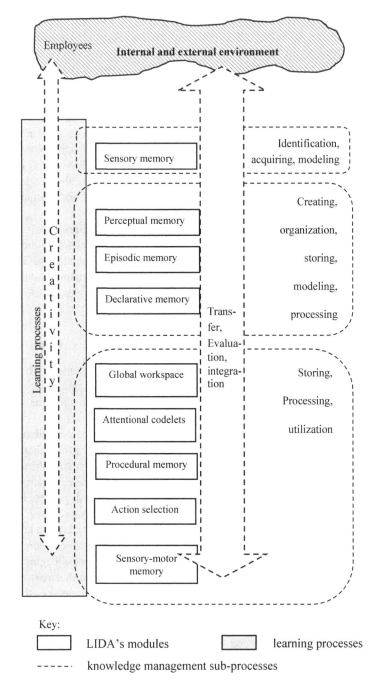

Fig. 5. Implementation of the knowledge management process using a cognitive agent. Source: own work on the basis of [169]

It should also be noted that the functioning of a cognitive agent enables creativity to be triggered in employees who, due to the fact that they are imputing their knowledge, have an important contribution to the learning process of the agent. Conversely, the knowledge gained by a cognitive agent influences the creativity of the employees. Furthermore, it is important for the agent to be able to anchor the symbols, i.e. assign specific symbols of the natural language to relevant objects in the real world. This is necessary to correctly process unstructured knowledge, mainly written in natural language (e.g. customer feedback on products) [169]. Through the implementation of the transfer sub-process, employees have the opportunity to acquire new knowledge generated by a cognitive agent while simultaneously carrying out a continuous process of evaluating this knowledge, which allows the improvement of the entire knowledge management process.

In a wider scope a cognitive agent can play a role of Chief Knowledge Officer (CKO). It have ability of intellectual capital managing in an organization. Cognitive agent can help an organization maximize the returns on investment in knowledge because it ensure a coherence between knowledge related with business processes realization and intellectual capital. It can to manage intangible assets of organization (know-how, patents, and customer relationships), share best practices, repeat successes, improve innovation, and avoid knowledge loss after organizational restructuring [171].

It is necessary to put stress, that cognitive agent uses the static and dynamic (real-time) knowledge during realization of knowledge management process (the static knowledge is stored mainly in episodic memory and it influence on creating agent's experience).

The processing of unstructured knowledge is conducted by using modular architecture, as presented in Fig. 6.

Document search agents browse the Internet for documents that meet certain criteria (according to the search query) and add full contents of those documents to the database.

Information extraction agents identify the relevant information in the text documents. For example, if customer feedback on mobile phones is to be analyzed, then only text snippets that contain feedback should be extracted from the text documents (stored in the database by document search agents), e.g. text ads. The results of the agents' operation are saved in the database in text form.

Text analysis agents, based on a set of text documents containing the information resulting from the operations of the information extraction agents, perform a shallow text analysis, which is characterized in further parts of this work.

In this work, the method of analyzing text documents will be presented in relation to one of the agent functions, which is the analysis of customer feedback on services/products. The main purpose of the analysis is to determine the characteristics that meet the needs of the customer, and the features that need to be improved to maximize the service's/product's ability to meet customer needs. Specific objectives of this analysis are defined as follows:

- defining a general sentiment of opinion, i.e. determining whether the opinion is positive, negative or neutral,
- extraction of service's'/product's characteristics,
- defining the sentiment of opinion regarding individual features of the service/product.

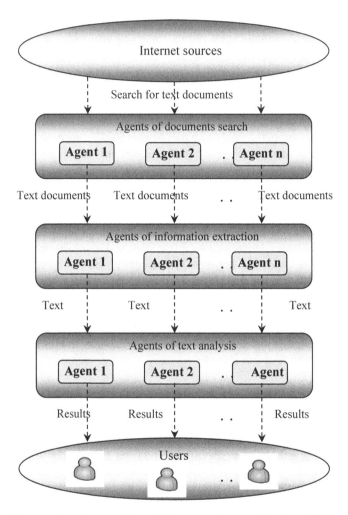

Fig. 6. Architecture of unstructured knowledge processing module in multi-agent integrated management system (on the basis of [172])

The operating environment of the text analysis agent is a collection of text documents containing this type of feedback (opinions can be found on online shops, forums or dedicated portals). The agent is searching for an opinion and then adds it to the repository (in the system database).

The analysis of text documents is carried out as follows:

1. Based on the learning set (opinions about services/products), a slipnet or slipnetplus is created in the perceptual memory, containing nodes and links (relations) between them. Perceptual memory also stores synonyms and variations of words.
2. The sensory memory (containing strings of characters) receives subsequently the respective opinions.

3. Feedback analysis is conducted by codelets, i.e. programs (implemented in the form of Java programming language classes) which search the text according to criteria defined by configuration parameters, whose value can be indicated by the user (parameters are written in the structure of the xml file and used in the codelets' program code). Codelets are divided into:
   - codelets for defining the opinion,
   - codelets for extraction of features and opinions about features.

   An example of codelet configurations that define the opinion is presented in Fig. 7.

```
<task name="positive_opinion">
<tasktype> CodeletObjectDetector </tasktype>
<param name="object" type="string">recommend</param>
<param name="noobject" type="string">not</param>
<param name="distance" type="int">1</param>
<param name="node" type="string"> positive_opinion </param>
</task>

<task name="negative_opinion">
<tasktype>CodeletObjectDetector</tasktype>
<param name="object" type="string">reccomend,not</param>
<param name="distance" type="int">1</param>
<param name="node" type="string">negative_opinion</param>
</task>
```

Fig. 7. An example of codelet configurations defining the opinion

The task name parameter (in the LIDA architecture, the codelet is configured as a task; the task can also be the refreshing of the GUI content and it is not implemented by the codelet) denotes the codelet's name, the *tasktype* parameter indicates the Java class name that contains the codelet's program code, the *object* parameter specifies which words (or expressions) are sought by the codelet in the sensory memory, the *noobject* parameter specifies which words (or expressions) cannot be in the text (for example, the opinion is positive when the text contains the word "recommend" without the word "not"); the *distance* parameter specifies the maximum distance between words or expressions, the *node* parameter determines which node to include in the working memory when the searched words (or expressions) are found.

4. The results of the analysis, in the form of a semantic network, are transferred to the workspace (the current situational model is created). Figure 8 presents an example of the results of the analysis for the following review of Product1: "I recommend it, feature1 and feature2 are good." The nodes are marked with a large circle symbol, while the links are marked with an arrow symbol. Dots indicate the levels of link activation (links can be specified with a certain level of probability). This network presents a situation in which both the general opinion of the product and the opinions about the individual characteristics of the product are positive.

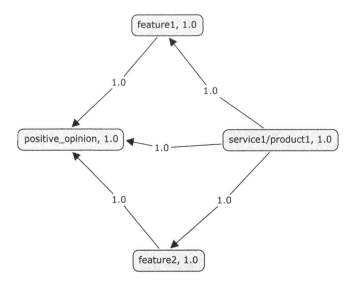

Fig. 8. Example of the results of analysis for the product opinion in the situation of a positive opinion on a product and its features

Figure 9 presents an example of the results of analysis for the following opinion: "I recommend it, feature1 is good, but feature2 is not good."

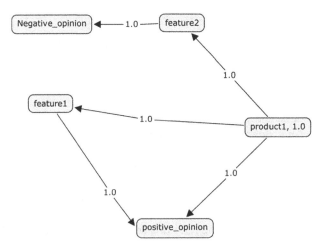

Fig. 9. Example of the results of analysis for the product opinion in the situation of a positive opinion of the product, but negative opinion about one of the features

5. In the next step, the situational model is transferred to the global workspace and from the procedural memory, the following action schemes are automatically selected: "save the results of the opinion analysis to the database" (noSQL-type database – analysis results – semantic network – are saved in the XML format), and "loading another opinion into sensory memory". It is also possible to choose the "statistical analysis" action, whereby the agent also points to the product characteristics that are most desirable by the customers.

Based on the analysis of text documents, cognitive agents can automatically make decisions and implement them. In order to perform these functions, appropriate action patterns should be implemented in the procedural memory (examples of activity patterns are presented in Sect. 4).

The presented method of analyzing textual documents by cognitive agents enables the representation of unstructured knowledge through the "slipnet" or "slipnetplus" semantic network. Consequently, cognitive agents can analyze the significance of phenomena occurring in the organization's environment. The results of the processing of unstructured knowledge are then used to make and implement decisions (automatically or by humans).

However, as already previously stated, due to the heterogeneity of knowledge sources and the variety of decision support methods, the functioning of cognitive agents is often associated with the occurrence of knowledge conflicts between them. These conflicts have been characterized in the next subsection.

3.4 Conflicts of Cognitive Agents' Knowledge

Conflicts of knowledge between cognitive agents in management information systems can be defined in various ways, including [173]:

1. The lack of compatibility of knowledge possessed by cognitive agents who are parties to the conflict.
2. The intentions of two (or more) agents cannot be fulfilled at the same time in the way as the agents would prefer.
3. A situation is considered a conflict when two independent agents have different opinions in a certain common theme.

These definitions complement one another, and it is enough that one of these definitions is fulfilled in the multi-agent management information system for the conflict to be present.

On the other hand, when there is a conflict of knowledge, there are three main ways to solve such a situation [174]:

1. Non-resolution of the conflict – the goals of the parties to the conflict have not been reached.
2. Power solution – every agent is fighting for their own purpose. There may appear the following results:
   - the goal has been achieved by one agent,
   - no agent has achieved their goal,
   - agents have only partially achieved their goals,
   - agents have achieved different goals than they intended.

3. Achieving agreement - Agents are jointly setting what goals can be achieved. There are two types of agreement:
   – concession – one of the agents resigns from achieving their goal, the second agent fulfils theirs goal in its entirety,
   – consensus or compromise – each agent modifies its purpose and these modified goals are achieved.

The best solution is to reach an agreement, especially consensus. Agreement can be achieved by considering context or other external knowledge.

In each conflict, including the conflict of knowledge, one can distinguish three main attributes [173]:

– subject – determines the participants, the perpetrators of the conflict,
– object – describes what the conflict is about,
– content – provides the subject's opinion on the object of the conflict.

In the considered systems, the subject of the conflict of knowledge are agents, the object of the conflict are events occurring in the organization's environment, while the content of the conflict is the knowledge of the individual agents about each event.

Conflicts of unstructured (as well as structured) knowledge of cognitive agents in management information systems arise from the inconsistencies or contradictions of the knowledge of these agents. Inconsistency occurs when one agent believes that a given attribute (feature) of the world in a given time interval exists or does not exist, while the other agent has no information or does not want to speak about this attribute [167]. Contradiction, on the other hand, occurs when one agent considers that a given world attribute in a given time interval exists, whereas another agent believes that the same attribute does not exist in the same time period [173]. To summarize, conflicts of knowledge occur when agents assign different attributes to the same world objects, or when agents assign different values to the same attribute [173]. Of course, the assumption is that the knowledge of agents is represented by a given method. In the case of unstructured knowledge, this may be, in particular, the semantic method.

It is important to note, however, that a semantic structure is most often required to record unstructured knowledge, allowing for the analysis of the significance of phenomena occurring in the organization's environment. For many years, conflicts of the knowledge of agents, including cognitive agents, were considered in the aspects of monovalent structures. Nguyen [7] proposed solving the conflicts of multivalued knowledge structures as well as conflicts of ontologies. In a multi-agent management information system, there is a particular semantic structure, because the knowledge of cognitive agents about real-world objects and the relationship between them can be expressed with a degree of probability (because economic decisions are always made under risk conditions or uncertainty). Detecting conflicts in such structures is not only about comparing nodes and links, but also about the comparison of probability values (link and nodes activation levels).

Taking into consideration the complexity of the cognitive agent's architecture and functionality, as well as the asynchronous nature of the cognitive cycle (5–10 cycles per second) having impact on the contents of particular architecture models, it may be concluded that they may constitute the reasons for the occurrence of knowledge conflicts. Potential places of these conflicts' sources may occur in the modules of the cognitive agent's architecture and be connected with:

- the domain of the value of objects stored in memory,
- the results of phenomena interpretation,
- events,
- rules,
- the perception of the current state of the environment (objects and links between them),
- the results of algorithm operation,
- the selection of the agent's actions.

Further in this work, there will be presented an example (on the basis of users' opinions about products) of conflicts in cognitive agents running in CIMIS in relation to agents' architecture (described in detail in Sub-sect. 3.1):

1. Sensory memory. As sales characteristics are stored, on regular basis, in the agents' sensory memory, the contents of these memories in particular agents may constitute the source of knowledge conflict. These conflicts are mainly connected with the domain of the value of objects stored in the memory. For instance, if it was adopted in the solution that the memory should include the users' opinions recorded in the text form, yet there occurred a situation in which the opinion contained graphic elements, their interpretation might be difficult or even impossible. As a consequence, the cognitive agents might incorrectly perceive the current state of the environment.

2. Perceptual memory. The knowledge conflicts occurring in the perceptual memory are thus connected with the results of the interpretation of its content. For example, if an opinion contains only the product characteristics such as the color, dimensions, function, it is difficult to determine the polarity of the opinion (state whether the opinion is positive or negative). Therefore, two or more agents may determine this polarity in different ways.

3. Workspace, episodic memory and declarative memory. The perception results in the form of objects or events are sent to the workspace, in which knowledge conflicts relate to the perception of the current state of the environment and are connected with the creation of local links with the use of events stored in the episodic memory and the rules stored in the declarative memory. Knowledge conflicts connected with the contents of episodic memory mainly relate to contradictory events which occurred as a result of an earlier event. For example, the earlier event recorded in the episodic memory of the first agent is: "two years before, the competition launched two products (which are also manufactured by the company in question) with better characteristics (product 1 and product 2)" and earlier events recorded in the episodic memory of the second agent are: "in the previous year, the sales of product 1 decreased" and "in the previous year, the sales of product 2 increased)". The knowledge conflicts occurring in the declarative memory are connected with the occurrence of the contradiction of rules (for instance "if the users' opinions are negative, the decrease in sales will take place", and "if the users' opinions are negative, the sales will remain at the same level").

4. Knowledge conflicts occurring in the workspace take place as a result of conflicts occurring in the episodic and declarative memory – the current situational model may contain incorrect objects or incorrect links between them.

5. Attentional codelets. In the attentional codelets module, there are significant elements of the situational model (the agent "rejects" insignificant elements of the situational model such as, for instance, "the drop of sales of products to client X occurred because this client liquidated their business" – this element is insignificant as no marketing actions can be taken with respect to client X anymore). The conflict of knowledge in the modules of particular agents relates to the results of algorithm actions determining which elements of the current situational model are insignificant.

6. Procedural memory. The procedural memory, in turn, contains specific action schemes – for instance "improving the product characteristics", "lowering the product price", "and launching the new product meeting the clients' expectations on the market". The conflict of knowledge relates to algorithms implemented as an action scheme, for instance determining what measures should be taken to launch a new product on the market.

7. Action selection module. The knowledge conflict in the action selection module relates to decisions which should be taken, for instance the first agent propose action: "lowering the product price" and the second agent propose action: "launching a new product meeting the clients' expectations" should be chosen.

8. Global workspace and sensory-motor memory. In the cognitive agents' architecture, there are also modules in which the sources of knowledge conflicts do not occur. They include: the global workspace (sources of knowledge conflicts do not occur in this module because there are significant elements of the situational model transferred from the module of current awareness for the purpose of initiating the phase of action selection) and sensory-motor memory (the sources of knowledge conflicts do not occur in this memory because it is a working module).

Conflicts of unstructured knowledge occurring at all modules of agents' architecture are reflected by a difference in knowledge representation structure, i.e. semantic net with nodes' and links' activation levels ("slipnet" or "slipnetplus"). Therefore, resolving these conflicts relies on determining (coordinating) such a structure which well represents all knowledge structures of conflict agents. The next sub-section presents current methods for resolving the analyzed conflicts.

3.5 Current Methods of Resolving the Analyzed Conflicts

Conflicts, including conflicts of unstructured knowledge, may be resolved at various stages, from the design stage of the system (situations that arise in the system are not always perceived as conflicting, as potential conflicts are resolved before they can occur), through the stage of planning objectives, tasks and individual actions by agents, as well as dynamically, during the operation of the system and the fulfilment of goals by the agents – when the conflict has already occurred.

The conflict resolution methods existing in multi-agent IT management systems to some extent rely on the stage at which the conflict is resolved. Conflicts can therefore be resolved:

1. Using methods in which agents have little involvement in conflict resolution. It can be conflict resolution by preventing or disallowing potential conflicts, or by avoiding conflicts – it is conflict resolution through prevention, also referred to in the literature as a method of arbitration by the system [174], for example, as in the physics-based model of cooperation described in the work [175]. It is very important to identify the potential conflict here. This identification has to be made at the design stage of the model, and the model includes the mechanisms for resolving such conflict situations. By resolving conflicts through arbitration, agents have a relatively minor personal role in solving them in comparison with other methods, as they do not resolve conflicts personally, but refer to arbitration on the part of the system; they are often "unaware" of the existing conflicts. The methods used by these models are primarily calculation methods (described later in this work). There may also occur different deductive methods, or strict rules imposed on agents' behavior. Such methods can be called methods of implicit conflict resolution.

2. Using methods in which the agents are active units participating in the conflict resolution process. Agents deal with conflicts both at the planning stage [176], where there are set the objectives, agents' actions, where there is regulated access to resources, and the knowledge agreed upon (this is also extremely important in identifying existing conflict situations), as well as dynamically, on a day-to-day basis when conflicts (of knowledge) occur [39]. Some conflicts may be impossible or difficult to resolve or identify at the planning stage, so they are resolved on a regular basis, when the system is running. The stages of planning can also be interwoven with the stages of operation. Agents resolving conflicts come to an open compromise, which can be realized by:

   (a) negotiation (also with argumentation, which is a special form of negotiation);
   (b) using deductive-computational methods, including, among others, the following methods:
      – based on game theory,
      – classical mechanics,
      – derived from the field of operational research,
      – derived from the field of constraint programming,
      – derived from behavioral sciences and sociology,
      – choice,
      – Consensus.

Negotiation methods are presented in numerous works [175, 177], and can be used to solve knowledge conflicts. Negotiation is a term completely separate and independent of the field of multi-agent systems, derived from everyday life. In general, to negotiate means to discuss with someone, to come to an agreement on a certain matter [178].

In multi-agent systems negotiations are often used to resolve conflicts of goals, plans and beliefs of agents as well as knowledge conflicts. An example of the use of negotiation in multi-agent decision support systems is the system described in the work [145]. In the literature, the definitions of negotiations in multi-agent systems vary. For example, in the work [177] negotiation means "*any communication process those results in a mutually acceptable agreement*". On the other hand, in the work [175], negotiations are defined as a process that takes place between two or more agents in which stakeholders communicate and exchange information (each of which evaluates the information from their own point of view) and communicate their endeavors in an attempt to arrive at a compromise and achieve a mutually profitable understanding, whether it is about beliefs, plans, or goals that they cannot or do not want to achieve on their own. By definition, we can infer that for an agent to be able to participate in the negotiation process, they must be able to submit bids (proposals), counter proposals, and accept or reject offers from other agents. It is important to note that the agents affect one another, so as to convince other agents to act in a certain way. Agents can generate arguments to support their viewpoint on a given matter, they can influence one another on their views, beliefs, preferences, and they can change their plans, goals, and beliefs. There is therefore a need to evaluate the relative value of the different offers made to the agent by other agents during negotiation, and the probable value of the agent's offers as perceived by other agents. In the negotiation process, an important factor is for the agents to possess information about other agents. If this information is incomplete, then the agent may present an incorrect offer to other agents. During negotiation, agents make proposals and accept or reject offers based on their information and beliefs. The minimum requirements for negotiation are (apart from, of course, communication ability) the ability of agents to submit proposals and counterproposals, and the ability to accept and reject offers from other agents.

The big problem in the negotiations is their time-consuming nature, because by devoting time to negotiations agents delay their tasks and the achievement of their goals. Thus, negotiation is a time-consuming and costly process (considering the computers increasing performances is it acceptable for users but the costs of multi-agent system are higher). Designers are trying to create multi-agent systems so that the time spent on negotiating is as short as possible, because any delay in achieving a goal by the agents results in measurable losses.

Negotiation processes can take place in one step, or on a multistep basis they can be completed in a single step, after the presentation and either rejection or acceptance of one offer, after one vote or one bid. They can also include numerous steps in which proposals and counterproposals are presented, or where the voting or bidding takes place repeatedly [175].

Designing the negotiation mechanism is a three-step process. In the first place, the designers of the agents must agree together on a specific definition of the field that will form the basis of both the whole model of cooperation and all mechanisms involved, including the negotiating mechanism. When the field is already defined, the next step is the exact specification of the negotiation protocol, which defines the rules of interaction between agents.

The characteristic feature of the negotiation is that the agent must allow changes in goals, plans, beliefs, or knowledge structures without any external influences.

In order to solve conflicts in multi-agent systems, deductive-computational methods are also used. This group includes, among others, methods derived from **game theory**. The field of science which is game theory is very similar to the problems of cooperation and conflict resolution in multi-agent systems. It is integrated part of artificial intelligence [176]. It examines mathematical models of conflict and cooperation between people. Game theory models are highly abstract representations of different classes of everyday situations in which individuals with different goals and preferences participate. An active unit in all game theory models is the player (decision-maker within context of management). These models are divided into two main types [177]:

- non-cooperative models, in which indivisible units are collections of possible actions (operations) undertaken by individual players,
- cooperative models, in which indivisible units are collections of possible common actions of groups of players.

Abstract game theory models can be used as the basis for agent interaction protocols in multi-agent systems. Agents must therefore agree in advance on the rules and protocols of agent interaction. Agents can be modelled by players in game theory models. Techniques in game theory are therefore used in systems where agents strive to maximize their profit, so they are most suitable for MA systems (as described in the previous section). These techniques are used in multi-agent systems in situations where each agent operates individually (using the first of the types of game theory models described here – the non-cooperative models), and in situations where tasks require cooperation between groups of agents (the cooperative models in game theory). Game theory models are only used where automatic agents have great computational capabilities and the ability to communicate. Because these models require a large number of often quite complex calculations and a lot of time is devoted to the communication between agents, the systems they use consist of a small number of agents, or there may be more agents in the system, but the interactions between them are limited to a small number. Non-cooperative game theory models are suitable for systems consisting only of several agents, while systems using cooperative models can consist of dozens of agents. The use of game theory in multi-agent systems does not necessarily mean the use of game theory models as the basis of agent interaction protocols. Conflict resolution models can be designed on a completely different basis, and only some elements derived from game theory may be used.

Another method belonging to the group of deductive methods of conflict resolution is the **classical mechanics** method [7]. It is used when there are situations where multi-agent systems require cooperation between very large numbers – i.e. hundreds and even thousands – of agents. These are typically situations where agents work together to achieve common, highly dispersive, often dynamically changing goals, so they are typically large-scale distributed problem solving (DPS) systems [177], less often MA systems. Designers of agents for these systems may in advance define certain rules and protocols for the interaction of agents. Conflict resolution methods based on agent communication are suitable for environments with relatively small numbers of agents. On the other hand, for very large groups of agents, these negotiating methods are usually too complicated to calculate and they consume too much time. [18]. In addition, even with a group of dozens of agents, direct high-speed communications between all agents can be simply impossible or too costly. The situation becomes even more difficult when in the system, in addition to a large number of agents, there are very frequent interactions between agents. For other large-scale multi-agent systems, other collaborative models are pursued, some which are not based on negotiation and which do not require communication links between agents and at the same time do not require very complicated and time-consuming calculations. Physical methods of intermolecular dynamics, which use mathematical equations to describe and predict the properties and evolution of various states of matter, have been very useful in this area. Effective techniques were developed for cooperation among hundreds of agents by adaptation of classical mechanics methods used by physicists to solve the problems of searching and describing the properties of interactions between numerous matter molecules. Although there is a multitude of differences between matter molecules and multi-agent systems, it is shown that such an approach enables efficient co-operation between agents in very large systems, providing mechanisms with low computational complexity, which is essential for such systems [179]. This approach is used, for example, in multi-agent systems that support large-scale production processes.

The basic idea of this type of model is that the units of the multi-agent system are modeled with molecules of matter, while the properties of the system and its units, as well as events occurring in the system, and are modeled by the properties of the corresponding state of matter, the properties of the molecules that build up that matter and interactions and events occurring between the matter molecules [180].

A feature of this type of approach is that the process of scheduling an action by the agents is intertwined with the task execution process. The agents continually calculate each successive movement, and immediately after the calculations have been made, there is movement (in physical or abstract sense) towards the goal, and then the agents calculate the next movement [181, 182].

The approach to a large scale physics based multi-agent system has several significant advantages. While most of the algorithms used in various other models require a thorough check of efficiency and optimality, either by formal proof or by simulation, models based on classical mechanics may rely on theoretical or experimental results well known in physics. Based on these results, it is possible to predict the evolution of the whole multi-agent model system, as it will evolve in a manner consistent with the already known physical model. Local interactions, which make it possible to draw conclusions about the global behavior of the system, provide low computational complexity of the model. No explicit communication between agents is required. For large scale multi-agent systems, this approach guarantees a model those results in efficient, low-cost, cost-effective cooperation. In addition, the properties of the system as a whole can be analyzed using statistical techniques (with the use of statistical mechanics techniques). It is also possible to draw conclusions about system properties as a whole based on the properties of system components.

Other methods of deductive and computational groups are methods of conflict resolution derived from the field of **operational research**. Operational research is about finding ways to best decision and then work on an organizational system that typically operates under limited resources [183]. Agents working in the DPS system can be considered as such an organizational system, so techniques and algorithms developed for human organizations through the field of operational research can be applied to this type of multi-agent environment. The computational complexity of these algorithms and techniques is usually high, and their performance drops significantly with the growth of the organization which uses them, so it is assumed that there will be a reduction in the number of agents and it is assumed that agents must be able to use high CPUs.

Operational research deals extensively with the problem of division and coverage of the set [184]. The solutions developed by this field apply to the problem of coalition formation in DPS systems, where the given set of agents and the set of tasks they have to perform together are looking for a way to assign each task to an agent group (alternatively, to a single agent, if it is able to do it by itself), which will fulfil this task.

The above-mentioned problem can be approached as an issue of division or coverage of a set. Because these problems belong to a group of NP-complete problems, different approximations of algorithms derived from operational research are used here.

Operational research methods cannot, of course, be applied directly to multi-agent systems. In order for this to be done, the following actions need to be undertaken [184]:

1. First, find the problem considered in the operational research that would be closest to the problem of the multi-agent system, and make a detailed match between the two problems.
2. Then adapt the operational research algorithms to the multi-agent system environment. In particular, because most of the operational research algorithms are centralized algorithms, moving to the distributed environments of distributed agent it is necessary to adapt the algorithms to be distributed algorithms.
3. It is also necessary to create the appropriate usability and cost features that agents can use and which provide the agents with efficient techniques for calculating them.

Constraint programming is a paradigm related to resolving combinatorial problems in artificial intelligence. Agents can be treated as constraints and multi-agent system as constraints network. Conflict resolving rely on "finding following the current partial instantiation from the leaf to the root of the search tree, the culprit decision that prevents the last variable from being assigned" [185]. This approach can be generalized so as to collect a set of incompatible variables that are together responsible for the last conflict [185]. It can lead to improve the solution in risky and uncertain environment.

Multi-agent environments are not always structured environments where agents' behaviors are fully predictable and where agents' designers are able to establish in advance strict rules of interaction and negotiation protocol for agents. Typically, automated agents of these systems interact with other automated agents as well as with people (often a person is perceived here from the system's perspective also as an agent) [186]. Agents in these systems most often (though not necessarily; it depends on the informal model used) have communicative abilities, because in the case of not strictly structuring the environment, communication is the best means which, on the one hand, does not restrict agents to strict, explicitly established interaction protocols, and on the other hand allows for conflict resolution and coordination of their actions. The number of agents in this type of environment cannot be large [186].

Due to the fact that unstructured environments cannot be based on overly formal methods, various kinds of informal methods can be found in such situations, which can be the basis for agent co-operation. It turned out that instead of creating such methods from scratch, it is beneficial to formalize (often using logic for this) and then implement in existing systems, informal **methods derived from behavioral sciences and sociology**. These studies deal with the analysis and investigation of human behavior, as well as the cooperation between people, the coordination of their actions. Communication and discovering of motivation. They have developed models of various organizations and human communities. In unstructured and unpredictable multi-agent environments, the use of heuristics of cooperation between agents and the coordination of their actions, based on proven human cooperation methods described by these models, turns out to be very relevant. However, there is always a need for simulations to assess the effectiveness of the methods used, since informal methods usually do not have formal methods for evaluating them and analyzing the behavior of systems based on these methods.

The main advantage of using these methods is that they are built on the experience and expertise provided by numerous scientists over the years and it does not require starting from scratch, based solely on one's own experience [187]. The validity of these applications is confirmed by simulations, especially by the successful attempt to create automatic negotiators.

The **theory of choice** is derived from sociological sciences [188], which have their roots in antiquity (it is, therefore, related to sociological methods of decision-making [189]) and deals with the following problem: the given set Z (e.g. a set of objects) is a subset of a set of objects X. Speaking of choice, according to certain criteria we select a certain subset Y of the set Z. In the decision-making process, the Z set is the set of decisions generated by the various methods, the X set is the set of permissible decisions, and the subset Y is the decision presented to the decision maker. Therefore, using the choice theory, the decision maker generated by one of the decision-support methods is presented to the decision maker. Other methods are not taken into consideration [29]. Methods of choice theory shorten the time needed to make a decision (the decision maker does not have to wonder which of the options to choose), but does not reduce the risk involved in decision making (one of the decisions is chosen, but it is not always the best decision).

The **consensus methods** have been detailed described in Sect. 4.

3.6 Premises for the Development of a New Method for Resolving Conflicts of Unstructured Knowledge of Cognitive Agents in the Investigated Systems

The conflict resolution methods in the multi-agent decision support system presented in the previous subsection, however, have some disadvantages. Negotiation methods guarantee the desired compromise between agents, but this is done at the expense of increased communication between agents, which obviously affects the speed of the system. On the other hand, deductive-computational methods do not significantly affect the speed of the system, but these methods, in addition to consensus methods, do not guarantee a good compromise. The decision maker requires a good performance system (real-time action) and a smooth conflict resolution between agents to obtain the best decision from the system.

Therefore, as methods of solving knowledge conflicts, better use the consensus methods (described in Sect. 4), which belong to the group of deductive-computational methods. Unlike other methods in this group, they guarantee a good compromise and are also a better way of negotiating methods because they allow to change the agent's knowledge in different conditions. In negotiation methods, two elements in an agent can only be changed if the agent considers the change to be appropriate without any external interaction. Consensus methods do not require high processing power of the processor and increased communication between agents, allowing for quick decision making.

It is clear from the considerations that there are conflicts in the analyzed systems that cannot always be solved easily. It is important to keep in mind that each conflict must be detected, classified and resolved in such a way that it does not disrupt the entire system. Only then can the system properly determine the decisions and present them to the decision maker. Generally speaking, the conflict of unstructured knowledge of cognitive agents results in different descriptions of a given phenomenon taking place in the organization's environment. Thus, resolving conflicts of unstructured (as well as structured) knowledge of cognitive agents in a management information system has a strong influence on the decision made by the decision maker, and hence on the functioning of the organization and the whole environment in which the decision maker operates. Resolving the conflicts also helps ensure that the system is functioning, ensuring that the decision generated by the system is the best one from the perspective of the criteria set by the decision maker, and thus gives the decision-maker satisfactory benefits.

It should also be emphasized that no consensus algorithms have been developed on the semantic net with links and nodes activation levels. The development of these algorithms will allow for solving conflicts of knowledge represented by the semantic method, taking into account the risks and uncertainty of economic decision-making.

The algorithms for detecting, classifying, and resolving conflicts should be implemented in the system and brought up after all agents have generated decisions. Of course, these algorithms are executed automatically by the system without the user. This does not exclude human participation in the knowledge management process [190]. It can supervise the results of the conflict of knowledge solution and supervise the course of business processes. If these aspects are ignored in the system, then the user or the decision-maker may have trouble making a quick and accurate decision, as the system may suggest an incorrect option, or may suggest several options, and the decision maker must then decide on the choice of one.

4 Consensus Theory in Resolving Conflicts of Unstructured Knowledge

4.1 The Essence of Consensus Theory

The consensus theory stems from choice theory. In its general meaning, consensus means agreement. Therefore, in consensus theory, choice does not have to be a subset of set Z, nor does it have to have the same structure as the elements of set Z [173].

Hence, the version of solution presented to the decision maker does not have to be a version determined by one of the agents. It can be a totally new version created on the basis of the said versions generated by individual agents. That is why all solution versions can be considered.

Initially, the consensus theory applied to structures[13] such as linear order or partial order. Later new and more complex structures were studied, such as divisions, hierarchies, n-trees. The papers [7, 137, 138, 172, 189–192] developed algorithms for determining consensus relating to multi-attribute and multi-value structures, as well as ontology, whereas the papers [135, 193] developed algorithms for determining consensus relating to structures that represent economic decisions. Therefore, the consensus theory applies to problems resulting from data analysis for extraction of useful information and knowledge – the same as in data exploration. However, while the purposes of data exploration methods apply to the search for cause-and-effect chains hidden in the data, the purposes of the consensus methods involve determining such version for a certain set of versions of data, information, or knowledge, that best represents the versions or is a compromise accepted by the parties that created the versions. In the paper [7], problems resolved with the consensus theory are included in the following groups:

1. Problems connected with discovering the hidden structure of an object. Managing an organization is very complicated, each management and decision-making support method may generate versions of solutions and decisions with different structure. Therefore, one must determine the structure of the version of a solution or decision determined by the consensus method.
2. Problems connected with agreeing inconsistent or conflicting data, information, or knowledge about the same object. The structure of knowledge in agents may differ in nodes, links (inconsistency), and/or values of activation levels of the nodes and/or links (conflict).

Determining consensus is divided into several steps (Fig. 10). First, one must study thoroughly the structure of set Z, being the set of all versions of solutions to a problem, generated by each management support method. Next, one must calculate the distances between individual subsets of set Z. Determining consensus involves selecting such set (version) that the distance between the set (consensus) and the sub-sets of set Z is minimal (according to various criteria).

The consensus theory is used, for example, to resolve conflicts of knowledge of experts, conflicts in temporal data bases[14], conflicts in multi-agent systems, to restore consistency of replicated data[15]. So far, however, it must be emphasized that the consensus theory has not been found useful in MIS where cognitive agents operate.

---

[13] A structure is a distribution of elements and a set of relations among them, characteristic for a given system as a whole, in other words it is a set of features of a given object.

[14] Temporal data base is a base where the time of an event and the time of saving data to base play an important role.

[15] Data replication is storing the same data on different servers to ensure the reliability of data read and save.

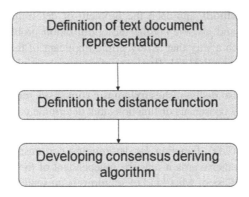

Fig. 10. The stages of consensus determining.

Consensus is always determined for a given profile, i.e. a set of opinions from cognitive agents. For instance, if five agents engage in conflict, the profile is composed of five elements. Naturally, the elements of the profile must be complex structures – 'slipnet' and 'slipnetplus' are two of such structures – and it is the type of the structures that determines the kind of consensus method to be used. The consensus methods are divided into constructive methods, optimization methods, Boolean inference methods, and axiomatic methods.

Constructive methods [138] involve resolving consensus problems on two levels: microstructure and macrostructure of universe U. The microstructure of set U is the structure of its elements. An example of a microstructure is linear order, divisions of different kinds (for example those characterized in papers by [8, 135, 137]). The macrostructure of set U is its structure. It can be a distance function, a relation. In constructive methods axioms to be met by the consensus are not formulated, instead they are defined immediately.

Optimizing methods [195] involve defining consensus functions with optimization rules. Quasi-median functions are very often used in the methods, hence the consensus is closer to all solutions it derives from, at the same time the distances between the consensus and individual solutions are even. The following optimization rules are used [196]:

1. Global optimality. The selected objects should be optimal in a global sense which means that if object a is regarded by all parties of the conflict as better than object b then object a should be in the consensus.
2. Condorcet optimality. The rule says that objects selected for consensus should be better from others in every comparison.
3. Median functions. Objects in the consensus should be as similar to profile elements as possible.
4. Quasi-median functions. Objects in the consensus should be as similar to profile elements as possible, and the distances between the consensus and profile elements should be as even as possible.

Booelan inference methods approach the problem of determining consensus as an optimization problem and involve coding the optimization problem in the form of a boolean formula in such a way that 'every prime implicant of the formula determines the solution to the problem' [137]. Boolean inference is useful when the number of variables and their domains are not big.

Subject literature also distinguishes **axiomatic consensus methods**. Axioms define conditions to be met by consensus or functions that determine consensus [139]. A total of eight requirements for determining consensus have been formulated [137]:

1. Unlimited domain (UD). Function for determining consensus must be defined for every situation, in other words it must be independent of the preferences of parties in a conflict. Regardless of what kind of solutions is presented by agents, consensus must be determined.
2. Order (P). If element a is better than element b in all profile elements, then element a should be in the consensus of this profile.
3. Independence of elements (IIA). Ordering two randomly selected elements (decisions) in consensus only depends on ordering these elements in the profile.
4. No Dictator (ND). Consensus cannot change when the order of conflict parties changes in the profile (all agents should be treated equally).
5. Neutrality (N). Consensus cannot change when the designation of conflict parties (agents) changes.
6. Symmetry (S). Functions for determining consensus are symmetrical.
7. Condorcet Consistency (Cc). If two groups of conflict parties (agents) have common preferences when expressing their opinions together, they also have the same preferences when expressing their opinions separately.
8. Condorcet Criterion (CC). If there are over 50% of situations where element a in the profile moves ahead of element b, then element a should also move ahead of element b in consensus (for a given order).

Constructive and optimization methods can be used in the analyzed systems because one must determine the macrostructure and microstructure of agent's knowledge and find solutions (decisions) that bring satisfactory benefits.

4.2   The Process of Determining Consensus

Consensus is always determined for a given profile – a set of knowledge structures that represent the opinions of conflict parties. They can also be semantic structures that represent the knowledge of cognitive agents. For instance, if there are five agents taking part in a conflict, then the profile consists of five elements. To determine consensus for a given profile, one must define a function that allows to calculate the distance between individual elements of the profile and the consensus. Assuming the opinions of conflict parties are represented with certain knowledge structures, the process of resolving conflict involves selecting a seub0set from the set of possible solutions. Therefore, we can define the following function of distance:

The set of versions of acceptable solutions (decisions) will be marked U.

Definition 10
The macrostructure of universe U is a certain function:

$$o : U \times U \to [0, 1], \qquad (13)$$

that meets the conditions:

$(\forall x, y \in U)(o(x, y) \geq 0),$
$(\forall x, y \in U)(o(x, y) = 0 \Leftrightarrow x = y),$
$(\forall x, y \in U)(o(x, y) = o(y, x)).$ ◆

These are typical conditions for a function of distance. Note, however, that we do not assume the condition of inequality of the triangle, so the function of distance does not have to be metric. The paper [7] states that metric conditions are often put on functions of distance but in some cases they are too strong. The pair (U, o) constitutes certain space, called space with distance.

Decision-making support systems find MK-class (minimizing costs) and OU-class (defining share) functions of distance to be the most useful. They are defined in the paper [7] and characterized in detail, for example, in the papers [8, 135, 191]. These functions are a generalization of functions defined earlier in other papers [197, 198]. MK-class function of distance between two sets of elements involves determining the minimum cost of transforming one set into the other. In other words, finding the lowest number of operations required for the transformation. Since this thesis assumes that agent knowledge is represented with 'slipnetplus' network, it becomes intentional to use a function of distance of this type in the analyzed systems. Since the structure of agent's knowledge also contains levels of activation of links and nodes, an OU-class functions of distance (defining share) must also be used between two sets of elementary values of a given attribute. The function defines the share of each elementary value in the difference.

Based on the presented functions of distance, one can formally define the function of consensus, using the following marks:

$\Gamma(U)$ – set of all non-void sub-sets of universe U (set of acceptable decisions),
$\Gamma'(U)$ – set of all non-void sub-sets with repetitions of universe U,
$\cup'$ – sum of sets with repetitions.

Let $X, X_1, X_2 \in \Gamma'(U)$, $x \in U$. The following parameters are also defined:

$$o(x, X) = \sum_{y \in X} o(x, y), \qquad (14)$$

$$o^n(x, X) = \sum_{y \in X} [o(x, y)]^n \text{ for } n \in \mathbb{N}. \qquad (15)$$

Note that the parameter $o(x, X)$ represents the sum of distances from elements x of universe U to the elements of profile X, and the parameter $o^n(x, X)$ represents the sum of nth powers of the distances. The value can be interpreted as the measure of evenness of distances from element x to elements of profile X. If lower value of n, then the more even are the distances. That is how to measure the distance from a giving knowledge structure to structures generated by cognitive agents.

Considering the parameters defined earlier, the function of consensus is defined in the following way [7]:

Definition 11

The function of consensus (or the function of selecting consensus) in space (U,o) is any function in the form:

$$c : \Gamma'(U) \rightarrow \Gamma(U). \blacklozenge \qquad (16)$$

For a profile (a set of knowledge structures $X \in \Gamma'(U)$ each element of set $c(X)$ is called its *consensus,* and the entire set $c(X)$ is called the representation of profile X.

The following part of this section will present the definitions of postulates that the function of distance should meet.

Postulates for function of consensus define individual classes of the functions of consensus. Besides, since postulates are intuitive conditions to be met by the function of consensus, they are the reason for using the functions in practice.

The following definition presents postulates for function of consensus [7, 137]:

Definition 12

Let X be any profile; we say the function of consensus $c \in C$ meets the postulate of:

1. Reliability (*Re*), if

$$C(X) \neq \varnothing. \qquad (17)$$

2. Consistency (*Co*), if

$$(x \in C(x)) \Rightarrow (x \in c(X \cup' \{x\})). \qquad (18)$$

3. Quasi-unanimity (*Qu*), if

$$(x \notin C(x)) \Rightarrow ((\exists n \in N)x \in c(X \cup' \{n * x\})). \qquad (19)$$

4. Proportionality (*Pr*), if

$$(X_1 \subseteq X_2 \wedge x \in c(X_1) \wedge y \in c(X_2)) \Rightarrow (o(x, X_1) \leq o(y, X_2). \qquad (20)$$

5. 1-Optimality (O_1), if

$$(x \in C(x)) \Rightarrow (o(x, X) = \min_{y \in U} o(y, X)). \qquad (21)$$

6. 2-Optimality (O_2), if

$$(x \in C(x)) \Rightarrow (o^2(x, X) = \min_{y \in U} o^2(y, X)). \blacklozenge \qquad (22)$$

The first postulate *(reliability)* assumes that consensus can always be determined for every profile. It corresponds to an optimistic approach that every conflict can be resolved. Reliability is a common criterion in the choice theory.

The postulate of *consistency* involves meeting the condition that if an element x is the consensus for profile X, then after expanding the profile by x (i.e. $X \cup' \{x\}$), the element should be the consensus for the new profile. Consistency is a very important property of the function of consensus because it allows the users to predict the actions of rules for determining consensus when the premises of independent choices are connected. The postulate guarantees that the knowledge structure determined by consensus will be consistent, meeting all conditions imposed by the user.

According to the postulate of *quasi-unanimity,* if an element x is not consensus for profile X, then it should be consensus for profile X^1 containing X and n occurrences of element x for certain n. In other words, every element of universe U should be selected as consensus for such profile, as long as the number of its occurrences is big enough. Therefore, if the knowledge structure of most agents is the same, it will be consensus.

The postulate of *proportionality* is a quite natural property, because the bigger the profile, the bigger the difference between its elements and the selected consensus.

The final two postulates are very particular. The first postulate of *1-optimality* requires the consensus to be as close (as similar) to the elements of profile as possible. Therefore, knowledge structure, being the consensus, must be similar to all decisions of a given profile. The postulate defines a specific class of functions called *medians.* On the other hand, the postulate of *2-optimality* requires that the sum of squared distances from consensus to the elements of a profile be as small as possible. The reason for introducing this postulate results from a very natural condition for defining the function of consensus: consensus should be as 'fair' as possible; it means that its distances from the elements of a profile should be as even as possible. Evenness means that the distance between a knowledge structure being the consensus and every other knowledge structure in the profile should be similar. Note that the number $o^n(x, X)$ defined above may be treated as a measure of evenness in distance between an object $x,$ and the elements of profile X. Therefore, the above condition requires that value o^n (consensus, X) be minimal. The paper [7] shows that functions which meet the postulate of *2-optimality* are better from the functions which meet the postulate of *1-optimality* due to higher evenness, and they differ from other functions of consensus with bigger similarity to the elements of profile. Hence, the postulate of *2-optimality* is a good criterion for selecting consensus.

Note that the first three postulates, i.e. *Re, Co* and *Qu*, are independent from the structure of universe U, which is the function of distance o, while the final three postulates (Pr, O_1 and O_2) are formulated with function o. The postulates *Re, Co* and *Qu* are also used in situations when the function of distance (or generally the macrostructure) for universe U cannot be defined. One can always define the function of distance for the 'slipnetplus' network, so one can use all the postulates.

In the process of management support, especially in an environment of risk and uncertainty, one good solution is the most even consensus that is a consensus that considers all possible solutions to the same degree. It lowers the risk of a given solution to a problem (a decision made). Therefore, if the postulate of *2-optimality* enables to reach a higher evenness than the postulate of *1-optimality*, then one should also define the postulate of *n-optimality* that allows to achieve a higher evenness of consensus for $n > 2$ than the postulate of *2-optimality*. This postulate have been developed in [199] and defined as follows:

Definitions 13

We say that the function of consensus $c \in C$ meets the postulate of *n-Optimality* (O_n), if

$$(x \in C(x)) \Rightarrow (o^n(x, X) = \min_{y \in U} o^n(y, X)). \blacklozenge \tag{23}$$

This postulate is a generalization of the postulates of *1-optimality and 2-optimality*.

Another extended postulate of determining consensus in MIS is the postulate of knowledge unconformity, defined as follows [199]:

Definition 14

We say that the functions of consensus $c \in C$ meets the postulate of knowledge unconformity (U_k), if

$$(x \in C(x)) \Rightarrow \left(o^n(x, X) > \min_{y \in U} o^n(\{X \backslash x\}, X) \right). \blacklozenge \tag{24}$$

The postulate states that there may be an element of a profile, whose distance from consensus is bigger than the sum of distances of other elements of the profile from consensus (in other words, one element of the profile is very distant from others). The reason of this situation can be inadequate level of knowledge in one conflict party (cognitive agent). In this case one should not consider the decision made by that party in the consensus. The solution to this problem is the use of multi-stage determination of consensus developed in the article by [200].

It must be noted, however, that the functions of determining consensus in relation to the processed structure of knowledge of a cognitive agent must meet both the general and the extended postulates, because otherwise the consensus might not guarantee that the determined solution (decision) fill bring satisfactory benefits to the user. For example, the consensus might excessively consider one cognitive agent whose knowledge is incorrect.

The paper [7] proves it is not possible for the function of consensus to meet all postulates at once. Therefore, detailed functions of consensus defined for various structures will differ depending on the postulates that they are supposed to meet. The postulates of the function of consensus define individual methods of determining consensus, so a function of consensus for decisions will differ from a function of consensus for a temporal database or an expert's opinion.

The use of the presented postulates on the process of developing consensus algorithms does not always guarantee the determination of a correct consensus. For example, one might determine a consensus where a given element of knowledge structure may be simultaneously used and not used – that is where contradiction occurs.

For every profile (a set of decisions) one can always determine consensus (according to postulates Q_n). However, the consensus does not always make sense and may not always be accepted as a resolution of the conflict. A solution to this problem is described in subject literature as testing the profile's susceptibility to consensus. Lack of profile's susceptibility to consensus may result in the decision maker's inability to obtain a correct solution from the system and their problem with making the right decision [135]. That is why it is important to test the susceptibility to consensus from the ensuing conflict. This will allow to take action leading to resolving the conflict and, consequently, making a quick and correct decision.

Consider the following example:

Space (U, o) is defined as follows: $U = \{a, b\}$ where a, b are decisions elements, and

$$o(x,y) = \begin{cases} 0 & for \quad x = y \\ 1 & for \quad x \neq y \end{cases} \tag{25}$$

for x, y that belongs to U.

For profile $X_1 = \{a, a, a, a, a, b, b, b, b, b\}$ consensus that meets the postulates O_n is equal a or b but it must be stated that neither a nor b is good consensus because only one element of the profile is considered in it, and therefore there is no consensus in such situation. However, if one modifies the profile in the following manner: $X_2 = \{a, a, a, a, a, a, b, b, b, b, b\}$. In this case the consensus that meets the postulates O_n is a and it is a good consensus. Therefore it is safe to say that profile X_2 is more susceptible to consensus.

The example above shows that a profile is not always susceptible to consensus, so it is worth to check, prior to selecting consensus, if a given profile is susceptible to consensus, because if it is not, then it must be modified so that it becomes susceptible.

In order to develop the definition of a profile's susceptibility to consensus, first one must define the following quantities:

Let there be a space of distances (U, o), $X \in \Gamma'(U)$, and card$(X) = k$.

Quantity:

$$o^n(X) = \frac{\sum\limits_{x,y \in X} (o(x,y))^n}{k(k+1)} \quad for \, n = 1, 2, \ldots \tag{26}$$

is the arithmetic mean of all possible distances in a given profile.

Quantity:

$$o_X^n(X) = \frac{\sum\limits_{y \in X} (o(x,y))^n}{k} \quad for \, n = 1, 2, \ldots \tag{27}$$

is the arithmetic mean of all distances from object x to elements of profile X.

Quantity:

$$o_{min}^n(X) = \min_{x \in U} o_X^n(X) \quad for \, n = 1, 2, \ldots \tag{28}$$

is a minimum value of expression $o_X^n(X)$.

Quantity:

$$o_{\max}^n(X) = \max_{x \in U} o_X^n(X) \quad \text{for } n = 1, 2, \ldots \tag{29}$$

is a maximum value of expression $o_X^n(X)$.

Next is the definition of a profile's susceptibility to consensus.

Definition 15

Let there be a profile $X \in \Gamma'(U)$. We say that profile X is susceptible to consensus in regard of postulate Q_n (or Q_n - susceptible to consensus) when and only when there is a following inequality:

$$o^n(X) \geq o_{\min}^n(X). \; \blacklozenge \tag{30}$$

Note that since the quantity $o_X^n(X)$ determines the average distance in profile X, and the quantity $o_{\min}^n(X)$ determines the average distance from consensus to the elements of this profile, then profile X is susceptible to consensus (i.e. it is possible to determine 'good' consensus for it), if the second number is not bigger than the first. Satisfying the above inequality proclaims that elements of profile X are concentrated 'densely enough' around the consensus.

Considering the above example and the postulate O_1, the defined quantities are as follows:

$$o^1(X_1) = \frac{2 * 5 * 5}{10 * 11} = \frac{5}{11}, \tag{31}$$

and

$$o_{\min}^1(X_1) = \frac{5}{10}. \tag{32}$$

These two quantities are compared: $\frac{5}{11} < \frac{5}{10}$, so profile X_1 is not susceptible to consensus in regard of postulate O_1.

Whereas for profile X_2 there is:

$$o^1(X_2) = \frac{2 * 5 * 6}{11 * 12} = \frac{5}{11}, \tag{33}$$

and

$$o_{\min}^1(X_1) = \frac{5}{11}. \tag{34}$$

These two quantities are compared: $\frac{5}{11} = \frac{5}{11}$, so profile X_2 is susceptible to consensus in regard of postulate O_1.

With the above analysis of profile's susceptibility to consensus, profile regularity can be defined as follows:

Definition 16

Let there be a profile $X \in \Gamma'(U)$. We say it is n-regular for $n = 1, 2, \ldots$ when and only when for both objects $x, y \in U$ there is:

$$o_x^n(X) = o_y^n(X). \ \blacklozenge \tag{35}$$

Therefore, if every element of the knowledge structure in a profile occurs as many times as other elements, the profile is n-regular.

Based on profile regularity, one can formulate theorems about profile's susceptibility to consensus [3, 148].

Theorem 1

Every n-regular profile X, where $\text{card}(X) > 1$, is not O_n-susceptible to consensus for $n = 1, 2, \ldots$

Theorem 2

Let there be profiles $X_1, X_2 \in \Gamma'(U)$, so that $X_2 = X_1 \cup \{x\}$ for a certain $x \in X_1$ and X_1 is i-regular, then profile X_2 is Q_n - susceptible to consensus for $n = 1, 2, \ldots$.

Therefore, if one element of decisions existing in the profile is added to the profile, it will be susceptible to consensus.

Theorem 3

In space (U, o) profile $X \in \Gamma'(U)$, is always Q_n - susceptible to consensus for $n = 1, 2, \ldots$ if $\text{card}(X)$ is an odd number.

This theorem claims that if a profile is composed of an odd number of knowledge structures, it is susceptible to consensus.

Profs for Theorems 1, 2, 3 are presented in papers [7, 200].

In a situation where profile X is not susceptible to consensus, but its context (profile Y) is worse or, in other words, the conflict involved in profile X is insignificant in relation to the conflict involved in profile Y, the following definition is useful:

Definition 17

Profile X is susceptible to consensus in the context of profile Y, if $X \subset Y$, X is not susceptible to consensus and

$$o_{\max}(X) \leq o_{\min}(Y). \ \blacklozenge \tag{36}$$

Therefore, in certain situations, if the profile is not susceptible to consensus, one must find its context in order to determine the consensus of the processed profile. In the process of decision making, it comes down to remaking a decision through given methods or increasing the number of methods used. The test for susceptibility to consensus should be conducted automatically, without any interference from the user. The procedure of testing for susceptibility to consensus must be implemented in computer-aided management systems where the consensus theory is used for resolving conflicts, because the results given by the system have big influence on the decisions made by the managing personnel, and, consequently, the operation of the entire organization. The test for susceptibility to consensus must be considered as early as in the system design phase, allowing smooth implementation of the procedures. Apart from cognitive agents performing their function of supporting management, unable to detect a conflict by themselves, the system must also be composed of conflict detection procedures, tests for susceptibility to consensus and, obviously, the methods for determining consensus. The elements should usually be implemented as a separate cognitive agent, operating within the system. Once a conflict is detected, the agent tests its susceptibility to consensus and, if it is susceptible, then consensus is determined. If the conflict is not susceptible to consensus, then it is modified to become susceptible and consensus is determined afterwards. This guarantees that the solution (decision) presented to the user is correct. All the procedures must work very quickly in close-to-real time because it is important for the user to make a decision as quickly as possible.

4.3 Analysis of the Existing Applications of the Consensus Theory in Resolving Conflicts of Unstructured Knowledge

Existing papers on resolving conflicts of unstructured knowledge mostly involved presentation of documents in the form of Term Frequency Matrix (TFM) [e.g. 201, 202], and ontology [137, 193].

Taking into consideration TFM, first it is necessary to define a profile. It needs to be noted that the profile is not made up of all text documents stored in the system, but documents connected with each other thematically, for example one profile may consist of documents containing opinions of users about a given $p1$ product, whereas another profile may consist of documents containing opinions of users about a $p2$ product.

The formal definition of a profile of the text documents is as follows:

Definition 18
Set of N index terms $T = \{t_1, t_2, \ldots, t_N\}$ is given, where $t_i = \{0, 1\}$.

A profile $D = \{d_1, d_2, \ldots, d_M\}$ is called set of M text documents described with the use of the index terms frequency vectors of finite set T, such, that:

$$
\begin{aligned}
d_1 &= \left\langle t_{1(d_1)}, t_{2(d_1)}, \ldots, t_{N(d_1)} \right\rangle \\
d_2 &= \left\langle t_{1(d_2)}, t_{2(d_2)}, \ldots, t_{N(d_2)} \right\rangle \\
&\ldots\ldots\ldots\ldots \\
d_M &= \left\langle t_{1(d_M)}, t_{2(d_M)}, \ldots, t_{N(d_M)} \right\rangle,
\end{aligned}
\tag{37}
$$

where $t_{i(d_x)}$ denotes value of the index term t_i at the document d_x. ♦

The main advantage of vector representation of documents over keywords-based representation is the possibility of defining measures of distance between documents or user's queries, which is the essence of the second stage of the process of deriving consensus. The distance may be conceptual (low, medium, high etc.) [177], but in this work we consider the quantitative distance due to developing a formal (mathematical) model of conflict resolving. If a vector document representation has been defined, documents of similar topic should be characterized by a similar frequency of occurrence of the same keywords. With a vector document representation at hand, any document may be interpreted as a point in T-dimension space whose dimensions match individual keywords.

Consequently, in order to evaluate distances between documents, and between documents and a query, one may use any measures used to measure distances in the Euclidean space. The measures always satisfy metric conditions (distance function is metrics). Adopting the Euclidean distance is connected with problems resulting from the great influence changes in the scale of coordinates have on results of grouping elements of space features, for example keywords (to avoid the problem the features value space has to be normalized, which results in a greater complexity of the distance calculation algorithm). Apart from the known measures of distance used in multidimensional Euclidean spaces, for the need of information searching systems a lot of specific measures have been devised, such as the cosine distance or Hamming distance [203]. In the article, in order to calculate distance, the metric measure of Hamming distance will be used. It has been claimed that the advantage of such a type of distance is the lack of influence of independent increase of coordinates on its value [203].

Hamming distance between two text strings of equal length is the number of positions in which their corresponding symbols are different. In other words, it measures the minimum number of substitutions required to change one string into the other, or the minimum number of errors that could have transformed one string into the other.

Hamming distance meets all metric and formal conditions, and in case of binary vectors, it is defined in the following way:

Definition 19

Let d_1, d_2 denote index terms frequency vectors characterized the text documents, then:

$$\omega(d_1, d_2) = \sum_{i=1}^{N} [d_1[i] \otimes d_2[i]] \tag{38}$$

where $d_x[i] = \{0, 1\}$ $(i = \{1, \ldots, M\})$ denotes a value of the ith index term of vector d_x, while the symbol $\otimes$ denotes an exclusive disjunction, operation means by which we obtain the following values:

$$[d_1[i] \otimes d_2[i]] = 0 \quad \Leftrightarrow \quad d_1[i] = d_2[i], \tag{39}$$

$$[d_1[i] \otimes d_2[i]] = 1 \quad \Leftrightarrow \quad d_1[i] \neq d_2[i]. \blacklozenge \tag{40}$$

Using presented definition of distance, the consensus function can be defined (third stage of consensus deriving). With regard to the representation of text documents using binary index terms frequency vectors this function is defined as follows:

Definition 20

Let D profile is given, and W denotes a set of all valuations of terms indexing T. The consensus of D is called following function:

$$Con(D) = \left\{ c \in W : \omega^2(c, D) = \min\left(\sum_{i=1}^{M} \omega(c, d_i)^2\right) \right\} \blacklozenge \qquad (41)$$

An algorithm which derives consensus according to a function specified in Definition 20 is a heuristic algorithm (as we are dealing with NP-complete problem) and it looks as follows:

Algorithm 1

```
Data:   A profile D = {d₁, d₂, ..., d_M} consists of M frequency
vectors characterized the text documents.
Result: Consensus c = Con(D) = ⟨t₁, t₂ ..., tₙ⟩ according D.
START
1: Let   j:=1.
         M
2: s =   Σ  dᵢ[j].
        i=1
3: If  s = M / 2 then  c[j] = random.
If s < M / 2 then  c[j] = 0.
If  s > M / 2 then  c[j] = 1.
4: If  j<N then  j=j+1, go to: 2.
If  j=N then go to: 5.
5: o = ω²(c, D).
6: Let j:=1.
7: c[j] = ¬c[j].
8: If ω²(c, D) < o  then  o = ω²(c, D).
   If ω²(c, D) > o  then  c[j] = ¬c[j].
9: If  j<N then  j=j+1, go to: 7.
If  j=N then END.
END.
```

The complexity of the algorithm amounts to $O(NM)$.

Taking into consideration resolving conflicts between ontologies, this is done on the concept level, instance level and relation level.

Considering the concept level, note that the same nodes can have different structures in different ontologies. Assuming that in ontology O_i the concept has a structure $\langle A^i, V^i \rangle$ for i = 1, ..., M (M – number of ontologies that require integration). The problem conflict's resolving on relations level can be presented as follows:

Algorithm 2

```
Input: Concept structures ⟨Aⁱ, Vⁱ⟩ for i = 1, ... , M .
```
$$\text{Input: Concept structures } \langle A^i, V^i \rangle \text{ for } i = 1, \ldots, M.$$

```
Output: Pair ⟨A*, V*⟩ as a result of the integration of
pairs.
START
```

1. Set $A^* = \bigcap_{i=1}^{M} A^i$.

2. For every pair of objects a, b from set A^* :
If $a \rightarrow b$ and b is not in relation with another object
from set A^* then set $A^* = A^* \setminus \{b\}$.

3. For every object a from set A^* determine its domain V_a
as a sum of its domains in pairs $\langle A^i, V^i \rangle$.

END

For a given set of pairs: $X = \{\langle A^i, V^i \rangle\}$ (where $\langle A^i, V^i \rangle$ is the structure of concept in ontology O_i) one must determine a pair $\langle A^*, V^* \rangle$ to represent a given set. This task is accomplished by Algorithm 2.

The algorithm referring to the instances level can be developed with the following assumptions:

1. Let there be a set of values $X = \{v_1, \ldots, v_M\}$, where v_i is the value of instance concept C_i and function of distance d between the values. Functions of distance are determined in relation to individual types of data structures. An easy example is the distance in Euclidean space. Distances in relation to more complex knowledge structures have also been defined. For instance, the paper [7] defines functions of distances for ordered divisions and coverings, while the paper [204] defines the

Algorithm 3

```
Input: set X = {v₁, ... , vₘ}.
Output: Value v as the result of integration.
START
1. Determine v, such, that:
```

$$\sum_{i=1}^{M} d(v, v_i) = \min_{v' \in type\,(C)} \sum_{i=1}^{M} d(v', v_i)$$

$$\text{where: } C = \bigcup_{i=1}^{M} C_i .$$

END

function of distance for hierarchy trees. Cosine distance was used as distance between text extracts (Hamming distance may also be used).

2. One must find the value v of a given type, that best represents set X.

In terms of relation level, consider a situation where relations between concepts c and c' differ in ontologies that knowledge conflicts appears. The problem of its resolving can be defined as follows:

For a given set $X = \{R_{O_i}(c, c')\}$ for i = 1, ..., M determine relations $R(c, c)$ that best represent set X.

Algorithm 4

```
Input: Set X = {R_{O_i}(c, c')} for i=1, ... , M.

Output: Relation R(c, c') as the result of integration.
START
```

1. Set $R(c, c') = \bigcup_{i=1}^{M} R_{O_i}(c, c')$.

2. For every arc $r \in R(c, c')$ determine the number $\tau(r)$ of its occurrence in set $R_{O_i}(c, c')$.

3. For every arc calculate:

$v(r) = \sum_{(1,1')} \tau(r')$.

4. Determine such r, that the number $v(r)$ is maximum, and $R(c, c') = R(c, c') \setminus r$.

```
END
```

In papers [205, 206] authors developed a framework of consensus-based method for fuzzy ontology integration. They proposed a conception for fuzzy ontology definition and three problems for fuzzy ontology integration on concept and relation levels and several algorithms for resolving these problems have been proposed.

The paper [148] developed the consensus algorithms for solving three levels of ontology conflicts: instance level, concept level and relation level.

In paper [207] authors developed a method for solving conflict on collaborative knowledge via social networking using consensus choice is presented. The structure of a collaborative group is distinguished by three types including centralized-, decentralized-, and distributed group. For each group type, a corresponding algorithm for conflict resolution using consensus choice has been developed.

In paper [208] a consensus theory has been used for resolving conflicts among users who describe the same wiki resources in different ways. Authors used measuring reputation scores of the wiki users for this purpose.

The paper [209] presents the hybrid architecture of web-based system user interface with application of consensus methods. The proposed architecture is based on the solution that there is some combination of collaborative filtering with elements of demographic recommendation solution with some elements of content-based approach.

4.4   Determinants of Using the Consensus Theory in Resolving the Analyzed Conflicts in Management Information Systems

The results obtained by using the consensus methods are a good representation of a given set of solutions or decisions because they consider virtually all subsets of the considered set of solutions or decisions, while choice methods, for example, consider only one subset of a given set of solutions or decisions to a large extent, and minimizing the consideration of other subsets of the analyzed set of solutions or decisions. Assuming that every method of decision making support is a conflict party, when the consensus method is used to resolve a conflict, the consensus will be a solution that brings the following benefits:

1. Every conflict party is considered in consensus.
2. Every conflict party 'loses' as little as possible.
3. Every conflict party brings its input in the consensus.
4. All parties accept the consensus.
5. The consensus is a representation of all conflict parties.

In conclusion, by using consensus methods, the manager (decision maker) uses results of several management support methods simultaneously, hence the decision maker saves time, not being forced to think about which method to choose. The risk of choosing the wrong management support method is also reduced. It enables a quick management and decision-making process at lower risk, which obviously leads to a better operation of the entire organization in the market economy.

Summarizing the considerations of this section, it is concluded that:

1. The consensus theory has properties which can be used in resolving conflicts in MIS.
2. So far, resolving conflicts with the consensus theory has not been applied in cognitive MIS.
3. The consensus theory may turn out to be useful because it reduces the risk of taking the wrong decisions to minimum, which results from the first property of the theory. Using the consensus theory, the decision maker does not have to reflect on choosing one of several solutions, instead he/she receive one solution, which obviously shortens the time necessary for making a decision, and, consequently leads to a more efficient operation of the entire organization.

Therefore, the consensus theory can also be used in resolving conflicts of unstructured knowledge of cognitive agents in MIS because consensus methods enable changing the state of knowledge of an agent in various conditions, not only when the agent allows that. Hence, a formal method for resolving conflicts of unstructured knowledge of cognitive agents will be developed in the next section.

5   The Use of Consensus Theory for Knowledge Conflicts' Resolving in the Considered Systems

5.1   Construction of a Method for Cognitive Agents' Unstructured Knowledge Conflicts Resolving

In general, the conflicts' resolving of unstructured knowledge of cognitive agents in management information systems concerns a situation in which there are a number of slipnetpluses representing the same piece of reality at a given time. The conflicts' resolving consists in determining the representation of these slipnetpluses'. In order to resolving these conflicts of knowledge, consensus deriving algorithms have been developed that refer to the levels of nodes, links axioms and instances.

Nodes Level
On this level it is assume that two nodes differ from each other in their structures (objects or values of objects, which their nodes represents or in activation level). That means these slipnetpluses can contain the same node but its structure is different in each slipnetpluses. The reason of this phenomenon is that these slipnetpluses come from different autonomous cognitive agents.

Algorithm 5

```
Input: Given set of structures of a node in M slipnet-
pluses
```
$$X = \left\{ \left\langle o^*, V^*, al^* \right\rangle : \left\langle o^*, V^*, al^* \right\rangle \text{ is a structure of node } n \right.$$
$$\left. \text{in slipnetplus } SN_i \text{ for } i = 1, ..., M \right\}$$
```
Output: Triple
```
$n^* = \left\langle o^*, V^*, al^* \right\rangle$ as a consensus of elements
```
from X.

START
1. Set
```
$o^* = o^i$.
```
2. Determine set
```
$X_V = \left\{ v^i : i = 1, ... M \right\};$
```
   Calculate
```
$v^* = \dfrac{1}{card(X_V)} \displaystyle\sum_{v \in X_v} v$;

```
3.    Determine set
```
$X_{al} = \left\{ al^i : i = 1, ... M \right\};$
```
      Order set X₀ in increasing order giving
```
$X = \left\{ al_1, al_2, ..., al_M \right\};$
```
2. Set interval
```
$\left\langle al_{\left\lceil \frac{M+1}{2} \right\rceil}, al_{\left\lceil \frac{n+2}{2} \right\rceil} \right\rangle$; Set al^* as value belong-
```
ing to the above defined interval
END
```

Definition 21

Let nodes SN_1 and SN_2 are in <O, V>-based slipnetpluses. Let node $\langle n_1, o^{n1}, V^{n1}, al^{n1} \rangle \in SN_1$ and node $\langle n_2, o^{n2}, V^{n2}, al^{n2} \rangle \in SN_2$. The conflict on node level take place if $n_1 = n_1$, but $o^{n1} \neq o^{n2}$ or $V^{n1} \neq V^{n2}$ or $al^{n1} \neq al^{n2}$. ◆

Definition 21 specifies such situations in which two slipnetpluses define the same node in different ways. For example node car in one slipnetplus may be defined by structure: Engine Production_year with weight 1.0, while in other agent it is defined by attributes: Engine, Production_year, and Color with weight 0.8. Thus on node level the problem of conflicts resolving is following:

For given a set of structures of the same node:

$X = \{\langle o^i, V^i, al^i \rangle : \langle o^i, V^i, al^i \rangle$ is a structure of node n in slipnetplus SN_i for $i = 1, \ldots, M\}$ is necessary to determine a pair $n^* = \langle o^*, V^*, al^* \rangle$ which best represent the given structures. Criterion "best represents" mean that one or more postulates should be satisfied by $n^* = \langle o^*, V^*, al^* \rangle$. This task is done by Algorithm 5.

The Algorithm 5 satisfying an O_2 postulate. The computation complexity of this algorithm is $O(M^2)$.

Links Level

Two kinds of slipnetplus conflicts on links level may occur. The first kind of conflict refers to situations where between the same node n and n' different slipnetpluses assign different links. As an example let's consider links Commodity and Customer, in one slipnetplus they are in link Buy, in another slipnetplus they are in link Complaint. Notice also that within the same slipnetplus two nodes may be in more than one link. Besides, the same pair of nodes can belong to the same link, but with different activation levels in different slipnetpluses. Let $L_{ij}(n, n')$ denotes the links between nodes n and n' within link L and slipnetplus SN_j for $i = 1, \ldots, K, j = 1, \ldots, M$, i.e.

$$L_{ij}(n, n') = \langle n, n', v \rangle \in L_i \tag{42}$$

where n and n' belong to slipnetplus SN_j.

We assume also that the set of nodes is the same for all slipnetpluses to be integrated.

Definition 22

Let nodes SN_1 and SN_2 are <O, V>-based slipnetpluses. Let nodes n and n' belong to both slipnetpluses. The conflict on links level take place if:

$$L_{i1}(n, n') \neq L_{i2}(n, n') \tag{43}$$

for some $i = 1, \ldots, K$. ◆

Based on the defined kinds of knowledge conflicts between slipnetpluses, we have the following problems of solving these conflicts:

1. For given $i = 1, \ldots, K$. and set $X = \{L_{ij}(n, n') : j = 1, \ldots, M\}$ of links between two nodes n and n' in M slipnetpluses it is needed to determine $L_i(n, n')$ of final links between n and n' which is consensus for given links.

In this problem all links are treated as independent on each other. However, it is always possible because some links can be, for example transitive, that is if pair $<n, n'>$ belongs to L_i with some activation level al_1 and pair $<n', n''>$ belongs to Li with activation level al_2 then pair $<n, n''>$ belongs to L_i with activation level $al = \min\{al_1, al_2\}$. In this case each pair of nodes cannot be treated separately.

In more general case where there are known the characteristics of links, for example symmetric, transitive, the problem conflict's resolving is more complex.

Algorithm 6
```
Input: Given set of  X = {L_{ij}(n, n') : j = 1, ... , M}
of links between two nodes n and n' in M slipnetpluses
Output: Pair  L_i(n, n') = (n, n', al) as a consensus of elements
from X.
START
1. Order set X in increasing order giving
     X = {x₁, x₂, ... , x_M};
```

2. Set interval $\left\langle x_{\left\lceil \frac{M+1}{2} \right\rceil}, x_{\left\lceil \frac{n+2}{2} \right\rceil} \right\rangle$;

```
Set al as value belonging to the above defined interval;
END
```

The Algorithm 6 satisfying an O_1 postulate. The computation complexity of this algorithm is $O(M^2)$.

2. The second kind of resolving conflict of knowledge is related to situations in which the same link is defined differently in different slipnetpluses. For example, for the same set of nodes {Value_of_sales, Income, Profit} link Influence can be transitive, that is if a value of sales influences on income and income influence on profit, then a value of sales also influence on profit to some degree. Besides, in one slipnetplus this relation occurs only between nodes Value_of_sales and Income, while in other slipnetplus it occurs between nodes Profit and Income. The conflict's resolving problem referring to this case is formulated as follows: For given $i = 1, \ldots, K$. and set of links $X = \{L_{ij} \subseteq N \times N \times (0, 1] : j = 1, \ldots, M\}$ it is needed to determine link $L_i \subseteq C \times C \times (0, 1]$ which is consensus for given links.

Algorithm 7

```
Input: Given set of X = {L_ij(n, n') : j = 1, ..., M}
of transitive links between two nodes n and n' in M slip-
netpluses
Output: Pair L_i(n, n') = (n, n', al) as a consensus of elements
from X.
START
1. Set L_i = ∅;
2. For each pair (n, n') ∈ C × C do
   Begin
   Determine multi-set
      X_(n,n') = {al : (c, c', al) ∈ L_ij for j = 1, ..., M};
   Order set X_(n,n') in increasing order giving
      X = {x_1, x_2, ..., x_M};
```

$$\text{Set interval} \left(x_{\left\lceil \frac{M+1}{2} \right\rceil}, x_{\left\lceil \frac{n+2}{2} \right\rceil} \right);$$

```
   Set al as value belonging to the above defined inter-
   val;
   Set L_i := L_i ∪ {(c, c', al)}
   End
   For each (c, c', c'') ∈ C × C × C do
   Begin
      If (c, c', al_1) ∈ L_i, (c, c', al_2) ∈ L_i and (c, c', al_3) ∈ L_i then
         change al_3 = min{al_1, al_2}
      If only (c, c', al_1) ∈ L_i and (c, c', al_2) ∈ L_i then set
      L_i := L_i ∪ {(c, c', al_3)} where al_3 = min{al_1, al_2}
END
```

The Algorithm 7 satisfying a O_1 postulate. The computation complexity of this algorithm is $O(M^2)$.

Axioms Level

The conflicts on axioms level is defined similar to links level. Also algorithms are similar.

Instances Level

An algorithm for instance level can be compiled assuming the following assumptions:

1. The set of values $X = \{v_1, \ldots, v_M\}$ is given, where v_i is the value of the object instance O_i and the distance function d between the values is also given. Distance functions are defined for each type of data structure. A simple example is the distance in the Euclidean space. Distance was also defined for more complex knowledge structures. For example, in [7], the distance functions for dividing and ordered partitions were defined, while in [194] the distance function for hierarchical trees was defined. The work [133] defines distance function for the structure of the financial decision (defined as the set of financial instruments. In this paper, as the distance between the parts of the text is used cosine distance (Hamming distance can also be used).
2. Find the value of v of the type that best represents the set X.

Algorithm 8

```
Input: The set X = {v₁, ... , v_M}.
Output: Value v as consensus.
START
1. Determine v, such, that:
```

$$\sum_{i=1}^{M} d(v, v_i) = \min_{v' \in type(O)} \sum_{i=1}^{M} d(v', v_i)$$

$$\text{where: } O = \bigcup_{i=1}^{M} o_i.$$

```
END
```

The Algorithm 8 satisfying an O_2 postulate. The computation complexity of this algorithm is $O(M^2)$.

5.2   Empirical Verification of the Developed Method

The empirical verification of the developed method has been performed with use CIMIS prototype (characterized in Sub-sect. 2.2) in relation to two areas:

- supporting trading decision on Forex (Foreign Exchange) market; functionalities related to Forex are placed in financial investment module (financial-accounting sub-system) of CIMIS,
- analysis users' opinions about selected products and services.

It is necessary to put stress, that the purpose of these experiments is evaluating an usability the developed method for unstructured knowledge resolving in relation to particular cognitive agents (which running on the basis of different sources of knowledge and different management or decision making support methods). Therefore in these experiments it is not evaluate to performance of particular methods of management supporting (decision supporting) in relation to another methods. For example it's not evaluate if technical analysis is better than fundamental analysis on Forex, or if cognitive agents are better in automatic users' opinion analysis than machine learning or rule-based methods (attempts of such evaluations are presented in several this work author's research papers and many others authors' research papers). The usability of system is assumed as usability of cognitive agents running in given area.

Verification on Forex

Verification of developed method has been performed taking into consideration a period D1 of Forex - currencies quotation exchange market. In order to perform this verification, a research experiment was conducted in which the following assumptions:

1. EUR/ USD pairs were quoted from three randomly selected periods:
   - 01-08-2016 h 0:00 to 31-08-2016 h 23:59,
   - 23-09-2016 h 0:00 to 22-10-2016 h 23:59,
   - 9-11-2016 h 0:00 to 9-12-2016 h 23:59,
2. The opinions of 4 experts (in Polish language) from financial portals were used for the verification. These opinions were analyzed by a cognitive agent and based on the results of the analysis, the agent determined what decisions should be made in the examined periods (buy-value 1, sell-value −1, leave unchanged-value 0). The knowledge conflicts between opinions have been resolved by Supervisor Agent (running on the basis of developed method, and based on the results of this process have also been identified buy-sell decisions).
3. It was assumed that the unit of measure of performance (relative measure) is the pips (price change by one "point" on the Forex market is referred to as pips).
4. Transaction costs are not included.
5. Money management – It is assumed that in each transaction the investor engages 100% of its capital. The capital management strategy can be set by the user. Performance analysis was conducted using the following measures (ratios):
   - rate of return (ratio x_1),
   - number of transactions,
   - gross profit (ratio x_2),
   - gross loss (ratio x_3),
   - total profit (ratio x_4),
   - the number of profitable transactions (ratio x_5),
   - the number of profitable consecutive transactions (ratio x_6),
   - the number of profitable consecutive transactions (ratio x_7),
   - Sharpe ratio(ratio x_8)

$$S = \frac{E(r) - E(f)}{|O(r)|} \cdot 100\%, \tag{44}$$

where:
$E(r)$ – arithmetic average of the rate of return,
$E(f)$ – arithmetic average of the risk-free rate of return,
$O(r)$ – standard deviation of rates of return.

– the average coefficient of volatility (ratio x_9) is the ratio of the average deviation of the arithmetic average multiplied by 100% and is expressed:

$$V = \frac{s}{|E(r)|} \cdot 100\%. \tag{45}$$

where:
V – average coefficient of variation,
s – average deviation of the rates of return,
$E(r)$ – arithmetic average of the rates of return
– the measure known as value exposed to the risk (Value at Risk – VaR) - that is the maximum loss of the market value of the financial instrument possible to bear in a specific timeframe and at a given confidence level [210].

$$VaR = P * O * k \tag{46}$$

where:
P – the initial capital,
O – volatility - standard deviation of rates of return during the period,
k – the inverse of the standard normal cumulative distribution.

6. The following usability function [211] has been used:

$$y = (a_1x_1 + a_2x_2 + a_3(1 - x_3) + a_4x_4 + a_5x_5 + a_6x_6 + \dots$$
$$+ a_7(1 - x_7) + a_8x_8 + a_9(1 - x_9) + a_{10}(1 - x_{10})),$$

where x_i denotes the normalized values of the ratios. Coefficients a_1 to a_{10} may be also determined by the investor in accordance with his/her preferences. The function is given the values from the range [0, 1], and the agent's usability is directly proportional to the function value.

7. The results obtained on the basis of individual opinions and Supervisor agent has been compared with the results of the strategy Buy-and-Hold (the investor makes a purchase decision at the beginning of the period, and the decision of sale at the end of the period).

Experiments were performed as follows:

1. Based on the opinions of the first period, the agent determined when to buy and when to sell the EUR/ USD.
2. In the next step, taking into account the results obtained from the individual agents', Supervisor Agent and the Buy-and-Hold method, the value of capital held and the rate of return were determined for each buy/sell transaction.

3. In the final stage, the value of performance indicators was calculated for the return rates resulting from all decisions (not only the final rate of return but the total return rate calculated after each sale decision). Usability functions were also calculated.
4. Then steps 1 to 3 were repeated using data from subsequent periods. Tables 1 and 2 show the results obtained in each period.

Generalizing the results of the usability analysis, it can be seen that in the analyzed periods the decisions made generated both profits and losses. The assessment of effectiveness should take into account not only the rate of return, but also other indicators, taking also into account the level of risk associated with the investment, which allows the assessment function. It can be seen that the ranking of decision evaluations generated on the basis of expert opinion, the results of the Supervisor Agent and the B & H method differs in particular periods. In the first period the best decisions were made as a result of Supervisor Agent, while the decisions generated on the basis of experts' opinions received a higher rating than the B & H benchmark. In the second period, the decisions generated on the basis of the opinions of Experts 2, Experts 3 and Experts 4 received lower scores than Supervisor agent, but the decisions generated on the basis of Experts 1 have been evaluated higher than Supervisor Agent. The Benchmark B & H received a higher score than the one generated on the basis of Expert 4's opinion. In the third period, the results achieved by Supervisor Agent were the best. The B & H benchmark was the lowest in this period. Therefore it can be concluded, that in more cases the developed method for unstructured knowledge resolving allow to increase the level of usability of considered system (the evaluation function's values were highest in all periods).

Table 1. Results of research experiment – part 1.

Ratio	Expert 1			Expert 2			Expert 3			Expert4		
	Period 1	Period 2	Period 3	Period 1	Period 2	Period 3	Period 1	Period 2	Period 3	Period 1	Period 2	Period 3
Rate of return [pips]	−65	1920	232	22	240	310	−35	311	420	−34	−94	411
The number of transactions	11	18	20	6	12	7	9	10	14	7	5	8
Gross profit [pips]	209	884	239	158	845	358	198	911	680	119	145	539
Gross loss [pips]	180	203	109	140	698	120	220	729	456	159	175	368
Total profit	186	2485	487	320	1024	485	256	1124	1230	238	1000	1230
The number of profitable transactions	6	15	14	4	7	6	5	6	8	3	2	5
The number of profitable consecutive transactions	3	6	6	2	3	5	2	3	3	1	1	3
The number of unprofitable consecutive transactions	2	1	3	2	2	1	1	1	2	1	1	1
Sharpe ratio	0.32	2.75	1.25	1.56	1.32	3.14	0.79	1.09	2.00	3.56	1.02	2.14
Value at risk	6.00	106.67	116.00	4.40	48.0	42.86	3.12	64.00	95.00	5.10	184.0	44.35
Average coefficient of volatility	11.80	9.73	12.75	9.76	15.60	17.87	23.01	21.87	7.30	11.45	25.70	22.34
Value of usability function (y)	0.18	0.43	0.17	0.32	0.31	0.21	0.23	0.33	0.28	0.19	0.11	0.22

Table 2. Results of research experiment – part 2.

Ratio	Consensus			B&H		
	Period 1	Period 2	Period 3	Period 1	Period 2	Period 3
Rate of return [pips]	15	430	538	−220	730	295
The number of transactions	4	5	6	1	1	1
Gross profit [pips]	186	834	735	0	730	295
Gross loss [pips]	120	468	532	−220	0	0
Total profit	234	1123	1431	0	0	0
The number of profitable transactions	3	4	4	0	1	1
The number of profitable consecutive transactions	2	3	3	0	1	1
The number of unprofitable consecutive transactions	1	1	1	1	0	0
Sharpe ratio	3.20	2.00	3.38	0.00	0.00	0.00
Value on risk	1.20	19.50	21.10	220.00	730.00	295.00
Average coefficient of volatility	2.17	6.35	4.45	0.00	0.00	0.00
Value of evaluation function (y)	0.28	0.44	0.54	0.12	0.23	0.18

Verification on Automatic Users' Opinions Analysis

In order to verify developed method, also the series of research experiments related to users opinions' analysis about products/services (in polish language), has been carried out. In these experiments the results of experiments presented in [54, 212, 213] (related to opinion about tv sets, mobile phones and hotels) have been extended about knowledge conflicts resolving method (Supervisor Agent). Also new experiment related to opinions about restaurants, has been carried out. In further part of this section this new research experiments and results related to all experiments, have been presented.

In this new experiment results of automatic analysis of opinions about the restaurants were compared with results of an analysis performed by a human (an expert), i.e. a manual analysis. The following assumptions were adopted in the experiment:

1. The three cognitive agents performing opinions analysis and Supervisor Agent performing unstructured conflicts resolving has been used.
2. The opinions about restaurants were received from web pages (each agent used a different webpage).
3. Number of analyzed opinions by each agent: 385. Because manual annotation (very time consuming process) has to be performed by human (expert), the number of opinion is limited. The opinions was randomly selected from several thousand opinions from several web pages in order to limit the possibilities of selection of large number of opinions from the same person (friend of hotel director or competitor, fake news to kill competitor, etc.).
4. If the numerical assessment appears, e.g. from 0 (very bad assesment) to 5 (very good assessment), then value less then 2.5 is assumed as negative opinion and value equals or greater than 2.5 is assumed as positive opinion.

5. For the needs of the experiment, five features of restaurants and their services were analyzed:
   – location,
   – food (meals),
   – price,
   – personnel.
6. If analyzed opinion did not contain information about given feature's sentiment then the sentiment of that feature was the same as overall sentiment of opinion.
7. A learning set consist of 80 opinions. Each agent was used a training set developed on the basis of the opinion from the website it used (the learning sets of particular agents differ in a certain degree).
8. In order to determine the accuracy of results of automatic analysis in relation to results of manual analysis, the effectiveness, the precision and the sensitivity measures was used.

Research experiment was carried out in the following way:

1. 385 randomly selected opinions about restaurants found on web sites were recorded in a data base by particular agents.
2. Manual annotation (by human) was performed.
3. The opinions were grouped according to the degree of difficulty (three groups – group 1 – sentiment of opinions and features easy to determine, group 3 - sentiment of opinions and features difficult to determine) of determining their sentiment and the sentiment of features of services offered by restaurants characterized in the opinions (Table 3).

Table 3. Types of opinions according the degree of difficulty of their analysis.

No.	Sample content of opinion (written in Polish language they was translated into English in this paper)
1	Very good restaurant, I recommend
2	Encouraging opinions prompted me to visit this place. Often passing by, I noticed there a lot of traffic, which was also to be a determinant of quality for me. The food was quite tasty and served reasonably. Ladies with nice and competent service. However, the prices are very high
3	We had to eat in an Italian restaurant, however, we came to this one. The restaurant has a family atmosphere, it is not feigned and force is sometimes found in Italian restaurants. Eat fresh, well-seasoned and most importantly tasty. The only minus is the price

Source: own work.

The opinions of the first group contain only text related to sentiment of opinions (individual features are not described), so it is easy to recognize the sentiment, however sentiment of individual features is treated as sentiment of opinions. The second group of opinions contains knowledge about sentiment of individual features. Recognizing of a particular feature can be difficult in this case. The third group of opinions is the most difficult to analyze as opinions belonging to the group contain descriptions of several restaurants in one opinion. It is difficult to determine to which restaurant sentiment of opinions should be assigned and to which restaurant/service should be assigned the features characterized in the opinion.

4. All the 385 opinions were loaded, one by one, into the sensory memory, analyzed, and saved results of the analysis in a database by particular cognitive agents.
5. Next, the knowledge conflicts resolving by Supervisor Agent have been done (separately in relation to each group of opinions).
6. Next measures of performance were calculated taking into consideration particular groups of degree of difficulty.

Table 4, 5, 6 presents the list of results obtained by particular agents.

Table 4. Results of the opinions' and features' sentiment analysis by agent 1.

Group of the opinion	Measure	Sentiment of opinions	Features			
			Food	Location	Price	Personnel
1	Effectiveness	0.8767	0.8767	0.8767	0.8767	0.8767
	Precision	0.8869	0.8869	0.8869	0.8869	0.8869
	Sensitivity	1.0000	1.0000	1.0000	1.0000	1.0000
2	Effectiveness	0.8751	0.7689	0.8120	0.7410	0.7832
	Precision	0.8942	0.6712	0.6585	0.5523	0.6556
	Sensitivity	1.0000	0.6867	0.6917	0.8468	0.7646
3	Effectiveness	0.6962	0.6923	0.6817	0.7126	0.7216
	Precision	0.7231	0.5556	0.7778	0.7300	0.5911
	Sensitivity	0.7612	0.5646	0.6439	0.8111	0.6665
Average	**Effectiveness**	**0.8160**	**0.7793**	**0.7901**	**0.7768**	**0.7938**
	Precision	**0.8347**	**0.7046**	**0.7744**	**0.7231**	**0.7112**
	Sensitivity	**0.9204**	**0.7504**	**0.7785**	**0.8860**	**0.8104**

Table 5. Results of the opinions' and features' sentiment analysis by agent 2.

Group of the opinion	Measure	Sentiment of opinions	Features			
			Food	Location	Price	Personnel
1	Effectiveness	0.8611	0.8611	0.8611	0.8611	0.8611
	Precision	0.8729	0.8729	0.8729	0.8729	0.8729
	Sensitivity	1.0000	1.0000	1.0000	1.0000	1.0000
2	Effectiveness	0.8624	0.7014	0.7120	0.7311	0.7724
	Precision	0.8812	0.6592	0.6467	0.5640	0.6530
	Sensitivity	1.0000	0.6750	0.6780	0.8386	0.7391
3	Effectiveness	0.6811	0.6819	0.6745	0.7050	0.7158
	Precision	0.7192	0.5675	0.7650	0.7247	0.5893
	Sensitivity	0.7587	0.5540	0.6556	0.7980	0.6565
Average	**Effectiveness**	**0.8015**	**0.7481**	**0.7492**	**0.7657**	**0.7831**
	Precision	**0.8244**	**0.6999**	**0.7615**	**0.7205**	**0.7051**
	Sensitivity	**0.9196**	**0.7430**	**0.7779**	**0.8789**	**0.7985**

Table 6. Results of the opinions' and features' sentiment analysis by agent 3.

Group of the opinion	Measure	Sentiment of opinions	Features			
			Food	Location	Price	Personnel
1	Effectiveness	0.8805	0.8805	0.8805	0.8805	0.8805
	Precision	0.8926	0.8926	0.8926	0.8926	0.8926
	Sensitivity	1.0000	1.0000	1.0000	1.0000	1.0000
2	Effectiveness	0.8789	0.7710	0.8120	0.7516	0.7910
	Precision	0.8996	0.6786	0.6614	0.5587	0.6616
	Sensitivity	1.0000	0.6792	0.6715	0.7129	0.7689
3	Effectiveness	0.6928	0.6817	0.6791	0.6840	0.6920
	Precision	0.7134	0.5685	0.7698	0.5382	0.5712
	Sensitivity	0.7681	0.5513	0.6469	0.6102	0.6558
Average	**Effectiveness**	**0.8174**	**0.7777**	**0.7905**	**0.7720**	**0.7878**
	Precision	**0.8352**	**0.7132**	**0.7746**	**0.6632**	**0.7085**
	Sensitivity	**0.9227**	**0.7435**	**0.7728**	**0.7744**	**0.8082**

Table 7 presents the average of measures obtained by agents 1–3.

Table 7. Average results of agents 1–3.

Group of the opinion	Measure	Sentiment of opinions	Features			
			Food	Location	Price	Personnel
1	Effectiveness	0.8728	0.8728	0.8728	0.8728	0.8728
	Precision	0.8841	0.8841	0.8841	0.8841	0.8841
	Sensitivity	1.0000	1.0000	1.0000	1.0000	1.0000
2	Effectiveness	0.8721	0.7471	0.7787	0.7412	0.7822
	Precision	0.8917	0.6697	0.6555	0.5583	0.6567
	Sensitivity	1.0000	0.6803	0.6804	0.7994	0.7575
3	Effectiveness	0.6900	0.6853	0.6784	0.7005	0.7098
	Precision	0.7186	0.5639	0.7709	0.6643	0.5839
	Sensitivity	0.7627	0.5566	0.6488	0.7398	0.6596
Average	**Effectiveness**	**0.8116**	**0.7684**	**0.7766**	**0.7715**	**0.7883**
	Precision	**0.8315**	**0.7059**	**0.7702**	**0.7023**	**0.7082**
	Sensitivity	**0.9209**	**0.7456**	**0.7764**	**0.8464**	**0.8057**

Table 8 presents results obtained by Supervisor Agent.

Table 8. Results of knowledge integration by Supervisor Agent.

Group of the opinion	Measure	Sentiment of opinions	Features			
			Food	Location	Price	Personnel
1	Effectiveness	0.8792	0.8792	0.8792	0.8792	0.8792
	Precision	0.8893	0.8893	0.8893	0.8893	0.8893
	Sensitivity	1.0000	1.0000	1.0000	1.0000	1.0000
2	Effectiveness	0.8756	0.7512	0.7806	0.7485	0.7822
	Precision	0.8986	0.6712	0.6587	0.5615	0.6612
	Sensitivity	1.0000	0.6816	0.6804	0.8120	0.7610
3	Effectiveness	0.6943	0.6894	0.6816	0.7045	0.7186
	Precision	0.7212	0.5631	0.7745	0.6682	0.5912
	Sensitivity	0.7685	0.5570	0.6514	0.7425	0.6612
Average	**Effectiveness**	**0.8164**	**0.7733**	**0.7805**	**0.7774**	**0.7933**
	Precision	**0.8364**	**0.7079**	**0.7742**	**0.7063**	**0.7139**
	Sensitivity	**0.9228**	**0.7462**	**0.7773**	**0.8515**	**0.8074**

On the basis on presented results we can state that effectiveness, precision and sensitivity of recognizing sentiment of opinions by all the agents, are high. The cause of this fact is that most often, users must obligatory determining sentiment of opinion. In case the features' sentiment analysis, the performance of this process is lower than the performance of recognizing sentiment of opinions, which means that not all words (expressions) indicating features' sentiment determined manually have been found by an agent. It caused mainly from the fact that not all of these words (expressions) were appearing in learning set. Low values of measures of group 3 opinions' sentiment analysis mean that the sentiment of the features in many cases had not been recognized correctly, i.e. many features having positive opinion had been recognized as features of a negative opinion or just the opposite.

Taking into consideration particular agents it can be state, that in relation to opinions sentiment analysis and in most cases of features sentiment analysis the third agent was the best. The results achieved by Supervisor Agent were better than results achieved by first and second agents and also were better than average results of agents' number 1 to 3.

Taking into consideration average values of particular measures, in relation to average of agents 1–3, one can see that the highest value of effectiveness has been obtained with respect to feature "personel" (0.7883), highest value of precision with respect to "location" (0.7702) and highest value of sensitivity with respect to feature "price" (0.8515). The lowest value of effectiveness has been obtained with respect to feature "food" (0.7684), lowest value of precision with respect to "price" (0.7063) and lowest value of sensitivity with respect to feature "food" (0.7456).

In case results achieved by Supervisor Agent the highest and the lowest values of particular measures are connected with the same features such in case average of agents 1–3.

On the basis of opinion analysis agents stated also that customers prefer to buy restaurant services paying attention mainly to the features of:

- food,
- personnel.

Therefore managers of restaurants must strive to improve the quality of service in these areas, as well as to take into consideration these areas during developing marketing strategies.

The limitation of this research is missing knowledge about participants (one like fusion cuisine, other may not). Also the number of opinions should be higher in order to make wider and precisely conclusions.

Taking into consideration a series of experiments the results are presented in Table 9 (in Table 1 experiments are numbered as follows: 1 - experiment related to opinions about restaurants, 2 - experiment related to hotels, 3 - experiment related to tv-set, 4 - experiment related to mobile phones). Due to in particular experiments the features sets differs, the averages values of effectiveness, precision and sensitivity of all the features has been calculated.

Table 9. Results series of experiments

Experiment number	Measure	Agent 1		Agent 2		Agent 3		Supervisor	
		Sentiment of opinions	Sentiment of features	Sentiment of opinions	Sentiment of features	Sentiment of opinions	Sentiment of features	Sentiment of opinions	Sentiment of features
1	Effectiveness	0.8160	0.7850	0.8015	0.7615	0.8174	0.7820	0.8164	0.7811
	Precision	0.8347	0.7283	0.8244	0.7218	0.8352	0.7149	0.8364	0.7256
	Sensitivity	0.9204	0.8063	0.9196	0.7996	0.9227	0.7747	0.9228	0.7956
2	Effectiveness	0.8345	0.8274	0.8185	0.7414	0.7240	0.7587	0.8236	0.7954
	Precision	0.8420	0.7324	0.8201	0.7020	0.8004	0.6980	0.8402	0.7386
	Sensitivity	0.9365	0.8276	0.9049	0.7786	0.8760	0.7347	0.9324	0.8201
3	Effectiveness	0.7245	0.7534	0.8136	0.7834	0.7543	0.7678	0.7745	0.7793
	Precision	0.7532	0.6346	0.8327	0.7632	0.7634	0.7735	0.8295	0.7683
	Sensitivity	0.8241	0.7563	0.9236	0.8236	0.8076	0.7826	0.8950	0.8124
4	Effectiveness	0.7680	0.7648	0.7456	0.7428	0.8328	0.7936	0.8268	0.7878
	Precision	0.8526	0.7038	0.8478	0.6450	0.8745	0.7247	0.8532	0.7134
	Sensitivity	0.9057	0.7765	0.8956	0.7547	0.9358	0.7875	0.9258	0.7794

In order to usability calculation, the following aggregated measures of effectiveness, precision and sensitivity of particular agents, have been calculated (Table 10):

- arithmetic average,
- average deviation,
- risk measure (the average coefficient of variation.

The following usability function, related to particular measures, has been developed:

$$y = (am + b(1 - r))$$

where m denotes the values given measure (effectiveness, precision, sensitivity) and r denotes the value of risk measure (due to these values are interval [0,1] it is not necessary to normalize them). Coefficients a and b may be also determined by the investor in accordance with his/her preferences. In these experiments these coefficient values are 0.5.

Taking into consideration results achieved by particular agents (Table 9) it can be stated, that in particular experiments different agents achieved the best results. In first experiment agent no 3 achieves the best result and agent no 2 achieves the worst results. In second experiment agent no 1 achieves the best result and agent no 3 achieves the worst results. In third experiment agent no 2 achieves the best result and agent no 1 achieve the worst results. In fourth experiment agent no 3 achieves the best result and agent no 2 achieves the worst results.

Table 10. Aggregated measures and usability function values.

Aggregated measures	Measure	Agent 1		Agent 2		Agent 3		Supervisor	
		Sentiment of opinions	Sentiment of features	Sentiment of opinions	Sentiment of features	Sentiment of opinions	Sentiment of features	Sentiment of opinions	Sentiment of features
Arithmetic Average	Effectiveness	0.7858	0.7827	0.7948	0.7573	0.7821	0.7755	0.8103	0.7859
	Precision	0.8206	0.6998	0.8313	0.7080	0.8184	0.7278	0.8398	0.7365
	Sensitivity	0.8967	0.7917	0.9109	0.7891	0.8855	0.7699	0.9190	0.8019
Average deviation	Effectiveness	0.0395	0.0236	0.0246	0.0152	0.0430	0.0123	0.0179	0.0057
	Precision	0.0337	0.0326	0.0090	0.0345	0.0365	0.0229	0.0069	0.0170
	Sensitivity	0.0363	0.0253	0.0107	0.0225	0.0437	0.0176	0.0120	0.0144
Risk measure	Effectiveness	0.0503	0.0301	0.0310	0.0201	0.0549	0.0159	0.0221	0.0072
	Precision	0.0411	0.0466	0.0108	0.0487	0.0446	0.0314	0.0082	0.0231
	Sensitivity	0.0405	0.0319	0.0117	0.0285	0.0494	0.0229	0.0131	0.0179
Usability function	Effectiveness	0.8677	0.8763	0.8819	0.8686	0.8636	0.8798	0.8941	0.8893
	Precision	0.8898	0.8266	0.9102	0.8296	0.8869	0.8482	0.9158	0.8567
	Sensitivity	0.9281	0.8799	0.9496	0.8803	0.9181	0.8735	0.9530	0.8920

Taking into consideration NLP issues and comparing to other methods of sentiment analysis (related to texts documents in Polish language) e.g. [214–216], the results achieved in experiments performed in this work are similar. However using cognitive agents in unstructured knowledge processing allows for achieve following benefits:

- taking into consideration risk and uncertainty level due to using nodes and links activation level,
- possibility of automatically decision making by cognitive agent on the basis of results of unstructured knowledge processing.

The Supervisor Agent was better than two agents and worse than one agent in each experiment. However the results achieved by Supervisor Agent have highest usability in each experiment mainly due to the low value of risk measure.

Therefore it can be concluded, that in more cases the developed method for unstructured knowledge resolving allow to increase the level of usability of considered system.

On the basic of performed research experiments it has been also state, that learning set have very big impact on the results of text documents analysis and, in consequence on usability of whole system. Therefore very important issue is to correct selection of learning set.

5.3 Conditions of Implementation of Developed Method

The developed method is general and can be used in every multi-agent management computer system. However, in order to implement it in a specific organization, one must particularly consider the needs of users, the nature of occurring problems and decisions made, the type of management support methods used, the size of the organization and the level of the computer technology utilized. The implementation of the method closely involves the implementation of MIS that uses cognitive agents, therefore the implementation determinants of the method should be connected with the implementation determinants of the system. The method can be implemented along with a new system or as an upgrade to an existing one. Note that the most effective solution is the implementation of the method in an integrated management information system such as CIMIS (characterized in Sect. 3.1.). Therefore, in order to implement MIS that uses cognitive agents and/or the method for resolving conflicts of knowledge developed in this thesis, organizational and technological determinants must be considered.

It is best to identify the organizational determinants in several stages:

1. Identify the needs.
2. Determine the necessary action.
3. Determine the types of decision supporting methods.
4. Set information sources.
5. Establish organization and information resources.
6. Determine the amount of financial means.
7. Select proper precautions.

First of all, in the first stage, one must determine the type of management problems and decisions to be supported by the system (or are supported by the existing system). It is influenced, among others, by the kind of business activity and organizational structure as well as the size of the organization. One must also consider whether to order the system from a software company or implement it on their own, provided the organization has a team of IT personnel. The cost of implementation is also a significant problem. Primarily, one must determine whether or not and to what degree the system will contribute to the effectiveness and competitiveness of the organization and whether the cost of creating and launching or upgrading the system will be commensurate with its decision supporting capabilities.

In the second stage, one should plan all the action and supervision of work in progress. It is best to allow possible modification and development of the system, since past experience in implementation of computer systems shows that additional needs may occur while the system is running. The most widely known methodologies of building the system are:

1. Incremental methodology which assumes that the system can be created in parts. Once the needs have been determined and documents created, particular parts of the system are developed according to the development plan. Once the design process, the implementation and testing is complete, overall tests are performed.
2. Iterative methodology which involves running a full development cycle of the system, from requirements to tests, and then repeating the cycle until the assumed results are achieved. It is used in situations when system requirements are not entirely known. An implementation example of such methodology is the Rational Unified Process developed by Rational Software Corporation (currently taken over by IBM). The process assumes four stages of process life: initiation, development, construction, and commissioning of the system. The initiation stage involves formulating the problem, determining the factors that affect success, developing the plan and description of the project and conducting initial risk analysis. In the second stage the basic system architecture is developed. The construction phase involves building particular components and other system functions as well as program writing. This phase may have a large number of iterations. In the final stage the system is commissioned by the software team to end users.
3. Incremental-iterative methodology that combines two methodologies: incremental and iterative.

Iterative methodology can be successfully used in the implementation of MIS that uses cognitive agents and the developed method for resolving conflicts of non-structuralized knowledge, since it often occurs that the decision maker specifies their requirements only after testing the initial version of the system. Incremental-iterative methodology can be used with the implementation of the analyzed system, provided that the decision makers change their requirements in a limited degree. Whereas, incremental methodology is used in situations when the requirements towards the developed systems are well known, so it is difficult to use it in the analyzed system because the management personnel of an organization do not always have the ability to specify their requirement at the design stage.

In the third stage one must determine the types of management and decision making support methods that will be utilized in the system. This is necessary because it determines the number of operating agents (each agent has a different method implemented in it). One can either use methods that were utilized in management without the system or augment the existing system with methods that have not been used before (e.g. due to lack of time or financial means). Naturally, methods that do not contribute to the management process due to their nature, should not be used.

The fourth stage involves setting knowledge sources (including non-structuralized knowledge) that the cognitive agents will use. The basic source is the Internet. Additionally, knowledge obtained from employees and organization managers is also used. The sources should be reliable and provide up-to-date knowledge because that guarantees proper operation of cognitive agents in the system. The agents should verify the credibility of the source, for instance by checking its certificates.

The fifth stage is about establishing organization and information resources. An analysis of the existing computer system in the organization must be conducted to determine areas that could supply knowledge for cognitive agents in MIS. Also, a team of employees must be assembled to implement (upgrade) the system and to operate it. Team leaders must be appointed as well.

In the sixth stage, the amount of financial means for the implementation (upgrade) of the system is determined. The means must be ready to cover, among others, hardware, software, employee salary, also training, system security, and maintenance and system administration after implementation.

The seventh stage involves security precautions. Like every other computer system, MIS that uses cognitive agents and a method for resolving conflicts of knowledge must properly secured, all the more that the system operates in a computer network. Otherwise it will cease to perform its function. The main problem could be the safety and security of sending and receiving data, information, and knowledge. This applies, among others, to the confidentiality of communication sent by cognitive agents and credibility of knowledge sources (the threat of 'posing' as a given server). Another problem is the physical security of the hardware, since malfunction is the most common cause of data loss. Also, if an unauthorized personnel has access to the system, they may alter or delete data used by the system, or modify the operation of individual agents. Such actions will cause the system to provide incorrect solutions and decisions which in turn may lead to faulty operation of the entire organization. Another major issue is managing the process of user authentication in the system.

Meeting the organizational conditions for implementing the system and method will not guarantee its correct operation. Technological requirements for method implementation must also be met, especially for IT tools used for implementing the model. Therefore, one must select the right hardware and software and use them effectively.

Various tools are used to implement cognitive agents, including complete platforms (e.g. LIDA, Cougaar) that allow for quick implementation of the agents. Such software may also be written from scratch in Java language. The Java language is perfect for creating cognitive agents because it allows for implementing their full mobility (agents can move around different hardware and software platforms). In small multi-agent decision-making support systems (several agents) where mobile agents do not need to be created, other programming languages can be used, such as C++, Delphi, Visual Basic, and PHP.

The knowledgebase management system is also very important. Due to processing unstructured knowledge, the best solution is using NoSQL database. The knowledgebase management system should have the following properties:

1. High capacity. Data, information and knowledge may be read and saved by agents with high frequency (agents must operate in near-real time).
2. The ability to build distributed knowledgebases, because data may be stored in different computers.

3. Servicing transactions. Data operations must be performed with transactions because this guarantees coherence of the knowledgebase.

The properties are very general and need to be put into more detail, depending on the needs of particular software environments or agent platforms.

Naturally, the question of selecting proper tools is open and largely depends on the individuals who create (upgrade) the system and implement the method for integration of knowledge. Note, however, that MIS that uses cognitive agents and the developed method for integration of non-structuralized knowledge should be as independent as possible from hardware and software platforms on which it operates.

6   Conclusions

This work addresses the problem of unstructured knowledge conflicts' resolving of cognitive agents running in management information systems. Consensus theory was used to solve this problem. The developed consensus algorithms allow for determining one consistent representation of knowledge presented by several agents. Consequently, it is possible to provide the user with a single, satisfactory solution on the basis of which decisions can be made. The developed consensus-based algorithms will further facilitate the work on multi-agent MIS as they can be directly implemented as an agent performing unstructured conflicts resolving into this type of system.

In recent works a lot of attention has been devoted to the problem of solving knowledge conflicts of cognitive agents, however, most publications mainly refer to structured-oriented knowledge. Due to the heterogeneity of knowledge sources and management methods, each agent can provide the user with a different solution to the problem. In other words, there is a conflict of unstructured knowledge between cognitive agents. Therefore, there was a need to develop a method for solving these conflicts of knowledge (which would allow the user to present one solution based on solutions generated by individual agents). This was the main aim of this work. The developed method for resolving cognitive agents' unstructured knowledge conflicts in the management system, which uses consensus theory, fulfills this task.

The conclusions can be generalized as follows:

1. An analysis of the functioning of MIS, including the use of cognitive agents, is a difficult and complex problem and so broad that it requires continuous analysis and improvement of these systems, especially in respect to knowledge management.
2. In analyzed systems, there are often conflicts of unstructured knowledge of cognitive agents and their resolving is one of the conditions for proper functioning of the system.
3. Based on the results analysis, it was concluded that the use of the developed method increase the usability of considered MIS (the evaluation function's value of Supervisor Agents was highest in performed research experiments), and in consequence enables the determination of satisfactory solutions for a given management problem. It allow for, among other, reducing risk level, costs and decisions making time.

4. The developed method extends the theory of consensus on the ability to solve conflicts of knowledge represented by slipnetplus. It also extends ways of resolving conflicts of knowledge in MIS.

On the basis of the literature analysis and the experimental results, it can be stated that the basic aim and the auxiliary and utilitarian aims have been achieved and hypothesis confirmed.

The presented method, due to its versatility and implemented tasks, will contribute to the efficient functioning of information management systems.

Presented solutions allow to fully automated decision making process without human participation. Such approach is necessary in the "Big Data" era, where processing big amount of structured and unstructured knowledge near real time is needed. As example may serve the investment decisions making on stock market or Forex market. In case high frequency trading making decision by humans is impossible because decision often must be take several times on a second.

However there also areas, where fully automated decision making cannot be performed. As example may serve research and development works. Artificial intelligence tools, including cognitive agents, are not able to carry out creative works as much as human [217].

The solutions proposed in this work, especially conception of CIMIS, can have a positive impact on corporate social responsibility and on green software development. The knowledge management process realized by CIMIS can helps to identify and manage risks related to social and environmental factors, engage in dialogue and engage stakeholders in dialogue and cooperation and increase the overall efficiency and effectiveness of the company by collecting and processing knowledge about its own activities, improvement cooperation and coordination between individual parts of the company and rationalization of expenses, lower costs of knowledge management, fewer crises and better knowledge of the market. The presented solutions may be delivered as cloud computing services (especially SaaS model). It may have a positive impact on lower energy consumption by reducing the number of servers needed to implementation of CIMIS.

The "knowledge thinking" has very strong influence on CIMIS developing. User's requirements analysis, system design, implementation and testing is performed in close coherence with knowledge management methods, techniques and tools.

The subject presented in the paper is so extensive that some of the issues discussed have been selectively treated and many important issues related to the functioning of MIS and conflict resolution of unstructured knowledge of cognitive agents have not been taken up. However, the subject matter and its interdisciplinary have forced a selective approach to the collected material.

The discussion in this paper does not exhaust the problem of resolving knowledge conflicts of cognitive agents in the MIS and impose further research objectives, including:

1. Performing the verification of developed method on existing multi-agent MIS in the real business conditions.

2. Extension of the method of representation of unstructured knowledge of cognitive agents by other methods, which will enable the use of knowledge of systems already functioning in the Internet.
3. Extend the method with the ability to personalize the system, so that each user can at any time determine according to what criteria is set consensus, and these settings would be assigned to a particular user.
4. Implementation a deep text analysis in the structure of cognitive agent.
5. Develop the methods for learning set selection.
6. Building a MIS, that use developed method and is used in practice in organizations.
7. Analysis of social aspects of human-agent interactions.
8. Integrating of KM principles to the eco design of future MIS.
9. Analysis how multi-agent systems could be used to educate Knowledge Cultivator culture.
10. Analysis how CIMIS can support the innovation processes.
11. Analysis how far the proposed system may influence a breakthrough innovation in the designing of MIS (new architectures).
12. Influence of the presented solution on the "green way" in CIMIS.
13. Using also other, than LIDA, cognitive architectures in CIMIS and to compare and to integrate results achieved by these architectures.
14. Verification of developed method on others area of management (such as CRM, logistics).

The results can be also used in further research on MIS.

References

1. Kisielnicki, J.: Management information systems. Placet, Warszawa (2013). (in Polish)
2. Wormell, I.: Databases as analytical tools. In: Dekker, M. (ed.) Encyclopedia of Library and Information Science, New York, vol. 70, no. 33, pp. 77–92 (2000)
3. Zins, C.: Conceptual approaches for defining data, information, and knowledge. J. Am. Soc. Inf. Sci. **58**, 479–493 (2007). https://doi.org/10.1002/asi.20508
4. Coulouris, G., Dollimore, J., Kindberg, T.: Distributed Systems: Concepts and Design, 5th edn. Pearson, London (2011)
5. Ferber, J.: Multi-Agent Systems: An Introduction to Distributed Artificial Intelligence. Addison Wesley, New York (1999)
6. Wooldridge, M.: An Introduction to MultiAgent Systems. Wiley, Hoboken (2002). p. 366
7. Nguyen, N.T.: Methods for deriving consensus and their application in conflict resolving in distributed systems. PWr Printing House, Wroclaw (2002). (in Polish)
8. Hernes, M., Nguyen, N.T.: Deriving consensus for hierarchical incomplete ordered partitions and coverings. J. Univ. Comput. Sci. **13**(2), 317–328 (2007)
9. Bush, P.: Tacit Knowledge in Organizational knowledge. IGI Global, Hershey, New York (2008)
10. Griffin, R.W.: Management, 11th edn. South-Western College Pub, Chula Vista (2012)
11. Drucker, P.F.: Management Challenges for 21st Century. Harper Business, New York (2000)
12. Duan, H., Zheng, Y.: A study on features of the CRFs-based Chinese named entity recognition. Int. J. Adv. Intell. Inform. **3**(2), 287–294 (2011)

13. Girdhar, J.: Management Information Systems. Oxford University Press, Oxford (2013)
14. Laudon, K.C., Laudon, J.P.: Management Information Systems: Managing the Digital Firm, 14th edn. Pearson, London (2015)
15. Burstein, F., Holsapple, C.W.: Handbook on Decision Support Systems. Springer, Berlin (2008). https://doi.org/10.1007/978-3-540-48713-5
16. Kendal, S.L., Creen, M.: An Introduction to Knowledge Engineering. Springer, London (2007). https://doi.org/10.1007/978-1-84628-667-4
17. Adamczewski, P.: Evolution in ERP-expanding functionality by bi-modules in knowledge-based management systems. In: Kubiak, B.F., Korowicki, A. (eds.) Information Management. Gdansk University Press, Gdańsk (2009)
18. Nycz, M.: Business intelligence as the exemplary modern technology influencing on the development on the enterprise. In: Kubiak, B.F., Korowicki, A. (eds.) Information Management. Gdansk University Press, Gdańsk (2009)
19. Sapkota, B., Roman, D., Kruk, S.R., Fensel, D.: Distributed web service discovery architecture. In: Advanced International Conference on Telecommunications and International Conference on Internet and Web Applications and Services (AICT-ICIW 2006), p. 136 (2006)
20. Ferreira, C.: Supporting unified distributed management and autonomic decisions: design, implementation and deployment. J. Netw. Syst. Manag. 25, 416–456 (2017). https://doi.org/10.1007/s10922-016-9398-4
21. Frank, L., Pedersen, R.U.: Integrated distributed/mobile logistics management. In: Hameurlain, A., Küng, J., Wagner, R. (eds.) Transactions on Large-Scale Data- and Knowledge-Centered Systems V. LNCS, vol. 7100, pp. 206–221. Springer, Heidelberg (2012). https://doi.org/10.1007/978-3-642-28148-8_9
22. Turban, E., King, D., Lee, J.K., Liang, T.-P., Turban, D.C.: Mobile commerce and ubiquitous computing. In: Turban, E., King, D., Lee, J.K., Liang, T.-P., Turban, D.C. (eds.) Electronic Commerce. STBE, pp. 257–308. Springer, Cham (2015). https://doi.org/10.1007/978-3-319-10091-3_6
23. Markoska, K., Ivanochko, I., Gregus ml., M.: Mobile banking services—business information management with mobile payments. In: Kryvinska, N., Gregus, M. (eds.) Agile Information Business. FSM, pp. 125–175. Springer, Singapore (2018). https://doi.org/10.1007/978-981-10-3358-2_5
24. Bytniewski, A. (ed.): An Architecture of integrated management system. Wydawnictwo Uniwersytetu Ekonomicznego we Wrocławiu, Wrocław (2015). (in Polish)
25. APICS Operations Management Body of Knowledge Framework, 3rd edn. http://www.apics.org/apics-for-individuals/apics-magazine-home/resources/ombok/apics-ombok-framework-table-of-contents/apics-ombok-framework-5.1. Accessed 10 Oct 2017
26. Plikynas, D.: Multiagent based global enterprise resource planning: conceptual view. WSEAS Trans. Bus. Econ. 5(6), 31–123 (2008)
27. Davenport, T.: Putting the enterprise into the enterprise system. Harv. Bus. Rev. 76, 121–131 (1998)
28. Better execute your business strategies - with our enterprise resource planning (ERP) solution. http://www.sap.com/pc/bp/erp/software/overview.html. Accessed 28 Nov 2017
29. Zhang, D.Z., Anosike, A.I., Lim, M.K., Akanle, O.M.: An agent-based approach for e-manufacturing and supply chain integration. Comput. Ind. Eng. 51(2), 343–360 (2006)
30. Boella, G., Hulstijn, J., Van Der Torre, L.: Virtual organizations as normative multiagent systems. In: Proceedings of the 38th Annual Hawaii International Conference on System Sciences, p. 192c (2005)
31. Hecker, A.: Knowledge beyond the individual? Making sense of a notion of collective knowledge in organization theory. Org. Stud. 33(3), 423–445 (2012)

32. Amidon, D.: The Innovation Strategy for the Knowledge Economy. Heinemann, Butterworth (1997)

33. Jakubczyc, J., Mercier-Laurent, E., Owoc, M.: What is Knowledge Management?. KAM, Wroclaw (1999)

34. Mercier-Laurent, E.: Artificial intelligence for successful Kflow. In: Mercier-Laurent, E., Boulanger, D. (eds.) AI4KM 2015. IAICT, vol. 497, pp. 149–165. Springer, Cham (2016). https://doi.org/10.1007/978-3-319-55970-4_9

35. Salojärvi, S., Furu, P., Sveiby, K.-E.: Knowledge management and growth in finnish SMEs. J. Knowl. Manag. **9**(2), 103–122 (2005)

36. Girard, J.P., Girard, J.L.: Defining knowledge management: toward an applied compendium. J. Appl. Knowl. Manag. **3**(1), 14 (2015)

37. Davenport, T.: Enterprise 2.0: the new, new knowledge management? Harv. Bus. Rev. (2008). http://discussionleader.hbsp.com/davenport/2008/02/

38. Newell, A., Shaw, J.C., Simon, H.A.: Report on a general problem-solving program. In: Proceedings of the International Conference on Information Processing, pp. 256–264 (1959)

39. Kingston, J., Shadbolt, N., Tate, A.: CommonKADS models for knowledge based planning. In: AAAI/IAAI, vol. 1, pp. 477–482 (1996)

40. Mercier-Laurent, E., Owoc, M.L., Boulanger, D. (eds.): AI4KM 2014. IAICT, vol. 469. Springer, Cham (2015). https://doi.org/10.1007/978-3-319-28868-0

41. Motta, E., Rajan, T., Eisenstadt, M.: A methodology and tool for knowledge acquisition in KEATS-2. In: Guida, G., Tasso C. (eds.) Topics in Expert Systems Design, North-Holland (1989)

42. Gruber, T.: Ontology. In: Liu, L., Özsu, M.T. (eds.) Encyclopedia of Database Systems. Springer, Boston (2009). https://doi.org/10.1007/978-0-387-39940-9_3200

43. Mercier-Laurent, E.: Innovation Ecosystems. Wiley, Hoboken (2011)

44. Mercier-Laurent, E., Boulanger, D. (eds.): AI4KM 2012. IAICT, vol. 422. Springer, Heidelberg (2014). https://doi.org/10.1007/978-3-642-54897-0

45. Owoc, M.L., Marciniak, K.: Knowledge management as foundation of smart university. In: Proceedings of the Federated Conference on Computer Science and Information Systems, Kraków, pp. 1267–1272 (2013)

46. Nonaka, I., Takeuchi, H.: The Knowledge-Creating Company. How Japanese Companies Create the Dynamics of Innovation. Oxford University Press, New York, Oxford (1995)

47. Katarzyniak, R.: Grounding modalities and logic connectives in communicative cognitive agents. In: Nguyen, N.T. (ed.) Intelligent Technologies for Inconsistent Knowledge Processing. Advanced Knowledge International, Australia, Adelaide, pp. 21–37 (2004)

48. Langley, P.: The changing science of machine learning. Mach. Learn. **82**(3), 275–279 (2011)

49. Sathish Babu, B., Venkataram, P.: Cognitive agents based authentication & privacy scheme for mobile transactions (CABAPS). Comput. Commun. **31**(17), 4060–4071 (2008)

50. Franklin, S., Patterson, F.G.: The LIDA architecture: adding new modes of learning to an intelligent, autonomous, software agent. In: Proceedings of the International Conference on Integrated Design and Process Technology. Society for Design and Process Science, San Diego (2006)

51. Hernes, M., Bytniewski, A.: Towards big management. In: Król, D., Nguyen, N.T., Shirai, K. (eds.) ACIIDS 2017. SCI, vol. 710, pp. 197–209. Springer, Cham (2017). https://doi.org/10.1007/978-3-319-56660-3_18

52. Bytniewski, A., Hernes, M.: The use of cognitive agents in the construction of an integrated information management system. In: Porębska-Miąc, T., Sroka, H. (eds.) Systemy Wspomagania Organizacji. Wydawnictwo Uniwersytetu Ekonomicznego w Katowicach, Katowice (2013). (in Polish)

53. Hernes, M.: A cognitive integrated management support system for enterprises. In: Hwang, D., Jung, J.J., Nguyen, N.-T. (eds.) ICCCI 2014. LNCS (LNAI), vol. 8733, pp. 252–261. Springer, Cham (2014). https://doi.org/10.1007/978-3-319-11289-3_26

54. Hernes, M.: Performance evaluation of the customer relationship management agent's in a cognitive integrated management support system. In: Nguyen, N.T. (ed.) Transactions on Computational Collective Intelligence XVIII. LNCS, vol. 9240, pp. 86–104. Springer, Heidelberg (2015). https://doi.org/10.1007/978-3-662-48145-5_5

55. Get ahead of the game with an enterprise resource planning system (ERP) from SAP. https://www.sap.com/products/enterprise-management-erp.html. Accessed 20 Nov 2017

56. Microsoft Dynamics 365 for Finance and Operations, Enterprise edition. https://www.microsoft.com/en-us/dynamics365/operations. Accessed 20 Nov 2017

57. Hernes, M., Matouk, K.: Knowledge conflicts in business intelligence systems. In: Annals of Computer Science and Information Systems, Proceedings of Federated Conference Computer Science and Information Systems (FedCSIS), Kraków (2013)

58. Zenkin, A.: Intelligent control and cognitive computer graphics. In: IEEE International Symposium on Intelligent Control, Montreal, Calfornia, pp. 366–371 (1995)

59. Pilipczuk, O., Eidenzon, D.: The application of cognitive computer graphics to economic data exploration. J. Autom. Mob. Robot. Intell. Syst. **7**(3), 3–9 (2013)

60. Rosenberg, J., Mateos, A.: The Cloud at Your Service, 1st edn. Manning Publications, New York (2010)

61. Kubiak, B.F., Korowicki, A. (eds.): Information Management. Gdansk University Press, Gdańsk (2009)

62. Oxford dictionaries, knowledge. http://www.oxforddictionaries.com/definition/english/knowledge. Accessed 20 Nov 2017

63. Owoc, M.L., Weichbroth, P., Zuralski, K.: Towards better understanding of context-aware knowledge transformation. In: Proceedings of FedCSIS 2017, pp. 1123–1126 (2017)

64. Dixon, N.: How to make use of your organization's collective knowledge - accessing the knowledge of the whole organization - Part I (2011). http://www.nancydixonblog.com/2011/01/how-to-make-use-of-your-organizations-collective-knowledge-accessing-the-knowledge-of-the-whole-orga.html

65. Chaffey, D., White, G.: Business Information Management. Prentice Hall, London (2011)

66. Kimmerle, J., Cress, U., Held, C.: The interplay between individual and collective knowledge: technologies for organisational learning and knowledge building. Knowl. Manag. Res. Pract. **8**, 33–44 (2010). https://doi.org/10.1057/kmrp.2009.36

67. Lindskog, H., Mercier-Laurent, E.: Knowledge management applied to electronic public procurement. In: Mercier-Laurent, E., Boulanger, D. (eds.) AI4KM 2012. IAICT, vol. 422, pp. 95–111. Springer, Heidelberg (2014). https://doi.org/10.1007/978-3-642-54897-0_6

68. Salaberry, M.R.: Declarative versus procedural knowledge. In: Liontas, J.I., DelliCarpini, M. (eds.) The TESOL Encyclopedia of English Language Teaching (2018). https://doi.org/10.1002/9781118784235.eelt0051

69. Furmankiewicz, M., Sołtysik-Piorunkiewicz, A., Ziuziański, P.: Artificial intelligence and multi-agent software for e-health knowledge management system. Bus. Inform. **2**(32), 51–63 (2014)

70. Karlsen, J.E.: Eur. J. Futures Res. **2**, 40 (2014). https://doi.org/10.1007/s40309-014-0040-y

71. Buzzetto-More, N.: Principles of Effective Online Teaching. Informing Science Press, Santa Rosa (2007)
72. Toffler, A.: Powershift: Knowledge, Wealth and Violence at the Edge of the 21st Century. Bantam Books, New York (1990)
73. Owoc, M.L. (eds.) Elements of expert systems. Wydawnictwo AE we Wrocławiu, Wrocław (2006). (in Polish)
74. Edvinsson, L., Kitts, B., Beding, T.: The next generation of IC measurement – the digital IC-landscape. J. Intell. Capital **1**(3), 263–273 (2000). https://doi.org/10.1108/14691930010350819
75. Chan, K.C., Mills, T.M.: Modeling competition over product life cycles. Asia-Pac. J. Oper. Res. **32**(4) (2015)
76. Fikes, R., Kehler, T.: The role of frame-based representation in reasoning. Commun. ACM **28**(9), 904–920 (1985). https://doi.org/10.1145/4284.4285
77. Kadhim, M.A., Afshar Alam, M., Kaur, H.: A multi-intelligent agent for knowledge discovery in database (MIAKDD): cooperative approach with domain expert for rules extraction. In: Huang, D.-S., Jo, K.-H., Wang, L. (eds.) ICIC 2014. LNCS (LNAI), vol. 8589, pp. 602–614. Springer, Cham (2014). https://doi.org/10.1007/978-3-319-09339-0_61
78. Palit, I., Phelps, S., Ng, W.L.: Can a zero-intelligence plus model explain the stylized facts of financial time series data? In: Proceedings of the Eleventh International Conference on Autonomous Agents and Multi-Agent Systems (AAMAS), vol. 2, pp. 653–660. International Foundation for Autonomous Agents and Multiagent Systems, Valencia (2012)
79. Zhang, X.F., Wang, G.J., Meng, G.W.: Theory of truth degree based on the interval interpretation of first-order fuzzy predicate logic formulas and its application. Fuzzy Syst. Math. **20**(2), 8–12 (2006)
80. Wang, X.Z., An, S.F.: Research on learning weights of fuzzy production rules based on maximum fuzzy entropy. J. Comput. Res. Dev. **43**(4), 673–678 (2006)
81. Zhu, G.J., Xia, Y.M.: Research and practice of frame knowledge representation. J. Yunnan Univ. (Nat. Sci. Ed.) **28**(S1), 154–157 (2006)
82. Zeng, Z.: Construction of knowledge service system based on semantic web. J. China Soc. Sci. Tech. Inf. **24**(3), 336–340 (2005)
83. Castells, P., Fernandez, M., Vallet, D.: An adaptation of the vector-space model for ontology-based information retrieval. IEEE Trans. Knowl. Data Eng. **19**(2), 261–272 (2007). https://doi.org/10.1109/tkde.2007.22
84. Keikha, M., Razavian, N.S., Oroumchian, F., Razi, H.S.: Document representation and quality of text: an analysis. In: Berry, M.W., Castellanos, M. (eds.) Survey of Text Mining II. Springer, London (2008). https://doi.org/10.1007/978-1-84800-046-9_12
85. Dudycz, H.: A topics map as a visual representation of economic knowledge. Wydawnictwo Uniwersytetu Ekonomicznego we Wrocławiu, Wrocław (2013). (in Polish)
86. Hofweber, T.: Logic and ontology. In: Zalta, E.N. (ed.) The Stanford Encyclopedia of Philosophy (Summer 2018 Edition) (2018). https://plato.stanford.edu/archives/sum2018/entries/logic-ontology/
87. Guarino, N., Oberle, D., Staab, S.: What is an ontology? In: Staab, S., Studer, R. (eds.) Handbook on Ontologies. International Handbooks on Information Systems. Springer, Berlin, Heidelberg (2009). https://doi.org/10.1007/978-3-540-92673-3_0
88. Fensel, D.: Ontologies: Silver Bullet for Knowledge Management and Electronic Commerce. Springer, New York (2001). https://doi.org/10.1007/978-3-662-09083-1
89. Sowa, J.F.: Semantic Networks. http://www.jfsowa.com/pubs/semnet.htm. Accessed 20 Oct 2017

90. Korczak, J., Dudycz, H., Dyczkowski, M.: Design of financial knowledge in dashboard for SME managers. In: Proceedings of the 2013 Federated Conference on Computer Science and Information Systems, Kraków, pp. 1111–1118 (2013)
91. Burger, W., Burge, M.J.: Principles of Digital Image Processing: Fundamental Techniques. Springer, London (2009). https://doi.org/10.1007/978-1-84800-191-6
92. Solomon, C.J., Breckon, T.P.: Fundamentals of Digital Image Processing: A Practical Approach with Examples in Matlab. Wiley, Hoboken (2010)
93. Murat Tekalp, A.: Digital Video Processing, 2nd edn. Prentice Hall, Upper Saddle River (2015)
94. Newmarch, J.: OpenMAX video processing on the Raspberry Pi. In: Newmarch, J. (ed.) Raspberry Pi GPU Audio Video Programming. Apress, Berkeley (2017)
95. Lin, H.-P., Hsieh, H.-Y.: On using digital speech processing techniques for synchronization in heterogeneous teleconferencing. In: Bartolini, N., Nikoletseas, S., Sinha, P., Cardellini, V., Mahanti, A. (eds.) QShine 2009. LNICST, vol. 22, pp. 679–695. Springer, Heidelberg (2009). https://doi.org/10.1007/978-3-642-10625-5_43
96. Baker, J., et al.: Developments and directions in speech recognition and understanding, part 1. IEEE Signal Process. Mag. **26**(3), 75–80 (2009)
97. Baldoni, M., Baroglio, C., Patti, V., Rena, P.: From tags to emotions: ontology-driven sentiment analysis in the social semantic web. Intelligenza Artificiale **6**(1), 41–54 (2012)
98. Potiopa, P.: Methods and tools for automatic text information processing and their use in the knowledge management process. Automatyka **15**(2), 409–419 (2011). http://journals.bg.agh.edu.pl/AUTOMATYKA/2011-02/Auto40.pdf
99. Tomassen, S.L.: Semi-automatic generation of ontologies for knowledge-intensive CBR. Norwegian University of Science and Technology, Trondheim (2002)
100. Pham, L.V., Pham, S.B.: Information extraction for Vietnamese real estate advertisements. In: Fourth International Conference on Knowledge and Systems Engineering (KSE), Danang (2012)
101. Balke, W.T.: Introduction to information extraction: basic notions and current trends. Datenbank-Spektrum **12**(2), 81–88 (2012)
102. Konchady, M.: Text Mining Application Programming. Cengage Learning India Private Ltd., New Delhi (2009)
103. Duan, R., Zhang, M.: Design of web-based management information system for academic degree & graduate education. In: Wang, W., Li, Y., Duan, Z., Yan, L., Li, H., Yang, X. (eds.) QShine 2009. IFIP International Federation for Information Processing, vol. 252, pp. 218–226. Springer, Boston (2007). https://doi.org/10.1007/978-0-387-75494-9_27
104. Banko, M., Cafarella, M., Soderland, S., Broadhead, M., Etzioni, O.: Open information extraction from the web. In: Proceedings of International Joint Conference on Artificial Intelligence (IJCAI), Hyderabad (2007)
105. Bekkerman, R., McCallum, A.: Disambiguating web appearances of people in a social network. In: Proceedings of International Conference on World Wide Web (WWW), Chiba (2005)
106. Hassell, J., Aleman-Meza, B., Arpinar, I.B.: Ontology-driven automatic entity disambiguation in unstructured text. In: Cruz, I., et al. (eds.) ISWC 2006. LNCS, vol. 4273, pp. 44–57. Springer, Heidelberg (2006). https://doi.org/10.1007/11926078_4
107. Chaudhuri, S., Ganti, V., Xin, D.: Mining document collections to facilitate accurate approximate entity matching. In: Proceedings of International Conference on Very Large Data Bases (VLDB), vol. 2, no. 1, Lyon (2009)
108. Dong, X., Halevy, A., Madhavan, J.: Reference reconciliation in complex information spaces. In: Proceedings of ACM International Conference on Management of Data, Baltimore (2005)

109. Cimiano, P., Handschuh, S., Staab, S.: Towards the selfannotating web. In: Proceedings of International Conference on World Wide Web (WWW), New York (2004)
110. Stoica, E., Hearst, M., Richardson, M.: Automating creation of hierarchical faceted metadata structures. In: Proceedings of Human Language Technology Conference of the Association of Computational Linguistics, Rochester (2007)
111. Carlson, A., Betteridge, J., Wang, R.C.: Coupled semi-supervised learning for information extraction. In: WSDM 2010, 4–6 February, New York (2010)
112. Etzioni, O., et al.: Unsupervised named-entity extraction from the web: an experimental study. Artif. Intell. **165**(1), 1–42 (2005)
113. Nenkova, A., McKeown, K.: Automatic summarization. Found. Trends Inf. Retr. **5**(2–3), 103–233 (2011)
114. Clahsen, F., Harald, C.: Grammatical Processing in Language Learners. Appl. Psycholinguist. **27**, 3–42 (2006)
115. Goldberg, Y.: A primer on neural network models for natural language processing. J. Artif. Intell. Res. **57**, 345–420 (2016)
116. Costa, F., Branco, A.: LXGram: a deep linguistic processing grammar for Portuguese. In: Pardo, T.A.S., Branco, A., Klautau, A., Vieira, R., de Lima, V.L.S. (eds.) PROPOR 2010. LNCS (LNAI), vol. 6001, pp. 86–89. Springer, Heidelberg (2010). https://doi.org/10.1007/978-3-642-12320-7_11
117. Pollard, C., Sag, I.: Head-Driven Phrase Structure Grammar. Chicago University Press and CSLI, Stanford (1994)
118. Sebastiani, F.: Machine learning in automated text categorization. ACM Comput. Surv. (CSUR) **34**(1), 1–47 (2002)
119. Wawer, A.: Mining opinion attributes from texts using multiple kernel learning. In: IEEE 11th International Conference on Data Mining Workshops, Vancouver (2011)
120. Wilson, T., Wiebe, J., Hoffmann, P.: Recognizing con-textual polarity: an exploration of features for phrase-level sentiment analysis. Comput. Linguist. **35**(3), 399–433 (2009)
121. Pang, B., Lee, L.: A sentimental education: sentiment analysis using subjectivity summarization based on minimum cuts. ACL, Stroudsburg (2004)
122. Turney, P.: Thumbs up or thumbs down? Semantic orientation applied to unsupervised classification of reviews. In: Proceedings of the 40th Annual Meeting of the Association for Computational Linguistics, Stroudsburg (2002)
123. Yu, H., Hatzivassiloglou, V.: Towards answering opinion questions: separating facts from opinions and identifying the polarity of opinion sentences. In: EMNLP, Stroudsburg (2003)
124. Riloff, E.: Learning extraction patterns for subjective expressions. In: Proceedings of the 2003 Conference on Empirical Methods in Natural Language Processing, Stroudsburg (2003)
125. Wiebe, J., Riloff, E.: Creating subjective and objective sentence classifiers from unannotated texts. In: Gelbukh, A. (ed.) CICLing 2005. LNCS, vol. 3406, pp. 486–497. Springer, Heidelberg (2005). https://doi.org/10.1007/978-3-540-30586-6_53
126. Michalski, R.S., Tecuci, G. (eds.): Machine Learning: A Multistrategy Approach, Volume IV. Morgan Kaufmann, Burlington (1994)
127. Vetulani, Z., Vetulani G., Kochanowski, B.: Recent advances in development of a lexicon-grammar of Polish: PolNet 3.0. In: Calzolari, N., et al. (eds.) Proceedings of the Tenth International Conference on Language Resources and Evaluation, LREC 2016, pp. 2851–2854. European Language Resources Association, Paris (2016)
128. Jackson, R.G., et al.: Natural language processing to extract symptoms of severe mental illness from clinical text: the Clinical Record Interactive Search Comprehensive Data Extraction (CRIS-CODE) project. BMJ Open **7**, e012012 (2017). https://doi.org/10.1136/bmjopen-2016-012012

129. Abramowicz, W., Bukowska, E., Filipowska, A.: Ensuring security through semantic monitoring of cyberspace. E-mentor **3**(50), 11–17 (2013)
130. Baptista, P., Cunha, T.R., Gama, C., Bernardes, C.: A new and practical method to obtain grain size measurements in sandy shores based on digital image acquisition and processing. Sed. Geol. **282**, 294–306 (2012)
131. Juang, B.H., Rabiner, L.R.: Automatic speech recognition-a brief history of the technology development.   http://www.ece.ucsb.edu/Faculty/Rabiner/ece259/Reprints/354_LALI-ASRHistory-final-10-8.pdf. Accessed 17 June 2017
132. Wilpon, J., Gilbert, M.E., Cohen, J.: The business of speech technologies. In: Benesty, J., Sondhi, M.M., Huang, Y.A. (eds.) Springer Handbook of Speech Processing. Springer, Heidelberg (2008). https://doi.org/10.1007/978-3-540-49127-9_34
133. Owoc, M.L., Ochmanska, M., Gladysz, T.: On principles of knowledge validation. In: Vermesan, A., Coenen, F. (eds.) Validation and Verification of Knowledge Based Systems. Springer, Boston (1999). https://doi.org/10.1007/978-1-4757-6916-6_2
134. Suh, Y.H., Murray, T.J.: A tree-based approach for verifying completeness and consistency in rule-based systems. Expert Syst. Appl. **7**(2), 199–220 (1994)
135. Hernes, M., Sobieska-Karpińska, J.: Application of the consensus method in a multiagent financial decision support system. IseB **14**(1), 167–185 (2016)
136. Korczak, J., Hernes, M., Bac, M.: Risk avoiding strategy in multi-agent trading system. In: Proceedings of Federated Conference Computer Science and Information Systems (FedCSIS), Kraków, pp. 1131–1138 (2013)
137. Nguyen, N.T.: Advanced Methods for Inconsistent Knowledge Management. Springer, London (2008). https://doi.org/10.1007/978-1-84628-889-0
138. Mirkin, B.G., Shestakov, A.: Least square consensus clustering: criteria, methods, experiments. In: Serdyukov, P., et al. (eds.) ECIR 2013. LNCS, vol. 7814, pp. 764–767. Springer, Heidelberg (2013). https://doi.org/10.1007/978-3-642-36973-5_79
139. Sobieska-Karpińska, J., Hernes, M.: Value of information in distributed decision support system. In: Pańkowska, M. (ed.) Infonomics for Distributed Business and Decision-Making Environments: Creating Information System Ecology. IGI Global, Hershey, New York (2009)
140. Albus, J.S., Barbera, A.J.: RCS: a cognitive architecture for intelligent multi-agent systems. Ann. Rev. Control **29**(1), 87–99 (2005)
141. Kollmann, S., Siafara, L.C., Schaat, S., Wendt, A.: Towards a cognitive multi-agent system for building control. Procedia Comput. Sci. **88**, 191–197 (2016)
142. Iantovics, B.: Cognitive medical multiagent systems. BRAIN. Broad Res. Artif. Intell. Neurosci. **1**(1), 12–21 (2010). Happy BRAINew Year!
143. Acampora, G., Vitiello, A.: Learning of fuzzy cognitive maps for modelling gene regulatory networks through Big Bang-Big Crunch algorithm. In: 2015 IEEE International Conference on Fuzzy Systems (FUZZ-IEEE), Istanbul, pp. 1–6 (2015)
144. Glaser, N., Chevrier, V., Haton, J.P.: Multi-agent modeling for autonomous but cooperative robots. In: Proceedings of 1st DIMAS, Cracow, Poland, pp. 175–182 (1995)
145. Korczak, J., Lipiński, P.: Agent systems in decision support on the securities market. In: Stanek, S., Sroka, H., Paprzycki, M., Ganzha, M. (eds.) Rozwój informatycznych systemów wieloagentowych. Wydawnictwo Placet, Warszawa (2008)
146. Duch, W., Oentaryo, R.J., Pasquier, M.: Cognitive architectures: where do we go from here? In: Wang, P., Goertzel, P., Franklin, S. (eds.) Frontiers in Artificial Intelligence and Applications, vol. 171, pp. 122–136. IOS Press, Amsterdam (2008)
147. Goertzel, B., Wang, P.: Introduction: what is the matter here? In: Goertzel, B., Wang, P. (eds.) Foundations of Artificial General Intelligence. Atlantis Press, Paris (2012)

148. Duch, W.: Artificial Intelligence. Knowledge Representation II: Semantic Networks. https://www.fizyka.umk.pl/~duch/Wyklady/AI/AI06-1.ppt. Accessed 23 Jan 2017

149. Douglas Bernheim, B., Rangel, A.: Behavioural public economics. In: Durlauf, S.N., Blume, L.E. (eds.) The New Palgrave Dictionary of Economics, 2nd edn. Palgrave Macmillan, Basingstoke (2008)

150. Hawkins, J., Blakeslee, S.: On Intelligence: How a New Understanding of the Brain will Lead to the Creation of Truly Intelligent Machines. Times Books, New York (2004)

151. Hecht-Nielsen, R.: Confabulation Theory: The Mechanism of Thought. Springer, Heidelberg (2007). https://doi.org/10.1007/978-3-540-49605-2

152. Laird, J.E.: Extending the SOAR cognitive architecture. In: Wang, P., Goertzel, B., Franklin, S. (eds.) Frontiers in Artificial Intelligence and Applications, vol. 171 (2008)

153. Kieras, D., Meyer, D.E.: An overview of the EPIC architecture for cognition and performance with application to human-computer interaction. Hum.-Comput. Interac. **12**, 391–438 (1997)

154. Hofstadter, D.R., Mitchell, M.: The copycat project: a model of mental fluidity and analogy-making, chap. 5. In: Hofstadter, D. (ed.) The Fluid Analogies Research Group, Fluid Concepts and Creative Analogies. Basic Books, New York (1995)

155. Wang, P.: Rigid Flexibility. The Logic of Intelligence. Springer, Dordrecht (2006). https://doi.org/10.1007/1-4020-5045-3

156. Langley, P.: An adaptive architecture for physical agents. In: Proceeding of the 2005 IEEE/WIC/ACM International Conference on Intelligent Agent Technology. IEEE Computer Society Press, Compiegne (2005)

157. Edelman, G.M.: Second Nature: Brain Science and Human Knowledge. Yale University Press, New Haven (2006)

158. Rohrer, B.: An implemented architecture for feature creation and general reinforcement learning. In: Workshop on Self-Programming in AGI Systems, Fourth International Conference on Artificial General Intelligence, Mountain View, CA. http://www.sandia.gov/rohrer/doc/Rohrer11ImplementedArchitectureFeature.pdf. Accessed 01 Apr 2017

159. Anderson, J.R., Lebiere, C.: The Newell test for a theory of cognition. Behav. Brain Sci. **26**, 587–601 (2003)

160. Sun, R., Zhang, X.: Top-down versus bottom-up learning in cognitive skill acquisition. Cogn. Syst. Res. **5**, 63–89 (2004)

161. Goertzel, B.: OpenCogBot: achieving generally intelligent virtual agent control and humanoid robotics via cognitive synergy. In: Proceedings of ICAI 2010, Beijing (2010)

162. Nestor, A., Kokinov, B.: Towards active vision in the DUAL cognitive architecture. Int. J. Inf. Theor. Appl. **11**, 9–15 (2004)

163. Just, M.A., Varma, S.: The organization of thinking: what functional brain imaging reveals about the neuroarchitecture of complex cognition. Cogn. Affect. Behav. Neurosci. **7**, 153–191 (2007)

164. Goertzel, B., et al.: An integrative methodology for teaching embodied non-linguistic agents, applied to virtual animals in second life. In: Wang, P., Goertzel, B., Franklin, S. (eds.) Artificial General Intelligence 2008. IOS Press, Amsterdam (2008)

165. Hensinger, A., Thome, M., Wright, T.: Cougaar: a scalable, distributed multi-agent architecture. In: IEEE International Conference on Systems, Man and Cybernetics (2004)

166. Cognitive Computing Research Group. http://ccrg.cs.memphis.edu/. Accessed 02 Nov 2017

167. Katarzyniak, R.: Priming the modal language of communication in agent systems. Akademicka Oficyna Wydawnicza EXIT (2007). (in Polish)

168. Pulvermuller, F.: The Neuroscience of Language. On Brain Circuits of Words and Serial Order. Cambridge University Press, Cambridge (2003)

169. Hernes, M.: The semantic method for agents' knowledge representation in the cognitive integrated management information system. In: Proceedings of Federated Conference Computer Science and Information Systems (FedCSIS), Łódź (2015)

170. Dalkir, K.: Knowledge Management in Theory and Practice. Elsevier Inc., Jordan Hill, Oxford (2005). p. 330

171. Snaider, J., McCall, R., Franklin, S.: The LIDA framework as a general tool for AGI. In: Schmidhuber, J., Thórisson, Kristinn R., Looks, M. (eds.) AGI 2011. LNCS (LNAI), vol. 6830, pp. 133–142. Springer, Heidelberg (2011). https://doi.org/10.1007/978-3-642-22887-2_14

172. Hernes, M.: Using cognitive agents for unstructured knowledge management in a business organization's integrated information system. In: Nguyen, N.T., Trawiński, B., Fujita, H., Hong, T.-P. (eds.) ACIIDS 2016. LNCS (LNAI), vol. 9621, pp. 344–353. Springer, Heidelberg (2016). https://doi.org/10.1007/978-3-662-49381-6_33

173. Nguyen, N.T.: Conflicts of ontologies – classification and consensus-based methods for resolving. In: Gabrys, B., Howlett, R.J., Jain, Lakhmi C. (eds.) KES 2006. LNCS (LNAI), vol. 4252, pp. 267–274. Springer, Heidelberg (2006). https://doi.org/10.1007/11893004_34

174. Ferber, J.: Multi-agent concepts and methodologies. In: Phan, D., Amblard, F. (eds.) Agent-Based Modelling and Simulation in the Social and Human Sciences. Bardwell Press, Oxford (2007)

175. Rosenfeld, A., Agmon, N., Maksimov, O., Kraus, S.: Intelligent agent supporting human-multi-robot team collaboration. Artif. Intell. **252**, 211–231 (2017)

176. Gaudel, R., Sebag, M.: Feature selection as a one-player game. In: ICML (2010)

177. Hemsley, G., Holm, A., Dodd, B.: Conceptual distance and word learning: patterns of acquisition in Samoan-English bilingual children. J. Child Lang. **40**, 799–820 (2013). https://doi.org/10.1017/S0305000912000293

178. Basheer, G.S., Ahmad, M.S., Tang, A.Y.C.: A framework for conflict resolution in multi-agent systems. In: Bǎdicǎ, C., Nguyen, N.T., Brezovan, M. (eds.) ICCCI 2013. LNCS (LNAI), vol. 8083, pp. 195–204. Springer, Heidelberg (2013). https://doi.org/10.1007/978-3-642-40495-5_20

179. Dyk, P., Lenar, M.: Applying negotiation methods to resolve conflicts in multi-agent environments. In: Zgrzywa, A. (ed.) Multimedia and Network Information Systems, MISSI 2006. PWr Publishing house, Wroclaw (2006)

180. Jennings, N.R., Faratin, P., Lomuscio, A.R., Parsons, S., Sierra, C., Wooldridge, M.: Automated negotiation: prospect, methods and challenge. J. Group Decis. Negot. **10**(2), 199–215 (2001)

181. Niazi, M., Hussain, A.: Agent-based computing from multi-agent systems to agent-based models: a visual survey. Scientometrics **89**(2), 479–499 (2011)

182. Kielar, P.M., Borrmann, A.: Auton. Agents Multi-Agent Syst. **32**, 387 (2018). https://doi.org/10.1007/s10458-018-9383-2

183. Li, G., Whiteson, S., Knox, W.B., et al.: Auton. Agents Multi-Agent Syst. **32**, 1 (2018). https://doi.org/10.1007/s10458-017-9374-8

184. Gabel, T., Riedmiller, M.: On a successful application of multi-agent reinforcement learning to operations research benchmarks. In: IEEE International Symposium on Approximate Dynamic Programming and Reinforcement Learning, Honolulu, pp. 68–75 (2007)

185. Doniec, A., Mandiau, R., Piechowiak, S., Espié, S.: A behavioral multi-agent model for road traffic simulation. Eng. Appl. Artif. Intell. **21**(8), 1443–1454 (2008)

186. Lecoutre, Ch., Saïs, L., Tabary, S., Vidal, V.: Reasoning from last conflict(s) in constraint programming. Artif. Intell. **173**(18), 1592–1614 (2009)

187. Abbas, J.: Social software use in public libraries. In: Dumova, T., Fiordo, R. (eds.) Handbook of Research on Social Interaction Technologies and Collaboration Software: Concepts and Trends. IGI Global, Hershey, New York (2009)

188. Uden, L., Eardley, A.: The usability of social software. In: Dumova, T., Fiordo, R. (eds.) Handbook of Research on Social Interaction Technologies and Collaboration Software: Concepts and Trends. IGI Global, Hershey, New York (2009)

189. Mirkin, B., Shestakov, A.: A note on the effectiveness of the least squares consensus clustering. In: Aleskerov, F., Goldengorin, B., Pardalos, P.M. (eds.) Clusters, Orders, and Trees: Methods and Applications. SOIA, vol. 92, pp. 181–185. Springer, New York (2014). https://doi.org/10.1007/978-1-4939-0742-7_11

190. Mercier-Laurent, E.: Knowledge management and risk management. In: Proceedings of Federated Conference on Computer Science and Information Systems (FedCSIS), Gdansk, pp. 1369–1373 (2016)

191. Domenach, F., Tayari, A.: Implications of axiomatic consensus properties. In: Lausen, B., Van den Poel, D., Ultsch, A. (eds.) Algorithms from and for Nature and Life. Studies in Classification Data Analysis and Knowledge Organization. Springer, Cham (2013)

192. Castano, S., Ferrara, A., Montanelli, S.: Designing crowdsourcing tasks with consensus constraints. In: International Conference on Collaboration Technologies and Systems (CTS), Orlando, FL, pp. 97–103 (2016)

193. Kozierkiewicz-Hetmańska, A., Pietranik, M.: The knowledge increase estimation framework for ontology integration on the relation level. In: Nguyen, N.T., Papadopoulos, G.A., Jędrzejowicz, P., Trawiński, B., Vossen, G. (eds.) ICCCI 2017. LNCS (LNAI), vol. 10448, pp. 44–53. Springer, Cham (2017). https://doi.org/10.1007/978-3-319-67074-4_5

194. Sobieska-Karpińska, J., Hernes, M.: Consensus determining algorithm in multiagent decision support system with taking into consideration improving agent's knowledge. In: Federated Conference Computer Science and Information Systems (FedCSIS) (2012)

195. Condorcet, M.: Essai sur l'application de l'analyse a la probabilite des decisions rendues ala prularite des voix. Chelsea Published, no. 6, New York (1974)

196. Maleszka, M., Nguyen, N.T.: Integration computing and collective intelligence. Expert Syst. Appl. **42**(1), 332–340 (2015)

197. Barthlemy, J.P.: Dictatorial consensus function on n-trees. Math. Soc. Sci. **25**, 59–64 (1992)

198. McMorris, F.R., Powers, R.C.: The median function on weak hierarchies. DIMACS Ser. Discret. Math. Theoret. Comput. Sci. **37**, 265–269 (1997)

199. Sobieska-Karpińska, J., Hernes, M.: The postulates of consensus determining in financial decision support systems. In: Proceedings of Federated Conference Computer Science and Information Systems (FedCSIS), Kraków (2013)

200. Hernes, M., Sobieska-Karpińska, J.: Susceptibility to consensus of conflict situation in intelligent multi-agent decision support system. In: Kubiak, B.F., Korowicki, A. (eds.) Information Management. Gdansk University Press, Gdańsk (2009)

201. Bytniewski, A., Hernes, M.: Algorithm for determining consensus in a situation of conflict of unstructured knowledge in distributed IT systems supporting management. Ekonometria **4**(42), 153–164 (2013). (in Polish)

202. Hernes, M.: Deriving consensus for term frequency matrix in a cognitive integrated management information system. In: Núñez, M., Nguyen, N.T., Camacho, D., Trawiński, B. (eds.) ICCCI 2015. LNCS (LNAI), vol. 9329, pp. 503–512. Springer, Cham (2015). https://doi.org/10.1007/978-3-319-24069-5_48

203. Hamming, R.W.: Error detecting and error correcting codes. Bell Syst. Tech. J. **29**(2), 147–160 (1950)

204. Maleszka, M., Mianowska, B., Nguyen, N.T.: A method for collaborative recommendation using knowledge integration tools and hierarchical structure of user profiles. Knowl.-Based Syst. **47**, 1–13 (2013)

205. Truong, H.B., Nguyen, N.T.: A multi-attribute and multi-valued model for fuzzy ontology integration on instance level. In: Pan, J.-S., Chen, S.-M., Nguyen, N.T. (eds.) ACIIDS 2012. LNCS (LNAI), vol. 7196, pp. 187–197. Springer, Heidelberg (2012). https://doi.org/ 10.1007/978-3-642-28487-8_19

206. Truong, H.B., Quach, X.H.: An overview of fuzzy ontology integration methods based on consensus theory. In: van Do, T., Thi, H.A.L., Nguyen, N.T. (eds.) Advanced Computational Methods for Knowledge Engineering. AISC, vol. 282, pp. 217–227. Springer, Cham (2014). https://doi.org/10.1007/978-3-319-06569-4_16

207. Nguyen, Q.U., Duong, T.H., Kang, S.: Solving conflict on collaborative knowledge via social networking using consensus choice. In: Nguyen, N.-T., Hoang, K., Jędrzejowicz, P. (eds.) ICCCI 2012. LNCS (LNAI), vol. 7653, pp. 21–30. Springer, Heidelberg (2012). https://doi.org/10.1007/978-3-642-34630-9_3

208. Jung, J.J., Nguyen, N.T.: Consensus choice for reconciling social collaborations on semantic wikis. In: Nguyen, N.T., Kowalczyk, R., Chen, S.-M. (eds.) ICCCI 2009. LNCS (LNAI), vol. 5796, pp. 472–480. Springer, Heidelberg (2009). https://doi.org/10.1007/978-3-642-04441-0_41

209. Sobecki, J.: Hybrid adaptation of web-based systems user interfaces. In: Bubak, M., van Albada, G.D., Sloot, P.M.A., Dongarra, J. (eds.) ICCS 2004. LNCS, vol. 3038, pp. 505–512. Springer, Heidelberg (2004). https://doi.org/10.1007/978-3-540-24688-6_66

210. Jajuga, K.: Managing risk and investment in small business. In: Porada-Rochoń, M., Mifsud, J., Pittella, G. (eds.) Managing a Small Business in the Contemporary Environment, pp. 175–194 (2012)

211. Korczak, J., Hernes, M., Bac, M.: Performance evaluation of decision-making agents' in the multi-agent system. In: Proceedings of Federated Conference Computer Science and Information Systems (FedCSIS), Warszawa, pp. 1177–1184 (2014)

212. Hernes, M., Chojnacka-Komorowska, A., Matouk, K.: Analysis of text documents in a multi-agent integrated management system. In: Porębska-Miąc, T. (ed.) Systemy Wspomagania Organizacji. Wydawnictwo Uniwersytetu Ekonomicznego w Katowicach, Katowice (2015). (in Polish)

213. Hernes, M., Chojnacka-Komorowska, A., Matouk, K.: External environment scanning using cognitive agents. In: Nguyen, N.T., Papadopoulos, George A., Jędrzejowicz, P., Trawiński, B., Vossen, G. (eds.) ICCCI 2017. LNCS (LNAI), vol. 10448, pp. 342–350. Springer, Cham (2017). https://doi.org/10.1007/978-3-319-67074-4_33

214. Bartusiak, R., Kajdanowicz, T.: Sentiment analysis based on collaborative data for Polish language. In: Luo, Y. (ed.) CDVE 2015. LNCS, vol. 9320, pp. 216–219. Springer, Cham (2015). https://doi.org/10.1007/978-3-319-24132-6_27

215. Piasecki, M.: Polish tagger TaKIPI: rule based construction and optimisation. Task Q. **11** (1–2), 151–167 (2007)

216. Sokołowska, W., Hossa, T., Fabisz, K., Abramowicz, W., Kubaczyk, M.: Sentiment analysis as a source of gaining competitive advantage on the electricity markets. J. Electron. Sci. Technol. **13**(3), 229–236 (2015)

217. Russel, S., Norvig, P.: Artificial Intelligence: A Modern Approach. Pearson, London (2009)

The Ins and Outs of Network-Oriented Modeling: From Biological Networks and Mental Networks to Social Networks and Beyond

Jan Treur[✉] iD

Behavioural Informatics Group, Vrije Universiteit Amsterdam,
Amsterdam, Netherlands
j.treur@vu.nl
https://www.researchgate.net/profile/Jan_Treur

Abstract. Network-Oriented Modeling has successfully been applied to obtain network models for a wide range of phenomena, including Biological Networks, Mental Networks, and Social Networks. In this paper it is discussed how the interpretation of a network as a causal network and taking into account dynamics in the form of temporal-causal networks, brings more depth. The basics and the scope of applicability of such a Network-Oriented Modelling approach are discussed and illustrated. This covers, for example, Social Network models for social contagion or information diffusion, adaptive Mental Network models for Hebbian learning and adaptive Social Network models for evolving relationships. From the more fundamental side, it will be discussed how emerging network behavior can be related to network structure.

1 Introduction

Network-Oriented Modeling is a relatively new way of modeling that is especially useful to model intensively interconnected and interactive processes. It has been applied to model networks for biological, mental, and social processes, and still more. The aim of this paper is to discuss the ins and outs of this modeling perspective in more detail. The paper is based on the contents of the Keynote Lecture with the same title at the 10th International Conference on Computational Collective Intelligence, ICCCI'18. It is discussed how the interpretation of a network as a causal network and taking into account dynamics brings more depth in the Network-Oriented Modeling perspective [18], leading to the notion of temporal-causal network. In a temporal-causal network, nodes represent states with values that vary over time, and connections represent causal relations describing how states affect each other. As these causal relations themselves also may change, adaptive networks are covered as well.

The wide scope of applicability [18, 19] of such a Network-Oriented Modelling approach will be discussed and illustrated. This covers, for example, network models for principles of social contagion (e.g., [24]) or information diffusion, and adaptive network models for principles of Hebbian learning in networks of mental states, but also adaptive network models for principles of evolving social networks, such as the

© Springer-Verlag GmbH Germany, part of Springer Nature 2019
N. T. Nguyen et al. (Eds.): TCCI XXXII, LNCS 11370, pp. 120–139, 2019.
https://doi.org/10.1007/978-3-662-58611-2_2

homophily principle. From the methodological side, it will be discussed how mathematical analysis can be used to identify the relation between emerging behaviour of the network and network structure.

In this paper, in Sect. 2 first the conceptual background of Network-Oriented Modeling is discussed, leading to a conceptual representation of a temporal-causal network, which defines such a network. Next, in Sect. 3 the numerical foundation is discussed, including a precise definition of a numerical representation by which a temporal-causal network model gets its intended semantics, and which can be used for simulation and analysis. In Sect. 4 the interesting challenge to determine how emerging network behaviour relates to network structure and some results on this relation are briefly discussed. In Sect. 5 the scope of applicability is discussed, thereby also addressing adaptive networks in which connections change over time. Finally, Sect. 6 is a discussion.

2   Network-Oriented Modeling: Conceptual Background

Network-Oriented Modeling is applied in a wide variety of areas. The general pattern is that some type of process in some domain X is described by a network structure, and then this type of network is called an X Network or X Network model. Note that such a network is considered as a modelling concept, not as reality. Some examples are:

- Modeling the dynamics of propagation of chemical activity in cells based on the concentration levels of chemicals by Biological Network models
- Modeling the dynamics of propagation of neural activity based on activation levels of neurons by Neural Network models
- Modeling the dynamics of propagation of mental activity based on engaging mental states by Mental Network models
- Modeling the dynamics of propagation of individual activity based on activation of personal states by Social Network models; e.g.,
  - Information diffusion; e.g., in social media
  - Opinion spread; e.g., in political campaigns
  - Emotion contagion; e.g., one smile triggering the other
  - Activity contagion; e.g., following each other as sheep.

These are just four types of domains X where processes in reality are modelled by network models, which then can be called X Networks with X = Biological, Neural, Mental, or Social.

2.1   The Unifying Potential of Networks

As an illustration, consider the following two examples, one for a Biological Network, and one for a Mental Network. The example of a Biological Network shown in Fig. 1 describes how bacteria generate and regulate their behaviour on the one hand based on their genetical background as encoded in their DNA, and on the other hand based on the situational context of the environment; see also [7]. For the general perspective on modelling the cell's metabolic and life processes as biochemical networks ('the dynamic biochemical networks of life'), see also [21, 22]. For example:

'Living organisms persist by virtue of complex interactions among many components organized into dynamic, environment-responsive networks that span multiple scales and dimensions. Biological networks constitute a type of information and communication technology (ICT): they receive information from the outside and inside of cells, integrate and interpret this information, and then activate a response. Biological networks enable molecules within cells, and even cells themselves, to communicate with each other and their environment.' [22], p. 1.

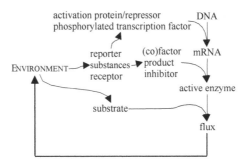

Fig. 1. Example of a Biological Network for bacterial behaviour based on its biochemistry; adapted picture from [7], Fig. 1 left hand side, p. 3.

As a second example, the Mental Network shown in Fig. 2 describes how human behaviour is generated and regulated by desires and intentions, and beliefs about the environment. Within Philosophy of Mind, Kim [8] describes Mental Networks based on causal relations as follows:

'Mental events are conceived as nodes in a complex causal network that engages in causal transactions with the outside world by receiving sensory inputs and emitting behavioral outputs' ([8], p. 104).

As can be noted similar network structures may describe different types of processes; see the isomorphic structures in Figs. 1 and 2, where actually the latter is a mirror image of the former. The Network-Oriented perspective provides a form of unification so that different types of processes become comparable, and we can, for example, compare the processes underlying human intelligence and behaviour to the processes underlying bacterial behaviour, as described in more detail in [6, 7, 22]. For example:

'We have become accustomed to associating brain activity – particularly activity of the human brain – with a phenomenon we call "intelligence." Yet, four billion years of evolution could have selected networks with topologies and dynamics that confer traits analogous to this intelligence, even though they were outside the intercellular networks of the brain. Here, we explore how macromolecular networks in microbes confer intelligent characteristics, such as memory, anticipation, adaptation and reflection and we review current understanding of how network organization reflects the type of intelligence required for the environments in which they were selected. We propose that, if we were to leave terms such as "human" and "brain" out of the defining features of "intelligence," all forms of life – from microbes to humans – exhibit some or all characteristics consistent with "intelligence". [22], p. 1.

The emphasis in this quote is on how not only in the brain, but even in the smallest life forms network structure, organisation and dynamics are used to realise many if not all aspects of intelligence.

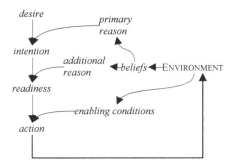

Fig. 2. Example of a Mental Network for behaviour based on Beliefs, Desires and Intentions (BDI); adapted picture from [7], Fig. 1 right hand side, p. 3.

As network structures for different domains may look similar, this suggests that there is a high potential for unification and exchange across different domains. For example, can we learn more about Mental Networks by studying Social Networks? Or can we develop Network Theory from a unified perspective that can be applied in both areas, or even more areas? These questions indicate some of the promises and challenges in what nowadays is called Network Science.

2.2   On the Meaning of the Basic Elements in a Network

There are, however, some issues that may have to be addressed to enable the further development of this perspective of a unified Network Science. A main issue is that not every network may have the same form concerning definition and semantics. Then unification may be not so easy. What actually is a network? What does a node mean? How should we interpret what a connection is or does? Are all connections considered equal? And what if there are multiple connections to one node? Should we interpret this as a kind of conjunction (AND), or disjunction (OR), or maybe something in between, like some average; then what kind of average?

Is a network just an abstract graph structure with nodes and connections and nothing more, and in particular no further semantics? Then in fact Network Science = Graph Theory, which is an already existing area within Mathematics, and Network-Oriented Modeling could also be called Graph-Oriented Modeling. This perspective may provide a relevant stream, but will not be all there is to further develop Network Science. For many applications, just a graph structure with only nodes and connections seems seriously underspecifying what is intended.

In many examples of applications of networks, such as those mentioned above, a notion of dynamics plays an important role. Shouldn't such dynamics be part of the definition or semantics of a network? These dynamics can concern dynamics of states (dynamics *within* a network: diffusion or contagion in a network), but also dynamics of the network structure itself (dynamics *of* a network: adaptive or evolving networks). Dynamics has a direct relation to causal relations describing how one state affects the other. The notions of dynamics and causality are fundamental for practically all scientific disciplines; these notions play an important unifying role in science and can be found in most of the scientific literature. Causal relations vary from how hitting a ball causes movement of the ball to how certain beliefs cause certain behaviour or how joining forces in a social movement causes change in a society, to name just a few cases.

2.3   Meaning as Defined by the Notion of Temporal-Causal Network

For the perspective on Network Science addressed in the current paper these notions of causality and dynamics have been incorporated and are part of a more refined structure and semantics of the considered networks. More specifically, the nodes in a network are interpreted here as states (or state variables) that vary over time, and the connections are interpreted as causal relations that define how each state can affect other states over time. To acknowledge this perspective of dynamics and causality on networks, this type of network has been called a *temporal-causal network* [18]. Many examples of applications have demonstrated that all types of domains as listed above can be covered in this way; e.g., [18]. In Sect. 5 below this wide applicability is briefly discussed; see also [19].

So, has the graph perspective disappeared now? Not really. A conceptual representation of a temporal-causal network model by a *labeled* graph still provides a fundamental basis. More specifically, a conceptual representation of a temporal-causal network model in the first place still involves representing in a declarative manner states and connections between them that now represent (causal) impacts of states on each other, as assumed to hold for the application domain addressed. This part of a conceptual representation is often depicted in a *conceptual picture* by a graph with nodes and directed connections. However, a full *conceptual representation* of a temporal-causal network model also includes a number of labels for such a graph. First, in reality not all causal relations are equally strong, so some notion of strength of a connection is used as a label for connections. Second, when more than one causal relation affects a state, some way to aggregate multiple causal impacts on a state is used as a label for states. Third, a notion of speed of change of a state is used for timing of the processes for that state. These three notions, called *connection weight* (denoted by $\omega_{X,Y}$), *combination function* (denoted by $c_Y(..)$), and *speed factor* (denoted by η_Y), which make the graph of states and connections a labeled graph (see Fig. 3), form the defining structure of a temporal-causal network model in the form of a conceptual representation; see also Table 1.

Note that combination functions in general are similar to the functions used in a static manner in the (deterministic) Structural Causal Model perspective described, for example, in [10, 12, 23], but in the Network-Oriented Modelling approach described here they are used in a dynamic manner. For example, Pearl [12], p. 203, denotes nodes by V_i and combination functions by f_i; he also points at the issue of underspecification for aggregation of multiple connections mentioned in Sect. 2.2 above, as in the often used graph representations the role of combination functions f_i for nodes V_i, is lacking:

'Every causal model M can be associated with a directed graph, $G(M)$ (…) This graph merely identifies the endogeneous and background variables that have a direct influence on each V_i; it does not specify the functional form of f_i.' [12], p. 203.

Therefore, if a graph representation is used, at least combination functions should be incorporated as labels, as is done for temporal-causal networks, in order to avoid this problem of under specification. That is the reason why combination functions are part of the definition of the network structure for temporal-causal networks, in addition to connection weights and speed factors.

Table 1. Conceptual representation of a temporal-causal network model

Concepts	Notation	Explanation
States and connections	$X, Y,$ $X{\rightarrow}Y$	Describes the nodes and links of a network structure (e.g., in graphical or matrix format)
Connection weight	$\omega_{X,Y}$	The *connection weight* $\omega_{X,Y} \in [-1, 1]$ represents the strength of the causal impact of state X on state Y through connection $X{\rightarrow}Y$
Aggregating multiple impacts on a state	$\mathbf{c}_Y(..)$	For each state Y (a reference to) a *combination function* $\mathbf{c}_Y(..)$ is chosen to combine the causal impacts of other states on state Y
Timing of the effect of causal impact	$\mathbf{\eta}_Y$	For each state Y a *speed factor* $\mathbf{\eta}_Y \geq 0$ is used to represent how fast a state is changing upon causal impact

Combination functions can have different forms, as there are many different approaches possible to address the issue of aggregating multiple impacts. For this aggregation a library is available with a number of standard combination functions as options, but also own-defined functions can be added.

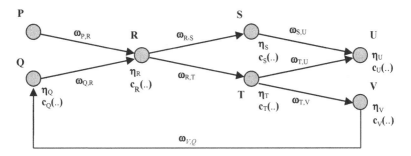

Fig. 3. Conceptual representation of a simple example temporal-causal network as a labeled graph, with states **P** to **V** and connection labels $\omega_{X,Y}$ for connection weights, state labels $\mathbf{c}_Y(..)$ for combination functions, and state labels $\mathbf{\eta}_Y$ for speed factors

2.4   Biological, Mental and Social Domains Ask for Networks

In Sect. 2.1 it already was discussed how 'the dynamic biochemical networks of life' [21] are fundamental to describe life forms in the biological domain. For the mental domain, the mechanisms found within the area of Cognitive and Social Neuroscience also show how many parts in the brain have connections that are adaptive and often form cyclic pathways; such cycles are assumed to play an important role in many mental processes; see also [2, 14]. It has been pointed out that to address such cyclic effects, a dynamic and adaptive perspective on causality is needed; e.g., [16]. Also by Kim [8] it is claimed that Mental Networks display cyclic network structures: ' (…) to explain what a given mental state is, we need to refer to other mental states, and explaining these can only be expected to require reference to further mental states, on so on – a process that can go on in an unending regress, or loop back in a circle.' [8], pp. 104–105).

For the social domain, intense interaction between persons also takes place based on mutual and usually cyclic relationships, by which they affect each other. Just one example from the context of modelling social systems or societies can be found in [11], where it is claimed that '*relational, network-oriented modelling approaches* are needed' to address human social complexity.

So, from the areas of biological processes [21, 22], mental processes [2, 8, 14, 16] and social processes [11], a notion of network is suggested as a basis of modeling, where connections between states or persons describe how they affect each other, thereby strongly suggesting causality and dynamics as crucial notions.

3   Numerical Representation of a Temporal-Causal Network

In this section the numerical-mathematical foundations of temporal-causal networks are discussed in more detail. In Sect. 2 the choice made on how networks are interpreted conceptually was discussed based on the notions of temporality and causality, thus indicating semantics for networks based on the notion of temporal-causal network.

3.1   Mathematical Formalisation of a Temporal-Causal Network

In the current section this interpretation based on temporality and causality is expressed in a formal-numerical way, thus associating semantics to any conceptual temporal-causal network specification in a detailed numerical-mathematically defined manner. This is done by showing how a conceptual representation as discussed in Sect. 2 (based on states and connections enriched with labels for connection weights, combination functions and speed factors), defines a numerical representation [18], Chap. 2; see also [26]. This is shown in Table 2; here Y is any state in the network and $X_1, ..., X_k$ are the states with outgoing connections to Y.

Table 2. Numerical representation of a temporal-causal network model.

Concept	Representation	Explanation
State values over time t	$Y(t)$	At each time point t each state Y in the model has a real number value in $[0, 1]$
Single causal impact	$\mathbf{impact}_{X,Y}(t)$ $= \omega_{X,Y}X(t)$	At t state X with connection to state Y has an impact on Y, using connection weight $\omega_{X,Y}$
Aggregating multiple impacts	$\mathbf{aggimpact}_Y(t)$ $= \mathbf{c}_Y(\mathbf{impact}_{X_1,Y}(t), \ldots, \mathbf{impact}_{X_k,Y}(t))$ $= \mathbf{c}_Y(\omega_{X_1,Y}X_1(t), \ldots, \omega_{X_k,Y}X_k(t))$	The aggregated causal impact of multiple states X_i on Y at t, is determind using combination function $\mathbf{c}_Y(..)$
Timing of the causal effect	$Y(t+\Delta t) = Y(t) + \eta_Y[\mathbf{aggimpact}_Y(t) - Y(t)]\Delta t$ $= Y(t) + \eta_Y[\mathbf{c}_Y(\omega_{X_1,Y}X_1(t), \ldots, \omega_{X_k,Y}X_k(t)) - Y(t)]\Delta t$	The causal impact on Y is exerted over time gradually, using speed factor η_Y; here the X_i are all states with connections to state Y

The difference equations in the last row in Table 2 form the numerical representation of a temporal-causal network model and can be used for simulation and mathematical analysis, and also be written in differential equation format:

$$Y(t+\Delta t) = Y(t) + \eta_Y[\mathbf{c}_Y(\omega_{X_1,Y}X_1(t), \ldots, \omega_{X_k,Y}X_k(t)) - Y(t)]\Delta t$$
$$\mathbf{d}Y(t)/\mathbf{d}t = \eta_Y[\mathbf{c}_Y(\omega_{X_1,Y}X_1(t), \ldots, \omega_{X_k,Y}X_k(t)) - Y(t)]$$

3.2   Options for Combination Functions

Often used examples of combination functions are the *identity* **id**(.) for states with impact from only one other state, the maximum and minimum **max**(..) and **min**(..), the *scaled sum* **ssum**$_\lambda$(..) with scaling factor λ, and the *advanced logistic sum* combination function **alogistic**$_{\sigma,\tau}$(..) with steepness σ and threshold τ:

$$\mathbf{id}(V) = V \qquad \mathbf{max}(V_1, \ldots, V_k) \qquad \mathbf{min}(V_1, \ldots, V_k)$$
$$\mathbf{ssum}_\lambda(V_1, \ldots, V_k) = (V_1, \ldots, V_k)/\lambda$$
$$\mathbf{alogistic}_{\sigma,\tau}(V_1, \ldots, V_k) = \left[(1/(1+e^{-\sigma(V_1 + \ldots + V_k - \tau)})) - 1(1+e^{\sigma\tau})\right](1+e^{-\sigma\tau})$$

Note that for $\lambda = 1$, the scaled sum function is just the sum function **sum(..)**, and this sum function can also be used as identity function in case of one incoming connection. In addition to the above functions, a *Euclidean combination function* is defined as

$$\mathbf{c}(V_1, \ldots, V_k) = \mathbf{eucl}_{n,\lambda}(V_1, \ldots, V_k) = ((V_1^n + \ldots + V_k^n)/\lambda)^{1/n}$$

where n is the order (which can be any nonzero natural number, but also any positive real number) and λ is a scaling factor. Note that for $n = 1$ (first-order Euclidean combination function) we get the scaled sum function:

$$\mathbf{eucl}_{1,\lambda}(V_1, \ldots, V_k) = \mathbf{ssum}_\lambda(V_1, \ldots, V_k)$$

For $n = 2$ it is the second-order Euclidean combination function $\mathbf{eucl}_{2,\lambda}(..)$ defined by:

$$\mathbf{eucl}_{2,\lambda}(V_1, \ldots, V_k) = \sqrt{(V_1^2 + \ldots + V_k^2)/\lambda}$$

This second-order Euclidean combination function is also often applied in aggregating the error value in optimisation and in parameter tuning using the root-mean-square deviation (RMSD), based on the Sum of Squared Residuals (SSR).

For proper functioning of Euclidean combination functions, some constraints are used. First, in general this function is only applied when all connection weights are positive, except in the specific case that n is an odd natural nunber. Moreover, also a constraint on the scaling factor λ is used. When no weights are negative, the maximal value of the outcome is achieved when for each X_i it holds $X_i(t) = 1$; then the maximal outcome is $((\sum_i \omega_{X_i,Y}^n)/\lambda)^{1/n}$. To keep the outcomes below 1, the scaling factor λ should be equal to or at least the sum of the nth powers of all weights: $\lambda \geq \sum_i \omega_{X_i,Y}^n$. In such cases the standard value $\lambda = \sum_i \omega_{X_i,Y}^n$ is often used as a form of *normalisation*. All this also applies to scaled sum functions, as this is the case $n = 1$. When n is an odd natural number, and also negative weights are involved the maximal outcome is $((\sum_{i,\omega_{X_i,Y} > 0} \omega_{X_i,Y}^n)/\lambda)^{1/n}$. Therefore, to keep the outcomes of the combination function below 1 in that case, the scaling factor λ should be at least the sum of the nth powers of the positive weights: $\lambda \geq \sum_{i,\omega_{X_i,Y} > 0} \omega_{X_i,Y}^n$. Again, as a form of *normalisation* the standard value $\lambda = \sum_{i,\omega_{X_i,Y} > 0} \omega_{X_i,Y}^n$ is often used.

4   Relating Emerging Network Behavior to Network Structure

The Network-Oriented Modeling approach based on temporal-causal networks does not only provide opportunities for simulation but also for mathematical analysis and to derive general theoretical results that predict or reflect behavior that is observed in specific cases of simulations. A general question for dynamic models is what patterns of behaviour will emerge, and how their emergence depends on the chosen network structure. Whether or not in general such relations between structure and emerging behavior can be found is sometimes a topic for discussion. However, in the context of the Network-Oriented Modeling approach based on temporal-causal networks considered here at least some results on this relation have been obtained.

Usually the structure of a network is described by a number of parameters. For temporal-causal networks in particular, such parameters are connection weights, combination functions and speed factors. So, the challenge is to find out how properties of connection weights, combination functions and speed factors relate to emerging behavior. Some results that have been found on this relation between structure and behavior, will be discussed below. In particular it will be addressed what limit behaviour emerges; for example:

- Will the values of different states eventually converge to a common value?
- Under which conditions on the structure of the network will this happen?

Such behaviour relates to what are called stationary points and equilibrium states, defined as follows:

Definition (stationary and equilibrium)
State Y (or connection weight ω) is *stationary* or *has a stationary point* at time t if $dY(t)/dt = 0$ (or $d\omega(t)/dt = 0$). The network is in an *equilibrium state* at t if all states (and connections) are stationary at t.

Note that for a temporal-causal network there is a simple *criterion* in terms of connection weights and combination functions (see also [17]): when $\eta_Y > 0$, state Y is stationary at t if and only if

$$\mathbf{c}_Y(\omega_{X_1,Y} X_1(t), \ldots, \omega_{X_k,Y} X_k(t)) = Y(t)$$

where $X_1, \ldots X_k$ are the states with outgoing connections to Y.

A number of properties of network structure have been identified such that they relate to similar emergent behavior. These network structure properties concern a connectivity property about how many states of the network are reachable from a given state, and some properties of combination functions.

4.1 Examples of Emerging Network Behaviour

To get the idea, first a few examples of a Social Network addressing social contagion are briefly discussed. Consider the (fully connected) network with connection weights and speed factors shown in Table 3. For this network, simulations have been performed for different combination functions. In Fig. 4 the three different simulations are shown. For the upper graph advanced logistic sum combination functions were used, for the middle graph normalized scaled sum functions, and in the lower graph scaled sum functions while two states remain constant (they have no incoming connections this time, so the cells in the columns for X_4 and X_8 in Table 3 all are 0 now). It turns out that in one case convergence to one common equilibrium value takes place, but in the other two cases that does not happen and instead some form of clustering seems to take place. How can we explain these differences in emerging behavior from the structure of the networks? This question will be answered in this section.

Table 3. Settings of the example Social Network: connection weights and speed factors

connections	X_1	X_2	X_3	X_4	X_5	X_6	X_7	X_8	X_9	X_{10}
X_1		0.1	0.2	0.1	0.2	0.15	0.1	0.25	0.25	0.1
X_2	0.25		0.25	0.2	0.1	0.2	0.15	0.25	0.25	0.25
X_3	0.1	0.25		0.1	0.2	0.15	0.1	0.25	0.1	0.15
X_4	0.25	0.15	0.25		0.15	0.8	0.25	0.15	0.25	0.25
X_5	0.25	0.2	0.1	0.2		0.25	0.2	0.1	0.2	0.15
X_6	0.25	0.1	0.25	0.25	0.25		0.1	0.25	0.25	0.1
X_7	0.2	0.1	0.2	0.15	0.2	0.2		0.2	0.15	0.25
X_8	0.1	0.25	0.1	0.25	0.05	0.15	0.25		0.1	0.25
X_9	0.25	0.15	0.25	0.15	0.2	0.1	0.2	0.15		0.15
X_{10}	0.2	0.25	0.2	0.2	0.1	0.2	0.15	0.8	0.2	
speed factors	0.8	0.5	0.8	0.5	0.5	0.5	0.8	0.5	0.5	0.5

4.2   Network Structure Properties Relevant for Emerging Network Behaviour

It has been found out that some properties of network structure (in particular concerning combination functions and connectivity) underlie the differences shown in Fig. 4. First relevant properties of combination functions.

Definition (properties of combination functions)

Let $c(V_1, \ldots, V_k)$ be a function of values $V_1, \ldots, V_k$
(a) $c(..)$ is called *nonnegative* if $c(V_1, \ldots, V_k) \geq 0$
(b) $c(..)$ *respects* 0 if $V_1, .., V_k \geq 0 \Rightarrow [c(V_1, \ldots, V_k) = 0 \Leftrightarrow V_1 = .. = V_k = 0]$
(c) $c(..)$ is called *monotonically increasing* if
  $U_i \leq V_i$ for all $i \Rightarrow c(U_1, \ldots, U_k) \leq c(V_1, \ldots, V_k)$
(d) $c(..)$ is called *strictly monotonically increasing* if
  $U_i \leq V_i$ for all i, and $U_j < V_j$ for at least one $j \Rightarrow c(U_1, \ldots, U_k) < c(V_1, \ldots, V_k)$
(e) $c(..)$ is called *scalar-free* if $c(\alpha V_1, \ldots, \alpha V_k) = \alpha c(V_1, \ldots, V_k)$ for all $\alpha > 0$.

The properties (a) to (c) are basic properties expected from most if not all combination functions. Properties (d) and (e) define a specific class of combination functions; this class includes all Euclidean combination functions, but logistic combination functions do not belong to this class as they are not scalar-free. Some theoretical results on emergent behaviour will be discussed for this class, but also some other network properties play a role.

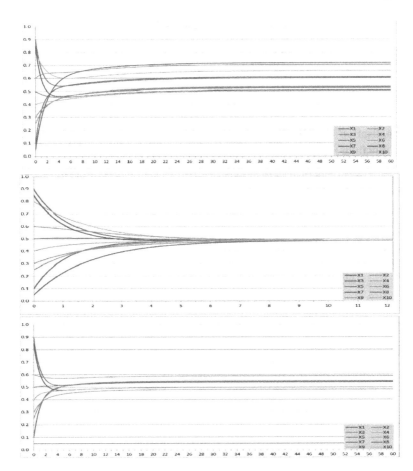

Fig. 4. The example network with (a) upper graph: advanced logistic sum combination functions with steepness $\sigma = 1.5$, threshold $\tau = 0.3$ (no convergence to one common value), (b) middle graph: normalised scaled sum functions (convergence to one common value), (c) normalised scaled sum functions with constant X_4 (at 0.8) and X_8 (at 0.05) (no convergence to one common value)

Definition (normalised network)

A network is *normalised* or uses normalised combination functions if for each state Y it holds $c_Y(\omega_{X_1,Y}, \ldots, \omega_{X_k,Y}) = 1$, where X_1, ..., X_k are the states with outgoing connections to Y.

Note that $c_Y(\omega_{X_1,Y}, \ldots, \omega_{X_k,Y})$ is an expression in terms of the parameter(s) of the combination function and $\omega_{X_1,Y}, \ldots, \omega_{X_k,Y}$. To require this expression to be equal to 1 provides a contraint on these parameters: an equation relating the parameter value(s) of the combination functions to the parameters $\omega_{X_1,Y}, \ldots, \omega_{X_k,Y}$. To satisfy this property, often the parameter(s) can be given suitable values. For example, for a Euclidean combination function, scaling factor $\lambda_Y = \omega_{X_1,Y}^n + \ldots + \omega_{X_k,Y}^n$ will provide a normalised network. This can be done in general:

(1) normalisation by adjusting the combination functions

If any combination function $c_Y(..)$ is replaced by $c'_Y(..)$ defined as

$$c'_Y(V_1, \ldots, V_k) = c_Y(V_1, \ldots, V_k)/c_Y(\omega_{X_1,Y}, \ldots, \omega_{X_k,Y})$$

then the network becomes normalised: indeed $c'_A(\omega_{X_1,Y}, .., \omega_{X_k,Y}) = 1$

(2) normalisation by adjusting the connection weights (for scalar-free combination functions)

For scalar-free combination functions also normalisation is possible by adapting the connection weights; define:

$$\omega'_{X_i,Y} = \omega_{X_i,Y}/c_Y(\omega_{X_1,Y}, .., \omega_{X_k,Y})$$

Then the network becomes normalised; indeed it holds:

$$c_Y(\omega'_{X_1,Y}, \ldots, \omega'_{X_k,Y}) = c(\omega_{X_1,Y}/c_Y(\omega_{X_1,Y}, .., \omega_{X_k,Y}), .., \omega_{X_k,Y}/c(\omega_{X_1,Y}, .., \omega_{X_k,Y})) = 1$$

Another important determinant for emerging behaviour is in how far the network has paths connecting any two states; for this, the following definition is used:

Definition
State Y is *backward reachable* from state X if there is a directed path from X to Y.

This property makes a difference between the third example simulation and the other two: no state is backward reachable from X_4 or X_8 in that third case as these states have no incoming connections.

4.3   Relating Network Structure Properies to Emerging Network Behaviour

Part of the mathematical analysis performed is summarised by the following proposition and the theorem that can be derived from this proposition.

Proposition 1 (equilibrium state values and connectivity)
Suppose a network with nonnegative connections is based on normalised, strictly monotonically increasing and scalar-free combination functions.
If in an equilibrium state, a state Y has highest state value or lowest state value, then all states backward reachable from Y have the same equilibrium state value as Y.

Theorem 1 (equal equilibrium state values)
Suppose a network with nonnegative connections is based on normalised, strictly monotonically increasing and scalar-free combination functions.

(a) Suppose for any state Y except at most one state, all other states X are backward reachable from Y. Then in an equilibrium state all states have the same state value.

(b) Under the conditions of (a) the equilibrium state is attracting, and the common equilibrium state value lies in between the highest and lowest previous or initial state values.

Theorem 1 can be used to prove for many cases that in an equilibrium all states have the same value. This includes cases in which the only combination functions used are Euclidean combination functions. This shows why for the second simulation in Fig. 4 convergence to one common value takes place, but not for the first and third case. The first case does not satisfy the scalar-free condition, and the third case does not satisfy the condition on backward reachability of (b) in Theorem 1; one exception is allowed but not two, as occurs in the third example in Fig. 4. In case of only one of X_4 and X_8 as exception, say X_4, there would be convergence to one common value: to the value of the one state that remains constant all the time. Note that these differences in emerging behaviour have no relation to linear or nonlinear equations, as Theorem 1 applies to, for example, all Euclidean combination functions, both to linear and nonlinear ones.

5   The Wide Applicability of Network-Oriented Modeling

Many applications of Network-Oriented Modeling exist: Biological Networks, Neural Networks, Mental Networks, and Social Networks. It sometimes is a silent assumption that a Network-Oriented Modeling approach can only work for such specific application domains, where networks are felt as more or less already given or perceived in the real world. From this perspective it was also discussed in Sect. 2 why biological, mental and social domains ask for Network-Oriented Modeling, domains where network structures are perceived, respectively, as networks of biochemical, mental, or social interactions. The question is whether the applicability of Network-Oriented Modeling goes beyond such domains where network structures seem to show themselves naturally.

5.1   Network-Oriented Modeling Applies Beyond Perceived Networks

In [19] it is shown that the above-mentioned silent assumption is not a correct assumption. It has been shown that the applicability of the Network-Oriented Modeling approach based on temporal-causal networks is much wider. For example, it has been proven that modeling by temporal-causal networks subsumes modelling approaches based on the dynamical system perspective [1, 13] or systems of first-order differential equations; see [19], Sect. 3. The dynamical system approach is not only often used to obtain dynamical cognitive models, but also to model processes in many other scientific domains, including biological and physical domains. Moreover, modeling by temporal-causal networks subsumes modelling approaches based on discrete (event) and agent simulation [15, 20], including very basic computational notions such as finite state machines and transition systems; see [19], Sect. 4.

This shows that temporal-causal network models do not just model networks considered as given in the real world, but can be applied to model practically any type of process. Therefore, indeed the modelling approach is not limited only to Biological Networks, Neural Networks, Mental Networks, and Social Networks, but applies far beyond those types of domains. Moreover, it shows that the specific temporal-causal interpretation and structure added to networks on top of a basic graph structure, as discussed in Sect. 2, which may seem to make it more specific, actually does not introduce serious limitations.

5.2   Network-Oriented Modeling Applies to Adaptive Networks

It may also be a question in how far adaptive networks can be modelled too: networks that change their structure over time. It has been shown that this question can also be answered in an affirmative manner, by addressing many examples varying from adaptive Mental Networks based on a Hebbian learning principle, to adaptive Social Networks based on a homophily principle or a preferential attachment principle; e.g., [18], Chap. 2, and Chap. 11, respectively. As an illustration, consider the way in which adaptive connection weights can be addressed as shown in Fig. 5; these weights are assumed ≥ 0 here. Here the network is extended by two additional states $\Omega_{X_1,Y}$ and $\Omega_{X_2,Y}$ for the connection weights $\omega_{X_1,Y}$ and $\omega_{X_2,Y}$. Both affect state Y; they themselves can be affected by other states as well. Note that in the extended network the connections get the default connection weights 1.

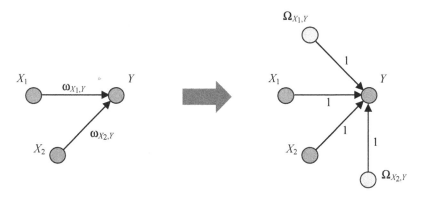

Fig. 5. Extending a temporal-causal network to model adaptive connections

In the original adaptive network the difference equation for Y is

$$Y(t + \Delta t) = Y(t) + \eta_Y[\mathbf{c}_Y(\omega_{X_1,Y}(t)X_1(t), \omega_{X_2,Y}(t)X_2(t)) - Y(t)]\Delta t$$

In the extended network obtained by adding states $\Omega_{X_1,Y}$ and $\Omega_{X_2,Y}$ the new combination function $\mathbf{c}'_Y(..)$ for state Y can be defined based on the original combination function $\mathbf{c}_Y(..)$ as follows:

$$\mathbf{c}'_Y(V_1, V_2, W_1, W_2) = \mathbf{c}_Y(W_1V_1, W_2V_2)$$

where V_i stands for the impact $X_i(t)$ from X_i on Y, and W_i for the impact $\Omega_{X_i,Y}(t)$ from $\Omega_{X_i,Y}$ on Y. Then

$$\mathbf{c}'_Y(X_1(t), X_2(t), \Omega_{X_1,Y}(t), \Omega_{X_2,Y}(t)) = \mathbf{c}_Y(\omega_{X_1,Y}(t)X_1(t), \omega_{X_2,Y}(t)X_2(t))$$

and

$$Y(t + \Delta t) = Y(t) + \eta_Y [\mathbf{c}'_Y(X_1(t), X_2(t), \Omega_{X_1,Y}(t), \Omega_{X_2,Y}(t)) - Y(t)]\Delta t$$
$$= Y(t) + \eta_Y [\mathbf{c}_Y(\omega_{X_1,Y}(t)X_1(t), \omega_{X_2,Y}(t)X_2(t)) - Y(t)]\Delta t$$

which indeed is the original equation.

This specific case can be applied, for example, both to adaptive Mental Networks based on a Hebbian learning principle, and to adaptive Social Networks based on a homophily principle. To define such an adaptation principle it has to be specified what other states affect the new states $\Omega_{X_1,Y}$ and $\Omega_{X_2,Y}$, and what combination functions are used for that impact. As a special case, assume that $\Omega_{X_i,Y}$ gets impact from just X_i and Y, then there are arrows to $\Omega_{X_i,Y}$ as shown in Fig. 6, all with weight 1.

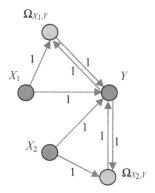

Fig. 6. Extended temporal-causal network to model connections affected by the connected states

In such cases of adaptation principles any differential equation may be assumed given for the adaptation of the connection weights. If, like above, the connection weight states $\Omega_{X_i,Y}$ depend on just X_i and Y this differential equation is

$$d\omega_{X_i,Y}(t)/dt = F(X_i(t), Y(t), \omega_{X_i,Y}(t))$$

for an arbitrary function $F(..)$. Then by a suitable combination function $\mathbf{c}'_{\Omega_{X_i,Y}}(..)$ for $\Omega_{X_i,Y}(t)$ this can be modeled as follows:

$$\mathbf{c}'_{\Omega_{X_i,Y}}(V_1, V_2, W) = W + F(V_1, V_2, W)$$

where V_1 stands for $X_i(t)$, V_2 for $Y(t)$ and W for $\Omega_{X_i,Y}(t)$. Then

$$\mathbf{c}'_{\Omega_{X_i,Y}}(X_i(t), Y(t), \Omega_{X_i,Y}(t)) = \Omega_{X_i,Y}(t) + F(X_i(t), Y(t), \Omega_{X_i,Y}(t))$$

Setting $\eta_{\Omega_{X_i,Y}} = 1$, the differential equation for $\Omega_{X_i,Y}(t)$ becomes

$$d\Omega_{X_i,Y}(t)/dt = \eta_{\Omega_{X_i,Y}}[\mathbf{c}'_{\Omega_{X_i,Y}}(X_i(t),\ Y(t),\Omega_{X_i,Y}(t))-\Omega_{X_i,Y}(t)\,]$$
$$= \Omega_{X_i,Y}(t)+F(X_i(t),\ Y(t),\Omega_{X_i,Y}(t))-\Omega_{X_i,Y}(t)$$
$$= F(X_i(t),\ Y(t),\Omega_{X_i,Y}(t))$$

This indeed is equal to the assumed differential equation for $\omega_{X_i,Y}(t)$, so the choice for this combination function

$$\mathbf{c}'_{\Omega_{X_i,Y}}(V_1,\ V_2,W)\ =\ W+F(V_1,\ V_2,W)$$

is correct for the considered type of adaptation principle. Specific examples of this type of adaptation principle are the following.

Hebbian learning principle in adaptive Mental Networks (e.g., [4, 5, 18]):

$$F(V_1,\ V_2,W) = V_1 V_2(1-W)-(1-\mu)W$$
$$\mathbf{c}'_{\Omega_{X_i,Y}}(V_1,\ V_2,W)\ =\ V_1 V_2(1-W)+\mu\,W$$

with μ a persistence parameter

Homophily principle in adaptive Social Networks (e.g., [3, 9]):

$$F(V_1,\ V_2,W) = \alpha(\tau-|V_1-V_2|)(1-W)W$$
$$\mathbf{c}'_{\Omega_{X_i,Y}}(V_1,\ V_2,W)\ =\ W+\alpha(\tau-|V_1-V_2|)(1-W)W$$

with τ threshold parameter and α an amplification parameter

Note that this illustrates once more how the Network-Oriented Modeling approach provides a unifying perspective across different domains, in this case the mental and social domain. Both are described in a unified manner by the picture in Fig. 6, and by a general combination function $\mathbf{c}'_{\Omega_{X_i,Y}}(V_1,\ V_2,W)$. Moreover, this also illustrates once more how arbitrary differential equations can be covered by the temporal-causal network format.

6   Discussion

In this paper the ins and outs of the Network-Oriented Modeling modeling perspective were discussed in some detail. By committing to an interpretation of networks based on the notion of a temporal-causal network, more structure and more depth is obtained, and more dedicated support is possible. At first sight it may suggest that it introduces a limitation to commit to a specific interpretation and structure of networks, but the proven wide scope of applicability of this Network-Oriented Modelling approach shows otherwise, as causality and temporality are very general concepts; e.g., see also [18, 19]. On the contrary, the specific added structures such as connection weights, combination functions and speed factors allow for a quite sensitive and unifying way of modeling realistic processes. These structures also allow more theoretical depth, which was illustrated by presenting some mathematical results on how emerging network behaviour relates to specific properties of the network structure.

By considering dynamics not only for states but also for characteristics of the network structure such as connection weights, also adaptive processes are covered in the form of adaptive networks. Examples of this have been used to illustrate the unifying role that temporal-causal network models can play, in particular by revealing similar structures in adaptive Mental Networks based on a Hebbian learning principle [4, 5], and adaptive Social Networks based on a homophily principle [9]. Again, the added structure provided by the notion of temporal-causal network provides the machinery to express such unified structures.

In further work a number of fundamental themes are being developed in more depth. One of them is the idea of *network reification*. This is what happens if the structure of a (base) network is itself represented in a network that extends the base network. For temporal-causal networks their structure is defined by their connection weights, speed factors, and combination functions. In a reified network all of these parameters are represented explicitly as additional states that have their effect on the states of the base network. A simple example of this for connection weights was already shown in Sect. 5.2 and Fig. 6. This provides a substantial enhancement of expressive power of the modelling format, in particular where it concerns adaptive networks where these parameters change over time. As a first step, in [25] (forthcoming) it is shown how this construction can be defined in general, and it is illustrated by several examples for Mental and Social Networks how any network adaptation principle can be defined within the reified network itself. In the forthcoming [30] it is shown how this reification construction can be repeated, thus obtaining *multilevel network reification* in which, for example, adaptive adaptation principles can be represented explicitly.

Another fundamental theme being developed further in more depth is the *relation between network structure and emerging network behaviour*. Keeping in mind that network structure is defined by connection weights, speed factors, and combination functions, in this theme it is analysed how certain properties of these parameters relate to certain limit behaviour. For example, can the limit values of the states for $t \rightarrow \infty$ be predicted from these parameters? And in which cases will all states end up with the same common value? This is addressed in the forthcoming [28] and [31], where in the latter the network is analysed based on its *strongly connected components* [33] and *stratification* [32] of the abstracted acyclic *condensation graph*. For adaptive networks based on Hebbian learning this is addressed in the forthcoming [27] and for bonding based on homophily this is addressed in the forthcoming [29], respectively.

A third area in which much development takes place is in the area of applications to certain psychological and/or social domains. The temporal-causal format makes it easy to represent causal domain knowledge in an understandable and executable manner. Several examples of applications in psychological and social domains illustrate this. In addition, it may be interesting to further investigate applications to the area of business economics, organisation modeling and management; e.g., [11].

References

1. Ashby, W.R.: Design for a Brain, 2nd edn. Wiley, New York (1960)
2. Bell, A.: Levels and loops: the future of artificial intelligence and neuroscience. Phil. Trans. R. Soc. Lond. B **354**, 2013–2020 (1999)
3. Blankendaal, R., Parinussa, S., Treur, J.: A temporal-causal modelling approach to integrated contagion and network change in social networks. In: Proceedings of the 22nd European Conference on Artificial Intelligence, ECAI 2016, pp. 1388–1396. IOS Press (2016)
4. Jonker, C.M., Snoep, J.L., Treur, J., Westerhoff, H.V., Wijngaards, W.C.A.: Putting intentions into cell biochemistry: an artificial intelligence perspective. J. Theoret. Biol. **214** (2002), 105–134 (2002)
5. Jonker, C.M., Snoep, J.L., Treur, J., Westerhoff, H.V., Wijngaards, W.C.A.: BDI-modelling of complex intracellular dynamics. J. Theoret. Biol. **251**, 1–23 (2008)
6. Kim, J.: Philosophy of Mind. Westview Press, Boulder (1996)
7. Gerstner, W., Kistler, W.M.: Mathematical formulations of Hebbian learning. Biol. Cybern. **87**, 404–415 (2002)
8. Hebb, D.: The Organisation of Behavior. Wiley, Hoboken (1949)
9. McPherson, M., Smith-Lovin, L., Cook, J.M.: Birds of a feather: homophily in social networks. Annu. Rev. Sociol. **27**, 415–444 (2001)
10. Mooij, J.M., Janzing, D., Schölkopf, B.: From differential equations to structural causal models: the deterministic case. In: Nicholson, A., Smyth, P. (eds.) Proceedings of the 29th Annual Conference on Uncertainty in Artificial Intelligence (UAI-13), pp. 440–448. AUAI Press (2013). http://auai.org/uai2013/prints/papers/24.pdf
11. Naudé, A., Le Maitre, D., de Jong, T., Mans, G.F.G., Hugo, W.: Modelling of spatially complex human-ecosystem, rural-urban and rich-poor interactions (2008). https://www.researchgate.net/profile/Tom_De_jong/publication/30511313_Modelling_of_spatially_complex_human-ecosystem_rural-urban_and_rich-poor_interactions/links/02e7e534d3e9a47836000000.pdf
12. Pearl, J.: Causality. Cambridge University Press, Cambridge (2000)
13. Port, R.F., van Gelder, T.: Mind as Motion: Explorations in the Dynamics of Cognition. MIT Press, Cambridge (1995)
14. Potter, S.M.: What can artificial intelligence get from neuroscience? In: Lungarella, M., Bongard, J., Pfeifer, R. (eds.) Artificial Intelligence Festschrift: The next 50 years, vol. 4850, pp. 174–185. Springer-Verlag, Berlin (2007). https://doi.org/10.1007/978-3-540-77296-5_17
15. Sarjoughian, H., Cellier, F.E. (eds.): Discrete Event Modeling and Simulation Technologies: A Tapestry of Systems and AI-Based Theories and Methodologies. Springer, Berlin (2001). https://doi.org/10.1007/978-1-4757-3554-3
16. Scherer, K.R.: Emotions are emergent processes: they require a dynamic computational architecture. Phil. Trans. R. Soc. B **364**, 3459–3474 (2009)
17. Treur, J.: Verification of temporal-causal network models by mathematical analysis. Vietnam J. Comput. Sci. **3**, 207–221 (2016)
18. Treur, J.: Network-Oriented Modeling: Addressing Complexity of Cognitive, Affective and Social Interactions. Springer, Heidelberg (2016). https://link-springer-com.vu-nl.idm.oclc.org/book/10.1007/978-3-319-45213-5
19. Treur, J.: On the applicability of network-oriented modeling based on temporal-causal networks: why network models do not just model networks. J. Inf. Telecommun. **1**, 23–40 (2017)

20. Uhrmacher, A., Schattenberg, B.: Agents in discrete event simulation. In: Proceedings of the European Symposium on Simulation, ESS 1998, Nottingham, England. Society for Computer Simulation, San Diego (1998)
21. Westerhoff, H.V., He, F., Murabito, E., Crémazy, F., Barberis, M.: Understanding principles of the dynamic biochemical networks of life through systems biology. In: Kriete, A., Eils, R. (eds.) Computational Systems Biology, 2nd edn, pp. 21–44. Academic Press, Oxford (2014)
22. Westerhoff, H.V., et al.: Macromolecular networks and intelligence in microorganisms. Front. Microbiol. **5**, Article 379 (2014)
23. Wright, S.: Correlation and causation. J. Agric. Res. **20**, 557–585 (1921)
24. Bosse, T., Duell, R., Memon, Z.A., Treur, J., van der Wal, C.N.: Agent-based modelling of emotion contagion in groups. Cogn. Comput. **7**(1), 111–136 (2015)
25. Treur, J.: Network reification as a unified approach to represent network adaptation principles within a network. In: Proceedings of the 7th International Conference on the Theory and Practice of Natural Computing, TPNC 2018. LNCS. Springer, Heidelberg (2018, to appear)
26. Treur, J.: Dynamic modeling based on a temporal-causal network modeling approach. Biol. Inspired Cogn. Architect. **16**, 131–168 (2016)
27. Treur, J.: Relating an adaptive network's structure to its emerging behaviour for Hebbian learning. In: Proceedings of the 7th International Conference on the Theory and Practice of Natural Computing, TPNC 2018. LNCS. Springer, Heidelberg (2018, to appear)
28. Treur, J.: Relating emerging network behaviour to network structure. In: Proceedings of the 7th International Conference on Complex Networks and Their Applications, Complex Networks 2018. SCI. Springer, Heidelberg (2018, to appear)
29. Treur, J.: Relating an adaptive social network's structure to its emerging behaviour based on homophily. In: Proceedings of the 7th International Conference on Complex Networks and Their Applications, ComplexNetworks 2018. SCI. Springer, Heidelberg (2018, to appear)
30. Treur, J.: Multilevel network reification: representing higher order adaptivity in a network. In: Proceedings of the 7th International Conference on Complex Networks and Their Applications, Complex Networks 2018. SCI. Springer, Heidelberg (2018, to appear)
31. Treur, J.: Mathematical analysis of a network's asymptotic behaviour based on its strongly connected components. In: Proceedings of the 7th International Conference on Complex Networks and Their Applications, Complex Networks 2018. SCI. Springer, Heidelberg (2018, to appear)
32. Chen, Y.: General spanning trees and reachability query evaluation. In: Desai, B.C. (ed.) Proceedings of the 2nd Canadian Conference on Computer Science and Software Engineering, C3S2E 2009, pp. 243–252. ACM Press (2009)
33. Harary, F., Norman, R.Z., Cartwright, D.: Structural Models: an Introduction to the Theory of Directed Graphs. Wiley, New York (1965)

Local Termination Criteria for Swarm Intelligence: A Comparison Between Local Stochastic Diffusion Search and Ant Nest-Site Selection

Andrew O. Martin[1], J. Mark Bishop[1(✉)], Elva J. H. Robinson[2], and Darren R. Myatt[3]

[1] TCIDA, Goldsmiths, University of London, New Cross, London, UK
{m.bishop,a.martin}@gold.ac.uk
[2] York Centre for Complex Systems Analysis and Department of Biology, University of York, York, UK
elva.robinson@york.ac.uk
[3] Acrefield House, Belle Vue Estate, London, UK
darren.myatt@googlemail.com
http://www.tungsten-network.com/tcida/
https://www.york.ac.uk/biology/research/ecology-evolution/elva-robinson/
https://www.linkedin.com/in/darren-myatt-0857b63

Abstract. Stochastic diffusion search (SDS) is a global Swarm Intelligence optimisation technique based on the behaviour of ants, rooted in the partial evaluation of an objective function and direct communication between agents. Although population based decision mechanisms employed by many Swarm Intelligence methods can suffer poor convergence resulting in ill-defined halting criteria and loss of the best solution, as a result of its resource allocation mechanism, the solutions found by Stochastic Diffusion Search enjoy excellent stability.

Previous implementations of SDS have deployed stopping criteria derived from global properties of the agent population; this paper examines new *local* SDS halting criteria and compares their performance with 'quorum sensing' (a termination criterion naturally deployed by some species of tandem-running ants). In this chapter we discuss two experiments investigating the robustness and efficiency of the new *local* termination criteria; our results demonstrate these to be (a) effectively as robust as the classical SDS termination criteria and (b) almost three times faster.

Keywords: Collective decision making · Ant nest selection
Stochastic Diffusion Search · Swarm Intelligence · Global Search

This paper offers extended discussion of results first presented at ICCCI 2016 (Halkidiki) and published in the conference proceedings [11].

1   Introduction

In recent years there has been growing interest in Swarm Intelligence (SI), a distributed mode of computation utilising interaction between simple agents [37]. Such systems have often been inspired by observing interactions between social insects: ants, bees, termites (cf. Ant Algorithms and Particle Swarm Optimisers) see Bonabeau [12] for a comprehensive review. SI algorithms also include methods inspired by natural evolution such as Genetic Algorithms [29,33] or indeed Evolutionary Algorithms [5]. The problem solving ability of SI methods emerges from positive feedback reinforcing potentially good solutions and the spatial/temporal characteristics of their agent interactions.

Independently of these algorithms, Stochastic Diffusion Search (SDS), historically positioned as the first Swarm Intelligence meta-heuristic, was initially described in 1989 as a population-based, pattern-matching algorithm [7,8]. Unlike stigmergic communication employed in Ant Algorithms, which is based on modification of the physical properties of a simulated environment, SDS uses a form of direct communication between the agents similar to the tandem running mechanism employed by some species of ants (e.g. *Temnothorax* species, [23]).

SDS is an efficient probabilistic multi-agent global search, optimisation and decision making technique [42] that has been applied to diverse problems such as site selection for wireless networks [74], mobile robot self-localisation [6], object recognition [9] and text search [7]. Additionally, a hybrid SDS and n-tuple RAM [1] technique has been used to track facial features in video sequences [9,31]. Previous analysis of SDS has investigated its global convergence [51], linear time complexity [52] and resource allocation [50] under a variety of search conditions. For a recent review of the theoretical foundations, and applications of SDS see Al-Rifaie and Bishop [2].

In arriving at a 'decision' - *halting* - standard implementations of SDS examine the *stability* of the agent population as a whole; in this manner halting is defined as a *global* property of the agent population. However such global mechanisms are both less biologically/naturally plausible and more complex to implement on parallel computational systems, than local decision making mechanisms.

The organisation of this paper is as follows. Firstly we outline *Swarm Intelligence* meta-heuristic and against the background of communication in the social insects. Next we describe how collective decision making occurs in nature by analysing the behaviour of house-hunting ants. We subsequently introduce the Stochastic Diffusion Search.

SDS has subsequently been thoroughly mathematically explored; it is not appropriate to include its full analysis herein (see [9,50–52,55] for detail), however a simplified description (under-pinning that suggested in [31]) and based on the 'practical' characterisation[1] from Myatt et al. [48] is included. Together these analyses make SDS one of the best characterised of all the SI meta-heuristics.

Finally this paper examines the local quorum sensing behaviour observed in some natural (ant) systems and uses this as the inspiration for two new local termination mechanisms - one mechanism, 'independent termination', seeks to implement a protocol in SDS that is as close as possible to the quorum sensing method used by real ants; a second method - confirmation termination - aims to implement a mechanism closely related to quorum sensing on a more conventional SDS architecture; both halting criteria are algorithmically outlined and their performance experimentally evaluated.

2   Swarm Intelligence

Natural examples of swarm intelligence systems that exhibit such forms of collective interactions and decision-making are: fish schooling, bird flocking, bacterial growth, animal herding, nesting and foraging in the social insects etc. and in recent years, abstractions of such natural behaviour have suggested several new meta-heuristics for use in modelling collective intelligence. The simple and often successful deployment of these new meta-heuristics on traditionally difficult optimisation problems has in turn generated increasing interest in the nascent field of swarm intelligence algorithms: nature-inspired algorithms instantiating distributed computation via the interaction of simple agents and their environment (e.g. ant algorithms [20,21] and particle swarm optimisation [38] etc.).

In this paper we will illustrate Stochastic Diffusion Search - in which interactions between agents cause a population of agents to evolve towards potential solution states - and show that it shares many of the characteristics and behaviours of classical swarm intelligence algorithms; furthermore, we show that core stochastic diffusion processes are illustrated in the behaviours of some social insects (e.g. bees in identifying potential new food sources and ants in choosing a new nest site location) in the following sections of the paper (Sects. 2.1 and 2.2); we explore SDS in this context.

2.1   Communication in Social Insects

In the study of interaction in social insects, two key elements are the individuals and the environment, which results in two modes of interaction: the first defines the way in which individuals interact with each other and the second defines the interaction of individuals with the environment [13]. Interaction between individual agents is typically carried out via agent recruitment processes and it has been demonstrated that various recruitment strategies are deployed by ants [15,32] and honey bees [30,67]. These recruitment strategies may be used, for example, to attract other members of the population to gather around one or

---

[1] The simplifying assumption is that, by considering only the mean transition of agents between different clusters of agents, rather than the full probability distribution (as investigated in [51]), a *sufficiently* accurate model of SDS may be obtained.

more desired areas in the search space, either for foraging purposes or in order to facilitate a colony relocation to a better nest site.

It has been observed that recruitment strategies in social insects may take the form of: localised or global recruitment; one-to-one or one-to-many recruitment; and may operate stochastically or deterministically. The nature of information exchange also varies in different environments and with different types of social insects. Sometimes the information exchange is quite complex and, for example, might communicate data about the direction, distance and suitability of the target; or sometimes the information sharing is relatively simple, for example, a stimulation forcing a particular triggered action. Nonetheless, what all recruitment and information exchange strategies have in common is an ability to distribute useful information across their community [42].

2.2   Methods of Communication

Chemical communication through pheromones forms the primary method of recruitment in many species of ants; however, in certain species a 'tandem running' mechanism (one-to-one communication) is used [23]. In this process, the scouting ant that finds the resource location attracts a single recruit upon its return to the nest (tandem calling) and physically leads the recruit to the resource (tandem running); by this action the location of the resource is physically publicised [75] to the population.

Conversely in group recruitment, one ant summons a group of ants, leading them to the resource location. Group recruitment may entail laying a pheromone trail from the resource to the nest; a more complex process in which the recruiting ant is no longer necessarily in physical contact with the recruited ants.

The largest-scale ant recruitment mechanism is called 'mass recruitment' [76]; in this mechanism, worker ants both follow the pheromone trail and incrementally add an amount of pheromone on their journeys to and from the resource location. In such 'mass recruitment', the concentration of pheromone plays an important role in attracting other ants to the resource trail.

Different recruitment and communication algorithms thus induce differing search performances. Ants communicating through group recruitment are faster than tandem running ants, and similarly, ants utilising mass recruitment are more efficient in their performances than the former recruitment strategies [15]. Ant algorithms have been successfully applied to hard optimisation and search problems such as travelling salesman problem and the quadratic assignment problem [22].

However, as mentioned in [17], the success of the ants in reaching the food they have been recruited to obtain, varies from one species to another. In another form of communication, indirect or stigmergic communication, the exchange of information is based on modifying the physical properties of the environment and its success lies in spatial and temporal attributes of mass recruitment and the positive feedback mechanism it employs. In this mode, which is based on using pheromone, short routes are loaded with more pheromone (because of the shorter time it takes the ants to travel back and forth between the source and target [34]).

An ant-like task allocation has been investigated in [35] where robots were used to simulate different non-communication and communication strategies, concluding that ant-inspired techniques of decentralised control, namely tandem running recruitment mechanism [75] shows better results than single robots doing the same task. This technique of information exchange is an instance of a broader type of recruitment strategy utilised in stochastic diffusion search [42], which will be discussed in more detail, later in this paper.

In honeybees, group recruitment is performed by means of waggle dances, in which the angle of the dance relative to gravity shows the direction of the resource, and the duration of the central part of the dance represents the distance to the target area. Each scouting bee can choose one of the dancing bees as a guide to a food source or a new nest.

3   Collective Decision-Making in House Hunting Ants

Quorum sensing is widespread throughout biological systems. When a collective decision is required, a quick and effective way of moving from an information-gathering phase to an implementation phase is to use a quorum threshold. A quorum response can be said to occur when an individual's probability of exhibiting a behaviour (e.g. choosing a given option) is a sharply nonlinear function of the number of other individuals already performing this behaviour (or having chosen that option) [72]. Quorum sensing is used by biological systems as diverse as bacteria, insects, fish, and primates - including humans [43,44,71,73]. A model system for collective decision-making and the use of quorum thresholds is provided by the process of house-hunting in social insects, such as honeybees and cavity-nesting ants. Ants that nest in fragile cavities in rocks or twigs have only limited scope to modify their nest-site, and readily relocate their entire colony when the need arises. The processes by which cavity-nesting ant colonies of the genus *Temnothorax* decide whether to emigrate, choose their new nest and implement that choice have been well-explored, both empirically and theoretically, as they provide a key model of animal collective decision-making.

The stages of an emergency emigration by a colony of cavity-nesting ants are summarised in Fig. 1. Even when no emigration is needed, scouts survey the surrounding area for potential new nest sites [25,70]. If the home nest cavity is damaged or degraded, then scouts leave the home nest and both visit the sites they already know and also search for new nest sites. Scouts assess the available nests across a number of metrics using a weighted additive strategy [27]. If a nest is judged as unsuitable, a scout continues searching; if a nest is assessed as suitable by a scouting ant (Scout A), this scout will return towards the home nest and recruit a second scout (Scout B) from in or near the home nest [64]. Scout A will lead Scout B to the new nest by a slow tandem-running process whereby Scout A moves slowly, with Scout B walking behind, making contact with its antennae and learning the route [23]. Scout B will then make an independent assessment of the nest, and will either reject it and keep searching, or accept the nest and spend some time in it, before returning home and recruiting a further scout. By this process of positive feedback, a good quality nest will accumulate ants [61,63]. Different ants appear to have differing thresholds for accepting a nest and starting to recruit; this means that even low quality nests can attract some ants, but scouts will accumulate more quickly and to a higher level at higher quality nests [62,70]. This assessment and recruitment process is terminated when a nest reaches a quorum of scouts. When scouts sense that a nest site has reached quorum, they change into a 'post-quorum' behavioural state [59]. From this point on they stop leading other scouts by tandem-running, and are no longer willing to be recruited by tandem-running themselves. Instead, they transport brood, queen, nest workers and other scouts to the chosen site. Transported workers do not learn the route between the home nest and the new nest, so are unable to return home, and thus cannot challenge the decision that has been implemented [59]. Transported ants therefore contribute strongly to the quorum by staying in the new nest, so once a few scouts have moved into a 'post-quorum' state and started transporting, other scouts will quickly follow suit.

4   Quorum Sensing in House Hunting Ants

The sensing of a quorum threshold is clearly central to the decision-making process, as it marks the transition from information-gathering and assessment, to implementation. Terminating information-gathering promotes cohesion, which is very important for ant colonies that only have one reproductively active queen. For cavity-nesting ants, quorum thresholds appear to be based on direct encounter rate, rather than any indirect cue such as pheromone concentration [61]. Scouts spend 1–2 min in a nest assessing the number of workers present via their encounter rate [58]. Quorum threshold as a proportion of colony size is remarkably constant across a range of colony sizes (3.5%) [19], and this is intriguing, because the relationship between colony size and cavity size is not simple positive correlation: although larger colonies do inhabit larger cavities in the wild, in laboratory tests both small and large colonies prefer larger cavities, presumably to allow for growth [14,39,45,60].

Quorum sensing is a separate process from quality assessment and recruitment. This means that the quorum sensing process in effect detects an average quality assessment across many scouts, and has the potential to smooth out differences in individual nest acceptance thresholds (or indeed, artificially-induced fluctuations in nest quality) [28]. Once quorum is reached and transport has begun, scouts do not re-assess quorum on subsequent visits - they will continue to bring brood even if the nest is artificially emptied of ants [58]. The quorum threshold itself is not modulated depending on the quality of the new nest [57]. If nest quality is artificially manipulated during the assessment phase of an emigration, the ants are able to respond flexibly to the new nest qualities; if quality is manipulated after quorum is reach and implementation has begun, then colonies often become 'trapped' in an inferior nest [26,65]. This indicates that quality is not re-assessed after quorum has been reached in these cavity-dwelling *Temnothorax* species. In contrast, a different ant species, *Diacamma indicum* recruits only by tandem-running with no clear quorum point and no adult transport [3]. Colonies of *Diacamma indicum* are able to respond flexibly to manipulated qualities at any stage of the emigration - but overall colony cohesion is lower, supporting the idea that using a quorum threshold increases cohesion, but at a cost to flexibility.

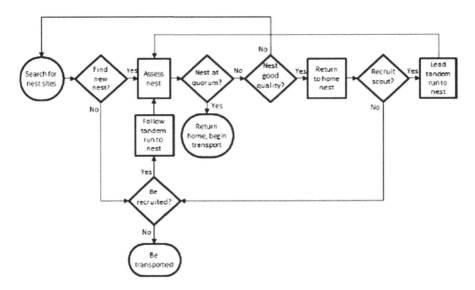

Fig. 1. The process of assessment and recruitment for an individual scouting ant of the genus *Temnothorax*, triggered by damage to the home nest. The scout starts by searching for new nest sites, and may finish by detecting quorum at a site and starting implementation of the decision to choose that site. Alternatively, if it is unable to recruit other scouts or be recruited by other scouts, this indicates that quorum has been reached at another site, and the scout will then be transported to that site and will cease to search. Non-emergency emigrations also occur, but in non-emergency situations scouts may spontaneously cease to search for a nest or attempting to recruit and instead enter a quiescent state. Probability of becoming re-activated is dependent on the home nest quality.

Although quorum sensing behaviour is not modulated by the quality of the options available, it is influenced by the scout's experience, and by the context of the emigration. Naive scouts use different quorum thresholds to those used by more experienced scouts, but the direction of this difference differs between species [57]. This suggests that there is a learning component to quorum sensing behaviour, but the mechanisms by which appropriate quorum thresholds are learnt is unknown. Figure 1 describes an emergency emigration, but cavity-nesting ants do also sometimes emigrate even when their home nest is undamaged, if a better nest is available in the neighbouring area. This is not due to direct comparison of the quality of the two nests, but due to quality-dependent nest leaving by scouts, and quality-dependent nest acceptance [63,70]. In these non-emergency migrations, scouts appear to use a quorum threshold around twice as high as in emergency migrations [18], suggesting that colonies prioritise speed over accuracy when conditions are harsher.

5   Stochastic Diffusion Search

SDS is based on distributed computation, in which the operations of simple computational units, or agents are inherently probabilistic. Agents collectively construct the solution by performing independent searches followed by diffusion of information through the population. Positive feedback promotes better solutions by allocating to them more agents for their exploration. Limited resources induce strong competition from which the largest population of agents corresponding to the best-fit solution rapidly emerges.

In many search problems the solution can be thought of as composed of many subparts and in contrast to most Swarm Intelligence methods SDS explicitly utilises such decomposition to increase the search efficiency of individual agents. In what is known as standard, *or vanilla*, SDS each agent poses a hypothesis about the possible solution and evaluates it partially. Successful agents repeatedly test their hypothesis while recruiting unsuccessful agents by direct communication. This creates a positive feedback mechanism ensuring rapid convergence of agents onto promising solutions in the space of all solutions. Regions of the solution space labelled by the presence of agent clusters *with the same hypothesis* can be interpreted as good candidate solutions. A global solution is thus constructed from the interaction of many simple, locally operating agents forming the largest cluster. Such a cluster is dynamic in nature, yet stable, analogous to, *"a forest whose contours do not change but whose individual trees do"*, [4,10,53,54]. Below the SDS mechanism is illustrated by analogy in 'The Restaurant Game'.

5.1   The Restaurant Game Analogy

A group of delegates attends a long conference in an unfamiliar town. Each night they have to find somewhere to dine. There is a large choice of restaurants, each of which offers a large variety of meals. The problem the group faces is to find the best restaurant, that is the restaurant where the maximum number of delegates would enjoy dining. Even a parallel exhaustive search through the restaurant and meal combinations would take too long to accomplish. To solve the problem delegates decide to employ a Stochastic Diffusion Search[2].

---

[2] It should be emphasised that this analogy is provided simply to illustrate the communication and feedback mechanisms at the heart of a stochastic diffusion search, and **not** as a heuristic to be employed by a group of hungry conference delegates.

Each delegate acts as an agent maintaining a hypothesis identifying the best restaurant in town. Each night each delegate tests his hypothesis by dining there and randomly selecting one of the meals on offer. The next morning at breakfast every delegate who did not enjoy his meal the previous night, asks one randomly selected colleague to share his dinner impressions. If the experience was good, he also adopts this restaurant as his choice. Otherwise he simply selects another restaurant at random from those listed in 'Yellow Pages'.

Using this strategy it is found that very rapidly significant number of delegates congregate around the best restaurant in town.

Abstracting from the above we get the algorithmic process defined in Table 1. By iterating through test and diffusion phases agents stochastically explore the solution space. However, since tests succeed more often on good candidate solutions than in regions with irrelevant information, an individual agent will spend more time examining 'good' regions, at the same time recruiting other agents, which in turn recruit even more agents. Candidate solutions are thus identified by concentrations of a substantial population of agents.

Table 1. Algorithmic description of the restaurant game

Initialisation phase
  whereby all agents (delegates) generate an initial hypothesis
  (select a restaurant at random)
loop
  Test phase
    Each agent evaluates evidence for its hypothesis (meal quality).
    Agents are partitioned into active (content) and inactive (disgruntled)
    groups (of diners).
  Diffusion phase
    Inactive agents adopt a new hypothesis by either communication with
    another agent or, if the selected agent is also inactive, there is no
    information flow between the agents; instead the selecting agent must
    adopt a new hypothesis (restaurant) at random.
endloop

Central to the power of SDS (see Algorithm 1) is its ability to escape local minima. This is achieved by the probabilistic outcome of the partial hypothesis evaluation in combination with reallocation of resources (agents) via stochastic recruitment mechanisms. Partial hypothesis evaluation allows an agent to quickly form its opinion on the quality of the investigated solution without exhaustive testing (e.g. it can find the best restaurant in town without having to try all the meals available in each).

Algorithm 1. Vanilla SDS

```
 1: procedure step(swarm, search_space)
 2:     for each agent in swarm do                                    ▷ Diffuse Phase
 3:         if not agent.active then
 4:             polled_agent = swarm.random_agent()
 5:             if polled_agent.active then
 6:                 agent.hypothesis = polled_agent.hypothesis
 7:             else
 8:                 agent.hypothesis = search_space.random_hypothesis()
 9:     for each agent in swarm do                                    ▷ Test Phase
10:         test_result = perform_random_test(hypothesis)
11:         agent.active = test_result
```

6   An Approximate Characterisation of the Stochastic Diffusion Search

Stochastic Diffusion Search has often been used for pattern matching; such problems can be more generally redefined in terms of an optimisation, by defining the objective function, $F(\mathbf{x})$, for a hypothesis, $\mathbf{x}$, as the similarity between the target pattern and the corresponding region at $\mathbf{x}$ in the search space and finding $\mathbf{x}$, such that $F(\mathbf{x})$ is maximised. In general SDS is most easily applied to optimisation problems where the objective function is decomposable into components that can be evaluated independently:

$$F\left(\mathbf{x}\right) = \sum_{i=1}^{n} F_i\left(\mathbf{x}\right), \qquad (1)$$

where $F_i(\mathbf{x})$ is defined as the ith partial evaluation of $F(\mathbf{x})$.

In a standard SDS a 'Test Function' returns boolean value indicating whether a randomly selected partial evaluation of the objective function is suggestive of a 'good' hypothesis. In pattern matching the Test Function may return True if the ith sub-feature of the target pattern is present at position $(\mathbf{x}, i)$ in the search space. Thus the *Test Score* for a given hypothesis is the probability that the Test Function will return true, and is hence indicative of the underlying value of the objective function.

6.1   Homogeneous Background Noise

In [50] Nasuto first derived a comprehensive analysis of SDS in which he presented several alternative noise cases and examined the resource allocation of SDS in each using an Ehrenfest Urn model. One of these cases was that of homogeneous noise, where there are a number of distractors with the same Test Score (the probability of an agent becoming active for a given hypothesis). However, practical issues in the selected experimentation domain of text search prevented the exploration of high values of both p_d, (the probability of selecting a distractor from the search space) and p^+ (the overlap of the distractor with the target).

Nonetheless, in many real-world situations there will be high values of p_d, in that any non-optimal hypothesis can be regarded as a significant distractor. In the brief and simplified analysis presented herein[3], we consider the case of 'homogeneous background noise', where $p_d \approx 1$ and the Test Score of each distractor is identical. Moreover, even if the distractors show significant deviation from homogeneity, some search space could be constructed that would produce the same mean response from SDS; hence in many real-world situations the homogeneous background noise model is both practical and useful.

In a typical convergence of SDS in the presence of homogeneous background noise it can be seen that before an optimal solution is found the proportion of active agents remains approximately constant [51]. Let this level of homogeneous background noise be called β, and be equal to the proportion of active agents given that the optimal solution has not yet been selected. Additionally, β is also equivalent to the Test Score of the homogeneous distractors, since if all agents are currently associated with distractors of Test Score β then the proportion of the agents active will also be β. Therefore, the noise parameter β replaces the two parameters p_d and p^+ used in previous analyses by Nasuto. It is noted that in practise the background noise of a search can be estimated simply by iterating SDS for a short time and taking the mean of the number of active agents per iteration.

6.2 Expected Cluster Size Formulation of SDS

In this section the minimum Test Score, $\alpha_{\min}$, for which a stable cluster of agents can form will be derived. A simplifying assumption is that, by considering only the mean transition of agents between different clusters, rather than the full probability distribution (as investigated in [50]), a *sufficiently accurate* characterisation of SDS can be produced. The noise model that will be assumed is that of 'homogeneous background noise', where every non-optimal hypothesis corresponds to a distractor of Test Score β. It is also assumed that there is a single optimal solution with Test Score α that has a negligible probability of being selected. Let $\bar{c}_i$ be the mean number of active agents with the optimal solution as a proportion of the total population.

Consider a function, f, that defines the mean transition between the size of a cluster of active agents with the optimal hypothesis, in consecutive iterations, as a proportion of the total number of agents. It can be seen that f is therefore a function of the current cluster size $\bar{c}_i$, the Test Score of the optimal solution α and the level of homogeneous background noise β.

$$\bar{c}_{i+1} = f\left(\bar{c}_i, \alpha, \beta\right). \tag{2}$$

---

[3] The material in Sect. 6 was included at the suggestion of one of the reviewers of this manuscript; it forms a much extended and adapted version of the 'practical' analysis of SDS behaviour first presented by Myatt et al. in [48].

By calculating f for a given variant of SDS it is possible to extract both the mean optimal cluster size once a stable convergence has occurred and also the minimum value of α for which a stable convergence can occur as a function of β, $\alpha_{\min}$. The stationary state γ occurs when the mean cluster size (the number of *active* agents with the same hypothesis) remains constant between successive iterations i.e.

$$\gamma = f\left(\gamma, \alpha, \beta\right). \tag{3}$$

It is apparent that (3) will have two solutions, one of which will be zero (when $\bar{c}_i = 0$). A cluster will, on average, increase in size if the constraint

$$\bar{c}_{i+1} > f\left(\bar{c}_i, \alpha, \beta\right) \tag{4}$$

holds. $\alpha_{\min}$ may therefore be found using the constraint

$$f\left(\frac{1}{k}, \alpha_{\min}, \beta\right) > \frac{1}{k}, \tag{5}$$

which assumes the worst case that only one agent has the correct hypothesis.

For a given value of $\alpha_{\min}$ SDS will then stably converge if the constraint

$$\alpha_{\min} < \alpha \leq 1 \tag{6}$$

is satisfied. For a non-negligible p_m, the value of $\alpha_{\min}$ derived will be artificially large but will still provide a useful guide.

6.3   Convergence Level of SDS

In the following analysis it is assumed that p_m is negligible and hence over a small number of iterations the optimal solution will not be found.

During the diffusion phase, the mean number of inactive agents selecting an agent within the optimal cluster is given by $g(\bar{c}_i, \alpha, \beta)\bar{c}_i$, where g yields the number of inactive agents for a given iteration. From Fig. 2 g can be immediately written as

$$g(\bar{c}_i, \alpha, \beta) = \frac{1-\alpha}{\alpha}\bar{c}_i + (1 - \beta)\left(1 - \frac{\bar{c}_i}{\alpha}\right). \tag{7}$$

Therefore, the function f that defines the mean 1-step optimal cluster size evolution is

$$\bar{c}_{i+1} = f(\bar{c}_i, \alpha, \beta) = \alpha\left(\bar{c}_i + g(\bar{c}_i, \alpha, \beta)\bar{c}_i\right). \tag{8}$$

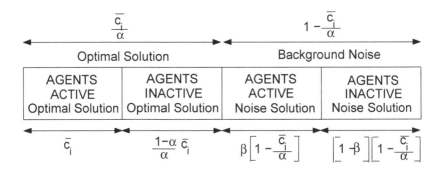

Fig. 2. Illustration of the current state of the agent population in iteration i in terms of $\bar{c}_i$, α and β

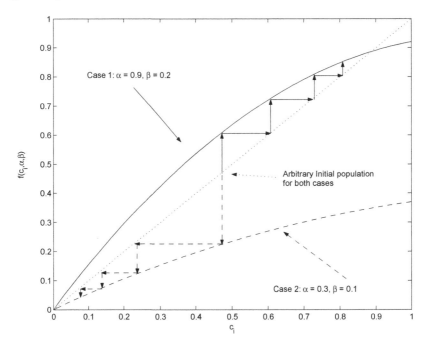

Fig. 3. A 1 dimensional iterated map showing how different values of α and β can either result in a stable optimal cluster or a return to zero.

and consequently

$$f(\bar{c}_i, \alpha, \beta) = \alpha \left[\bar{c}_i + \left(\frac{1-\alpha}{\alpha} \bar{c}_i + (1-\beta) \left(1 - \frac{\bar{c}_i}{\alpha} \right) \right) \bar{c}_i \right]. \tag{9}$$

Substituting this into (3) yields

$$\gamma = \frac{\alpha(2-\beta)-1}{\alpha-\beta}. \tag{10}$$

Similarly, substituting (9) into (5) gives

$$\alpha_{min} = \frac{1}{2 - \beta},\tag{11}$$

assuming that k is large. Figure 3 considers (9) as a 1 dimensional iterated map, and graphically it can be seen that for a non-zero attractor to exist the condition

$$\frac{df}{d\bar{c}_i} > 1 \tag{12}$$

must hold for $\bar{c}_i = 0$. Differentiating (9) wrt $\bar{c}_i$ yields

$$\frac{df}{d\bar{c}_i} = \alpha\,(2 - \beta) - 2\bar{c}_i\,(\alpha - \beta) \tag{13}$$

and it follows that the minimum value of α for which the constraint in (12) holds is

$$\alpha_{min} = \frac{1}{2 - \beta}.\tag{14}$$

Hence, for any $\alpha < \alpha_{min}$ the size of the cluster will tend to zero for *any* initial cluster size and the search will fail. NB. This maximum level of background noise is equal to the convergence level of SDS with $\beta = 0$.

6.4   Multiple Testing

In situations where the Test Score of the global optima cannot cause a stable convergence as defined by (5), the corresponding Test Function may be manipulated such that the Test Score of all hypotheses is boosted, thus allowing stable convergence. One simple of achieving this is the utilisation of *multiple testing*. If an agent performs t samples of the Test Function at a given hypothesis (rather than just one) and becomes active *iff* one or more of these tests are passed, then the Test Score α for all hypotheses will be increased, such that

$$\alpha' = 1 - (1 - \alpha)^t \tag{15}$$

Let $e = 1 - \alpha$, then

$$\frac{d\alpha'}{de} = -te^{t-1} \tag{16}$$

and

$$\frac{de}{d\alpha} = -1. \tag{17}$$

Therefore

$$\frac{d\alpha'}{d\alpha} = \frac{d\alpha'}{de} \cdot \frac{de}{d\alpha} \tag{18}$$

and thus

$$\frac{d\alpha'}{d\alpha} = t\,(1 - \alpha)^{t-1}. \tag{19}$$

Hence for $\alpha \in \mathbb{R}, 0 < \alpha < 1$ and $t \in \mathbb{I}, t > 0$,

$$\frac{d\alpha'}{d\alpha} > 0. \tag{20}$$

Therefore, because the increase of α' is monotonic with respect to α, the topology of the Objective Function landscape will be preserved (except as $t \to \infty$), and thus the optima of α' will still correspond to the optima of α. Multiple testing is therefore a generalisation of the standard testing technique in *Vanilla* SDS. Figure 4 shows the transformation applied by tuple testing for varying t (where t is the number of tests evaluated for each agent-hypothesis).

Considered in the domain of nest selection in social insects, multiple testing is analogous to a scout spending time at a potential nest site and evaluating it repeatedly using t *different* metrics, with the nest judged suitable if anyone of the metrics is positive[4].

Consequently, for sufficiently large t, SDS can be made to converge success-fully for any arbitrary optimal match. However, this may pose problems if such a value of t results in the *background noise*, β, of the search being greater than 50%, because it will be difficult to establish when convergence to the optimal solution has actually taken place (as the search will always be in some state of convergence). In such cases, it may be necessary to evaluate the search a num-ber of times (to a given termination criterion, say, a terminal number of search iterations, this number being selected to ensure a high probability of the search having located the optimal match). In summary we observe that the principle of *multiple testing* is robust and not domain specific (i.e. it may be applied to any problem in which the Test Score of the standard Test Function is not suffi-cient to ensure stable convergence); an example multiple testing SDS application (locating eyes in images of human faces) was outlined in [9].

7   Halting Criteria

The termination of SDS has historically been defined in terms of the *stability* of the population size of a group of active agents. Such methods are termed *global* halting criteria as they are a function of the total number of active agents within the global population of agents.

7.1   Global Halting Criteria

Two well documented global methods for determining when SDS should halt are the *Weak Halting Criterion* and *Strong Halting criterion* [50,51]; the former is a function of the *total* number of active agents and the latter the *total number of active agents sharing the same hypothesis*; the 'Weak' halting criterion is simpler to compute and from Fig. 5 can be broadly seen to demonstrate the same halting behaviour as the 'Strong'.

---

[4] Thus *multiple testing* is very similar to the *repeated metrics* strategy deployed by real scouts in nest selection, albeit in the latter case scouts assess potential nest sites across a number of metrics using a *weighted additive strategy* [27].

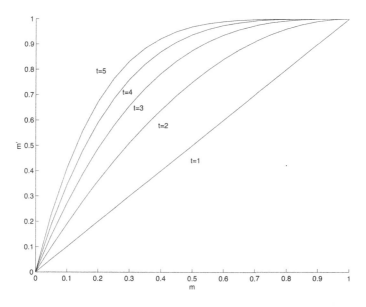

Fig. 4. The relationship between α and α' for varying tuple tests t

7.2 Local Halting Criterion

In order to approximate the behaviour of *Temnothorax* ants in their nest selection behaviour, the halting behaviour of SDS was redesigned such that it would emerge from purely *local* interactions of agents.

By analogy with the behaviour of tandem running *Temnothorax* ants (as outlined in Sects. 3 and 4 herein), in the following we propose two new variants of the process for determining when an agent should switch from the classical SDS *explore-exploit* behaviour to a new, so called, *'terminating'* behaviour which we term the *independent* and *confirmation* halting criteria.

In these variants agents can take on an additional behaviour in which they enter a new state we define 'Terminating', wherein their hypothesis becomes fixed and they subsequently seek to actively remove agents from the dynamic swarm[5] and give them their own (now fixed) termination hypothesis (analogous to the 'post-quorum' behavioural state in ants of the genus *Temnothorax*, wherein post-quorum ants literally carry other ants they encounter to the new nest site).

As this decision making process successively removes agents from the swarm we name the removal behaviour *Terminating*, and the whole process *Reducing SDS*. In this way a collective 'decision' is made (and the local halting condition met) when all agents are either active and/or have been removed from the swarm.

---

[5] Standard SDS has previously been shown to be a global search algorithm [51] - it will eventually converge to the global best solution in a given search space; by removing agents form the swarm, relative to standard SDS the number of potential agents remaining available for explore-exploit behaviour is reduced.

7.3   'Independent' Termination Behaviour

In *independent reducing SDS* we relax the assumption that all SDS agents update synchronously in iterative 'cycles' (wherein one such cycle corresponds to all agents being updated).

Algorithm 2. independent SDS

1: **procedure step**(*swarm, search_space*)
2:     *swarm = shuffle(swarm)*
3:     **for** each *agent* in *swarm* **do**
4:         *polled_agent = swarm.random_agent()*   ▷ *Diffusion behaviour*
5:         **if** Both agents are inactive **then**
6:             Both agents randomise hypothesis
7:         **else if** One agent is inactive and other is active but not terminating **then**
8:             Inactive agent assumes active agent's hypothesis
9:         **else if** One agent is terminating **then**
10:             Other agent is removed from the swarm
11:         **else if** Agents share a hypothesis **then**
12:             Both agents become terminating
13:         **if** not *agent.terminating* **then**   ▷ *Testing behaviour*
14:             *test_result = perform_random_test(hypothesis)*
15:             *agent.active = test_result*

In independent SDS agents update independently[6]; furthermore the diffusion process endeavours to mirror the behaviour of real ants when two ants 'meet':

- if neither agent is active both reselect new random hypotheses;
- one agent is inactive and other is active but not terminating then the inactive agent assumes active agent's hypothesis.
- one of the agents is in terminating mode then the other is 'removed' from the swarm and give (placed at) this hypothesis.
- if the two agents meet that both have the same hypothesis then both switch to *terminating* mode.

The above process is more fully outlined in Algorithm 2.

7.4   'Confirmation' Termination Behaviour

Since its inception in 1989 [7] a substantial body of algorithmic analysis (describing the theoretical behaviour of SDS), empirical studies and practical applications have been published (for a recent review see [2]). To more readily facilitate the future use of these results in both local termination variants and potentially

---

[6] To facilitate the use of homogenous performance metrics, we assume that in a population of k agents, k single asynchronous updates corresponds to one standard synchronous iteration cycle.

to extend this work to the analysis of real ants, we also present a further simplification of independent SDS to a second reducing behaviour that more closely aligns with that of standard SDS diffusion; we define this termination mode *confirmation reducing SDS*.

Algorithm 3. Confirmation SDS

 1: **procedure step**(*swarm*, *search_space*)
 2:     **for** each *agent* in *swarm* **do**   ▷ *Diffuse Phase*
 3:         *polled_agent = swarm.random_agent*()
 4:         **if** *agent.active* **then**
 5:             *hyp_1 = agent.hypothesis*
 6:             *hyp_2 = polled_agent.hypothesis*
 7:             **if** *polled_agent.active* and *hyp_1 == hyp_2* **then**
 8:                 *agent.terminating* == True
 9:         **else**
10:             **if** *polled_agent.active* **then**
11:                 **if** *polled_agent.terminating* **then**
12:                     *swarm.remove*(*agent*)
13:                 **else**
14:                     *agent.hypothesis = polled_agent.hypothesis*
15:             **else**
16:                 *agent.hypothesis = search_space.random_hypothesis*()
17:     **for** each *agent* in *swarm* **do**   ▷ *Test Phase*
18:         *test_result = perform_random_test*(*hypothesis*)
19:         *agent.active = test_result*

In confirmation reduction SDS agents are assumed to update synchronously and the diffusion of information is changed to more closely resemble that of classical dual mode (passive and active) recruitment SDS [49]. In *confirmation* SDS an active agent polls random agents in the diffusion phase. Active agents become *terminating* if their polled agent is also active and both agents share a hypothesis. The agent is then locked into being active, maintaining that hypothesis. If an inactive agent polls a terminating agent, the inactive agent is removed from the population (see Algorithm 3 for details).

Thus *independent* SDS has two major distinctions from confirmation SDS, firstly no distinction is made between the polling agent and the polled agent, the effect of their diffusion is resolved simultaneously; secondly, rather than alternating diffusion and test phases, agents are randomly selected to **individually** perform a *hypothesis diffusion* behaviour immediately followed by a *hypothesis test* behaviour. These two features are intended to more closely model the actual termination behaviour of real ants.

8   Experiments

A series of experiments was performed to investigate the diffusion behaviour of the two new halting criteria over a variety of search parameters to establish

(a) if the algorithms' gross behaviour remains characteristic of SDS and (b) to evaluate their robustness over a variety of search parameters (which effectively characterise the quality of the putative best solution, α ($0 \leq \alpha < 1$), relative to β, ($0 \leq \beta < 1$), the quality of the distractor solution[7]); in the 'ant migration' problem, α is analogous to a measure of the quality of the potential new nest site and β effectively a measure of the quality of the original nest.

In all experiments the population is initialised with one agent maintaining the hypothesis representing the potential best solution and the probability of an agent randomly selecting the hypothesis of the potential best solution is set to zero; this ensures that only the *diffusion* behaviour of the algorithm is explored[8].

In the first experiment each of the four termination functions (weak, strong, independent and confirmation) was modelled in a population of 10000 agents, one of which was active and at the solution hypothesis at time zero, with all other agents set inactive pointing to the 'noise' hypothesis. The algorithm was then evaluated 25 times from these conditions against a range of possible values of α and β (from 0 to 0.875 with a step of 0.125). The number of times the algorithm successfully halted within 250 iterations was recorded as was the mean average number of iterations before halting in these cases.

In the case of weak and strong halting SDS, halting was considered successful if the halting criterion was reached. All four algorithms would also halt if all agents were active at the solution hypothesis, as this is analogous to a successful migration of agents to an optimal state. Two further halting conditions were included, when the algorithm had run for more than a specified number of iterations and when all agents held the noise hypothesis. Any experiment that halted for these reasons was considered unsuccessful.

In a second experiment the four algorithms were run against fixed values of α and β which the first experiment had shown would be likely to successfully halt. The state of all agents was recorded at every iteration and number of agents (as a proportion of the total population) in various states was graphed over time to visualise the characteristic behaviour of the halting criteria (see Fig. 6).

8.1 Experiment 1

The graphs in Figs. 5 and 6 plot the cluster size of a population of 10,000 SDS agents over time using the four different halting criteria - weak, strong, independent and confirmation - with search parameters (solution hypothesis ($\alpha = 0.750$, noise hypothesis ($\beta = 0.375$); it is noted that the shapes of cluster sizes using all four termination criteria broadly follow the characteristic SDS S-shaped convergence curve.

---

[7] β defines a "uniform random noise" hypothesis; an aggregate of all the possible hypotheses an agent could have other than the putative solution hypothesis.

[8] These parameters define a problem analogous to the search space being infinitely large, wherein the only way an agent can adopt the 'best' solution is to receive it via diffusion from an active agent.

8.2   Experiment 2

Table 2 lists i the average number of iterations before halting and c the number of times that the algorithm successfully halted for a SDS experiment for all four algorithms using a population of 10,000 agents across a variety of parameter values of the noise hypothesis (β) and solution hypothesis (α).

NB. Pairs of values for α and β for which *all four* algorithms failed to converge 25 times out of 25 are not listed.

Examining the results presented in Table 2, the following comparative observations can be made:

weak versus strong halting the convergence time for weak and strong halting are almost identical whilst their robustness is similar (strong halting is more robust in 8 cases and less robust in 8);

strong halting versus independent reduction on average the convergence time is 3.3 times faster for independent whilst its robustness is similar (strong halting is more robust in 11 cases, less robust in 6);

strong halting versus confirmation reduction on average the convergence time is around 2.8 times faster for confirmation whilst its robustness is similar (strong halting is more robust in 8 cases, less robust in 6);

9   Comparison of Ant Quorum-Sensing and SDS Local Halting Criteria

The termination criterion of an SDS algorithm can be considered analogous to the ant quorum threshold, i.e. the point at which ants cease to search, and instead implement their chosen decision (Fig. 1). Once an ant has sensed that quorum is met, it does not re-visit that decision and is essentially committed to that hypothesis. This process can be compared to theoretical SDS local halting criteria that are able to terminate a decision-process rapidly. Specifically, the *independent SDS* termination criterion can be considered analogous to a process whereby an ant's decision to enter a post-quorum state is influenced by a one-to-one reinforcement of its own view. That is, Scout A will enter a post-quorum state (=terminating) for Nest A if Scout A has accepted nest A and returned to the home nest to recruit, but is instead itself then recruited by scout B back to nest A. This recruitment event would serve to reinforce Scout A's initial judgement. *Temnothorax* ants are indeed sometimes recruited back to nests they have already visited (Fig. 1), so there is potential for this 'reinforcement recruitment' process to play a role for ant colonies. For example, 'reinforcement recruitment' could cause ants to enter a post-quorum state at a lowered encounter rate. This would help extra rapid acceptance of a nest if there were only one new nest site available. This idea could be tested empirically, ideally in a complex arena that would promote tandem-running behaviour, allowing communication of preference.

Table 2. Mean average iterations before termination for three different halting criteria (*strong, independent and confirmation*) over varying quality of solutions

		Strong		Independent		Confirmation	
β	α	i	c	i	c	i	c
0.000	0.625	151.2	17	42.0	6	46.2	14
0.000	0.750	126.8	20	25.8	16	27.8	18
0.000	0.875	118.2	21	20.0	22	21.1	21
0.125	0.625	195.0	7	52.2	12	58.4	7
0.125	0.750	130.4	11	29.6	15	34.1	16
0.125	0.875	122.0	23	22.9	21	25.8	20
0.250	0.625	216.0	1	77.1	7	88.6	5
0.250	0.750	138.7	17	35.5	16	42.2	15
0.250	0.875	125.5	22	26.0	21	31.4	22
0.375	0.625	100.0	1	232.0	1	244.0	1
0.375	0.750	165.6	14	48.5	12	56.7	16
0.375	0.875	131.5	21	30.0	19	38.5	20
0.500	0.750	212.0	5	74.2	12	87.9	7
0.500	0.875	140.5	18	38.5	13	51.5	16
0.625	0.750	100.0	4	150.0	3	238.0	1
0.625	0.875	161.9	18	50.6	14	73.5	20
0.750	0.875	211.0	7	92.4	14	142.5	13
0.875	0.875	100.0	1	–	0	–	0

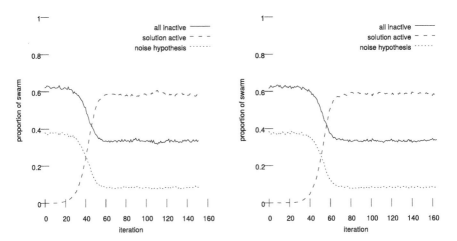

Fig. 5. Cluster size evolution over time for SDS using the *weak halting criterion* (left) and the *strong halting criterion* (right). The x-axis counts iterations, the y-axis shows cluster size as a proportion of the entire population. The behaviours are practically identical, the slightly later convergence of the strong halting SDS is a result of the inherent randomness. The positive feedback effect can be seen in the sharp S-curve of the solution cluster size.

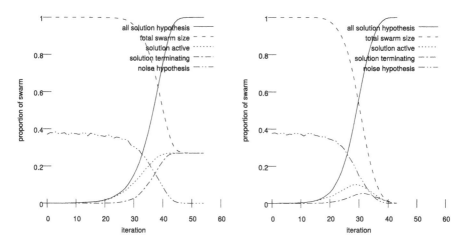

Fig. 6. Cluster size evolution over time for SDS using *confirmation SDS* (left) and *independent SDS* (right). The x-axis counts iterations, the y-axis shows cluster size as a proportion of the entire population. Both show an accelerating growth in the number of agents at the solution hypothesis followed by a similar growth of terminating agents at the solution hypothesis until the entire swarm is either active (in the case of confirmation SDS) or removed from the swarm (in the case of independent SDS).

The main limitation on the use of the *independent SDS* termination criterion by the ants is that the criterion relies on ants being able to communicate their current preference, which they are able to do only by the slow and fairly infrequent process of tandem-running. Empirical observations have shown that scouting ants can judge quorum to have been reached (through encounter rate) without having followed a tandem run, so clearly they are not relying solely on *independent*-like rules. An analogous - Swarm Intelligence - process has however been observed in house-hunting honeybees.

Honeybees, in contrast to ants, are able to directly 'poll' another scouting bee for its preference, without having to actually visit that bee's preferred site. This is because honeybees communicate the location of their preferred site using a waggle-dance performed back at the main swarm and honeybees are able to determine whether a waggle-dance indicates their chosen site or not, without flying to the location indicated by the dance ([69]). This gives the bees more power to use *independent*-like rules in their decision-making - and honeybees do indeed use the unanimity of the waggle-dances in their assessment of when to terminate the search and relocate to a new site ([68]). While in this way, honeybee decision-behaviour is closer to *confirmation SDS* than *Temnothorax* house-hunting is, on the other hand we note that bees use a one-to-many broadcasting communication when they waggle-dance, rather than pair-wise communication as used by tandem running ants and SDS agents.

10   Conclusion

This paper has looked at cooperative decision making in house-hunting ants and in the Stochastic Diffusion Search algorithm. Decision making in standard SDS is typically based on the use of one of two well established 'halting' functions - the Strong and Weak Halting criteria - both of which entail *global* access to the activity of the SDS population as a whole. Conversely in this paper, inspired by the quorum sensing mechanism deployed by some species of ants in nest moving, we have successfully demonstrated two new *local* termination criteria for SDS which have broadly been demonstrated to have similar behaviour to the standard SDS meta-heuristic using strong and weak halting criteria (in terms of their robustness to noise). Furthermore, it is observed that the use of a local halting mechanism substantially speeds up the collective decision making time; both independent and confirmation terminate are around three times faster than via the use of the strong halting criterion.

Although the independent and confirmation termination processes described in this paper found inspiration from the nest hunting behaviour of *Temnothorax* ants, we do not claim that the nest selection behaviour of these ants is isomorphic to SDS:- one critical difference between the two systems is that SDS relies on its agents being easily able to communicate their current hypothesis to each other, whereas *Temnothorax* ants are only able to do this by the slow [and relatively infrequent] process of tandem-running. Empirical observations have shown that scouting ants can judge quorum to have been reached (through encounter rate) without having followed a tandem run, so clearly *Temnothorax* ants do not solely rely on *independent*-SDS like termination rules. In this context, future research will investigate the degree to which appropriately modified SDS characterisations can be used to describe the behaviour of *Temnothorax* ants.

In conclusion we suggest that the successful deployment of local halting criteria (a) significantly simplifies the implementation of SDS on parallel computational hardware and (b) potentially open up analogical study of ant and honeybee decision-making behaviour through the transformational lens of SDS theory, where there is a significant extant body of proven mathematical results; for example outlining: speed of convergence, robustness, time complexity, stability of solutions etc. [2]; further mathematical study aims to better understand the empirical performance of the local termination criteria described herein, using extant mathematical models of SDS behaviour (ibid).

References

1. Aleksander, I., Stonham, T.J.: Guide to pattern recognition using random access memories. Comput. Digit. Tech. **2**(1), 29–40 (1979)
2. Al-Rifaie, M.M., Bishop, J.M.: Stochastic diffusion search review. J. Behav. Robot. **4**(3), 155–173 (2013)
3. Anoop, K., Sumana, A.: Response to a change in the target nest during ant relocation. J. Exp. Biol. **218**(6), 887–92 (2015)

4. Arthur, W.B.: Inductive reasoning and bounded rationality (The El Farol Problem). Amer. Econ. Rev. **84**, 406–411 (1994)
5. Back, T.: Evolutionary Algorithms in Theory and Practice. Oxford University Press, Oxford (1996)
6. Beattie, P.D., Bishop, J.M.: Self-localisation in the 'SENARIO' autonomous wheelchair. J. Intell. Robot. Syst. **22**, 255–267 (1998)
7. Bishop, J.M.: Stochastic Searching Networks. In: Proceedings of 1st IEE International Conference on Artificial Neural Networks. IEE Conference Publication (313), pp. 329–331. IEE, London (1989)
8. Bishop, J.M.: Anarchic techniques for pattern classification. Ph.D. thesis, Reading University, UK (1989)
9. Bishop, J.M., Torr, P.H.S.: The stochastic search network. In: Linggard, R., Myers, D.J., Nightingale, C. (eds.) Neural Networks for Images, Speech and Natural Language. Chapman Hall, New York (1992)
10. Bishop, J.M., Nasuto, S.J., De Meyer, K.: Dynamic knowledge representation in connectionist systems. In: Dorronsoro, J.R. (ed.) Artificial Neural Networks ICANN. LNCS, vol. 2415, pp. 308–313. Springer, Heidelberg (2002). https://doi.org/10.1007/3-540-46084-5_51
11. Bishop, J.M., Andrew, O.M., Robinson, E.J.H.: Local termination criteria for stochastic diffusion search: a comparison with the behaviour of ant nest-site selection. In: Nguyen, N., Iliadis, L., Yannis, M., Bogdan, T. (eds.) Computational Collective Intelligence. Lecture Notes in Computer Science, vol. 9875, pp. 474–486. Springer, Heidelberg (2016). https://doi.org/10.1007/978-3-319-45243-2_44
12. Bonabeau, E., Dorigo, M., Theraulaz, G.: Swarm Intelligence: From Natural to Artificial Systems. Oxford University Press, Oxford (1999)
13. Bonabeau, E., Dorigo, M., Theraulaz, G.: Inspiration for optimisation from social insect behaviour. Nature **406**, 3942 (2000)
14. Cao, T.T.: High social density increases foraging and scouting rates and induces polydomy in Temnothorax ants. Behav. Ecol. Sociobiol. **67**(11), 1799–1807 (2013)
15. Carroll, C.R., Janzen, D.H.: Ecology of foraging by ants. Annu. Rev. Ecol. Syst. **4**, 231–257 (1973)
16. Chadab, R., Rettenmeyer, C.: Mass recruitment by army ants. Science **188**, 1124–1125 (1975)
17. Deneubourg, J.L., Pasteels, J.M., Verhaeghe, J.C.: Probabilistic behaviour in ants: a strategy of errors? J. Theor. Biol. **105**(2), 259–271 (1983)
18. Dornhaus, A., Franks, N.R., Hawkins, R.M., Shere, H.N.S.: Ants move to improve: colonies of Leptothorax albipennis emigrate whenever they find a superior nest site. Anim. Behav. **67**(5), 959–963 (2004)
19. Dornhaus, A., Holley, J.A., Pook, V.G., Worswick, G., Franks, N.R.: Why do not all workers work? Colony size and workload during emigrations in the ant Temnothorax albipennis. Behav. Ecol. Sociobiol. **63**(1), 43–51 (2008)
20. Dorigo, M., Maniezzo, V., Colorni, A.: Positive feedback as a search strategy, Dipartimento di Elettronica e Informatica, Politecnico di (1991)
21. Dorigo, M.: Optimisation, learning and natural algorithms. Politecnico di Italy, Milano (1992)
22. Dorigo, M., Caro, G.D., Gambardella, L.M.: Ant algorithms for discrete optimisation. Artif. Life **5**(2), 137–172 (1999)
23. Franklin, E.L.: The journey of tandem running: the twists, turns and what we have learned. Insectes Sociaux **61**, 1–8 (2014)

24. Franks, N.R., Dornhaus, A., Metherell, B., Nelson, T., Lanfear, S.A., Symes, W.: Not everything that counts can be counted: ants use multiple metrics for a single nest trait. Proc. R. Soc. Lond. Ser. B **273**, 165–169 (2006)
25. Franks, N.R., Hooper, J.W., Dornhaus, A., Aukett, P.J., Hayward, A.L., Berghoff, S.M.: Reconnaissance and latent learning in ants. Proc. R. Soc. Lond. Ser. B **274**(1617), 1505–1509 (2007)
26. Franks, N.R., et al.: Moving targets: collective decisions and flexible choices in house-hunting ants. Swarm Intell. **1**(2), 81–94 (2007)
27. Franks, N.R., Mallon, E.B., Bray, H.E., Hamilton, M.J., Mischler, T.C.: Strategies for choosing between alternatives with different attributes: exemplified by house-hunting ants. Anim. Behav. **65**, 215–223 (2003)
28. Frank, N.R., et al.: How ants use quorum sensing to estimate the average quality of a fluctuating resource. Sci. Rep. **5**, 11890 (2015)
29. Goldberg, D.: Genetic Algorithms in Search, Optimisation and Machine Learning. Addison Wesley, Reading (1989)
30. Goodman, L.J., Fisher, R.C.: The Behaviour and Physiology of Bees. CAB International, Oxon (1991)
31. Grech-Cini, E.: Locating facial features. Ph.D. dissertation, University of Reading, Reading UK (1995)
32. Holldobler, B., Wilson, E.O.: The Ants. Springer, Heidelberg (1990)
33. Holland, J.H.: Adaptation in Natural and Artificial Systems. The University of Michigan Press, Ann Arbor (1975)
34. Fan, H., Hua, Z., Li, J.J., Yuan, D.: Solving a shortest path problem by ant algorithm. In: Proceedings of 2004 International Conference on Machine Learning and Cybernetics, vol. 5, pp. 3174–3177 (2004)
35. Krieger, M.J., Billeter, J.B., Keller, L.: Ant-like task allocation and recruitment in cooperative robots. Nature **406**(6799), 992–995 (2000)
36. Iosifescu, M.: Finite Markov Processes and Their Applications. Wiley, Chichester (1980)
37. Kennedy, J., Eberhart, R.C., Shi, Y.: Swarm Intelligence. Morgan Kauffman, San Francisco (2001)
38. Kennedy, J., Eberhart, R.C.: Particle swarm optimisation. In: Proceedings of the IEEE International Conference on Neural Networks IV, pp. 1942–1948 (1995)
39. Kramer, B.H., Scharf, I., Foitzik, S.: The role of per-capita productivity in the evolution of small colony sizes in ants. Behav. Ecol. Sociobiol. **68**(1), 41–53 (2013)
40. De Meyer, K.: Explorations in stochastic diffusion search: soft and hardware implementations of biologically inspired spiking neuron stochastic diffusion networks. Technical report KDM/JMB/2000-1. University of Reading, Reading UK (2000)
41. De Meyer, K., Bishop, J.M., Nasuto, S.J.: Small world network behaviour of stochastic diffusion search. In: Dorronsoro, J.R. (ed.) Artificial Neural Networks, ICANN, Madrid. LNCS, vol. 2415, pp. 147–152. Springer, Heidelberg (2002). https://doi.org/10.1007/3-540-46084-5_25
42. De Meyer, K., Nasuto, S.J., Bishop, J.M.: Stochastic diffusion optimisation: the application of partial function evaluation and stochastic recruitment. In: Abraham, A., Grosam, C., Ramos, V. (eds.) Stigmergic Optimisation. SCI, vol. 31, pp. 185–207. Springer, Heidelberg (2006). https://doi.org/10.1007/978-3-540-34690-6_8
43. Kurvers, R.H.J.M., Wolf, M., Krause, J.: Humans use social information to adjust their quorum thresholds adaptively in a simulated predator detection experiment. Behav. Ecol. Sociobiol. **68**(3), 449–456 (2014)
44. Miller, M.B., Bassler, B.L.: Quorum sensing in bacteria. Annu. Rev. Microbiol. **55**(1), 165–199 (2001)

45. Mitrus, S.: The cavity-nest ant Temnothorax crassispinus prefers larger nests. Insectes Sociaux **62**(1), 43–49 (2015)
46. Moglich, M., Maschwitz, U., Holldobler, B.: Tandem calling: a new kind of signal in ant communication. Science **186**(4168), 1046–1047 (1974)
47. Mugford, S.T., Mallon, E.B., Franks, N.R.: The accuracy of Buffon's needle: a rule of thumb used by ants to estimate area. Behav. Ecol. **12**, 655–658 (2001)
48. Myatt, D.M., Bishop, J.M., Nasuto, S.J.: Minimum stable convergence criteria for stochastic diffusion search. Electron. Lett. **22**(40), 112–113 (2004)
49. Myatt, D., M., Nasuto, S.J., Bishop J.M., : Alternative recruitment strategies for SDS. In: Proceedings of AISB06: Symposium on Exploration vs. Exploitation in Naturally Inspired Search, Bristol, UK, pp. 181–187 (2006)
50. Nasuto, S.J.: Analysis of resource allocation of stochastic diffusion search. Ph.D. dissertation. University of Reading, Reading UK (1999)
51. Nasuto, S.J., Bishop, J.M.: Convergence of the stochastic diffusion search. Parallel Algorithms Appl. **14**, 89–107 (1999)
52. Nasuto, S.J., Bishop, J.M., Lauria, S.: Time complexity of stochastic diffusion search. In: Heiss, M. (ed) Proceedings of International ICSC/IFAC Symposium on Neural Computation, Vienna (1998)
53. Nasuto, S.J., Dautenhahn, K., Bishop, J.M.: Communication as an emergent metaphor for neuronal operation. In: Nehaniv, C. (ed.) Computation for Metaphors, Analogy, and Agents. LNCS, vol. 1562, pp. 365–379. Springer, Heidelberg (1999). https://doi.org/10.1007/3-540-48834-0_19
54. Nasuto, S.J., Bishop, J.M., De Meyer, K.: Communicating neurons: a connectionist spiking neuron implementation of stochastic diffusion search. Neurocomputing **72**(4–6), 704–712 (2008)
55. Nasuto, S.J., Bishop, J.M.: Steady state resource allocation analysis of the stochastic diffusion search. Biol. Inspired Cogn. Arch. **12**, 65–76 (2015)
56. Neumaier, A.: Complete search in continuous global optimisation and constraint satisfaction. In: Isereles, A. (ed.) Acta Numerica 2004. Cambridge University Press, Cambridge UK (2004)
57. Pratt, S.C.: Behavioural mechanisms of collective nest-site choice by the ant Temnothorax curvispinosus. Insectes Sociaux **52**, 383–392 (2005)
58. Pratt, S.C.: Quorum sensing by encounter rates in the ant Temnothorax albipennis. Behav. Ecol. **16**, 488–496 (2005)
59. Pratt, S.C., Mallon, E.B., Sumpter, D.J.T., Franks, N.R.: Quorum sensing, recruitment, and collective decision-making during colony emigration by the ant Leptothorax albipennis. Behav. Ecol. Sociobiol. **52**(2), 117–127 (2002)
60. Pratt, S.C., Pierce, N.E.: The cavity-dwelling ant Leptothorax curvispinosus uses nest geometry to discriminate among potential homes. Anim. Behav. **62**, 281–287 (2001)
61. Pratt, S.C., Sumpter, D.J.T., Mallon, E.B., Franks, N.R.: An agent-based model of collective nest site choice by the ant Temnothorax albipennis. Anim. Behav. **70**, 1023–1036 (2005)
62. Robinson, E.J.H., Feinerman, O., Franks, N.R.: How collective comparisons emerge without individual comparisons of the options. Proc. Royal Soc. B **281**, 20140737 (2014). https://doi.org/10.1098/rspb.2014.0737
63. Robinson, E.J.H., Franks, N.R., Ellis, S., Okuda, S., Marshall, J.A.R.: A simple threshold rule is sufficient to explain sophisticated collective decision-making. PLoS One **6**, e19981 (2011)
64. Robinson, E.J.H., Smith, F.D., Sullivan, K.M.E., Franks, N.R.: Do ants make direct comparisons? Proc. Royal Soc. B **276**, 2635–2641 (2009)

65. Sasaki, T., Colling, B., Sonnenschein, A., Boggess, M.M., Pratt, S.C.: Flexibility of collective decision making during house hunting in Temnothorax ants. Behav. Ecol. Sociobiol. **69**, 707–714 (2015)

66. Sasaki, T., Pratt, S.C.: Emergence of group rationality from irrational individuals. Behav. Ecol. **22**(2), 276–281 (2011)

67. Seeley, T.D.: The Wisdom of the Hive. Harvard University Press, Cambridge (1995)

68. Seeley, T.D., Visscher, P.K.: Quorum sensing during nest-site selection by honeybee swarms. Behav. Ecol. Sociobiol. **56**, 594–601 (2004)

69. Seeley, T.D., Visscher, P.K., Schlegel, T., Hogan, P.M., Franks, N.R., Marshall, J.A.R.: Stop signals provide cross inhibition in collective decision-making by honey bee swarms. Science **335**, 108–111 (2012)

70. Stroeymeyt, N., Robinson, E.J.H., Hogan, P.M., Marshall, J.A.R., Giurfa, M., Franks, N.R.: Experience-dependent flexibility in collective decision-making by house-hunting ants. Behav. Ecol. **22**(3), 535–542 (2011)

71. Sueur, C., Deneubourg, J.L., Petit, O.: Sequence of quorums during collective decision making in macaques. Behav. Ecol. Sociobiol. **64**, 1875–1885 (2010)

72. Sumpter, D.J.T., Pratt, S.C.: Quorum responses and consensus decision making. Proc. R. Soc. B **364**(1518), 743–753 (2009)

73. Ward, A.J.W., Sumpter, D.J.T., Couzin, I.D., Hart, P.J.B., Krause, J.: Quorum decision-making facilitates information transfer in fish shoals. Proc. Nat. Acad. Sci. **105**(19), 6948–6953 (2008)

74. Whitaker, R.M., Hurley, S.: An agent based approach to site selection for wireless networks. In: Proceedings of 2002 ACM Symposium on Applied Computing (Madrid), pp. 574–577. ACM, New York (2002)

75. Wilson, E.O.: Communication by tandem running in the ant genus Cardiocondyla. Psyche **66**(3), 29–34 (1959)

76. Wilson, E.O.: Chemical communication among workers of the fire ant Solenopsis saevissima (Fr. Smith) 1. The organisation of mass-foraging. Anim. Behav. **10**, 134–147 (1962)

Towards Large-Scale Optimization of Iterated Prisoner Dilemma Strategies

Grażyna Starzec[1], Mateusz Starzec[1], Aleksander Byrski[1(✉)],
Marek Kisiel-Dorohinicki[1], Juan C. Burguillo[2], and Tom Lenaerts[3,4]

[1] Department of Computer Science, AGH University of Science and Technology,
Al. Mickiewicza 30, 30-059 Krakow, Poland
{grazyna.starzec,mateusz.starzec}@iisg.agh.edu.pl,
{olekb,doroh}@agh.edu.pl
[2] Escuela de Ingeniería de Telecomunicación,
Campus Universitario Lagoas-Marcosende, University of Vigo, 36310 Vigo, Spain
J.C.Burguillo@uvigo.es
[3] Machine Learning Group, Université Libre de Bruxelles,
Boulevard du Triomphe CP212, 1050 Brussels, Belgium
tlenaert@ulb.ac.be
[4] Artificial Intelligence Laboratory, Vrije Universiteit Brussel,
Pleinlaan 2, 1050 Brussels, Belgium
tlenaert@vub.be

Abstract. The Iterated Prisoner's Dilemma (IPD) game is a one of the most popular subjects of study in game theory. Numerous experiments have investigated many properties of this game over the last decades. However, topics related to the simulation scale did not always play a significant role in such experimental work. The main contribution of this paper is the optimization of IPD strategies performed in a distributed actor-based computing and simulation environment. Besides showing the scalability and robustness of the framework, we also dive into details of some key simulations, analyzing the most successful strategies obtained.

Keywords: Iterated prisoner dilemma · Parallel simulation
Optimization

1 Introduction

The prisoner's dilemma was first described in the 1950s. It is a two-person game modelling a situation in which the opponents are given a choice to either cooperate with each other or defect and although the second option can lead to the maximum payoff, mutual defection results in the minimum payoff. Such model is a very interesting topic in social or biological research as it might serve as an abstraction of various real-world situations such as arms race, market competition, use of banned substances in sports and others [1].

In real-life, the individuals make the choices repeatedly and this observation lead to extending the simple prisoner's dilemma (PD) into the iterated prisoner's

© Springer-Verlag GmbH Germany, part of Springer Nature 2019
N. T. Nguyen et al. (Eds.): TCCI XXXII, LNCS 11370, pp. 167–183, 2019.
https://doi.org/10.1007/978-3-662-58611-2_4

dilemma (IPD) in which the game is repeated multiple times. Consecutive choices allow the opponents to penalize each other for previous defections [2]. Such model is a popular subject of study in the academia due to its wide applicability, thus numerous implementations have been created, usually built on a similar bases - a population of individuals repeatedly playing one-on-one games (see, e.g. [3–7]).

Extending IPD experiments (or other similar simulations) from simple modeling to practical experiments requires huge amount of computational resources. In order to perform empirical game-testing analysis (as defined by Wellman [8]) either the problem itself has to be modified to limit the time in which satisfactory results can be obtained (see e.g., deviation-preserving reduction [9]) or an efficient, i.e., distributed or parallel, framework has to be developed in order to utilize the HPC infrastructure.

After developing many computing and simulation frameworks based on Java technology (see, e.g. [10,11]) we have decided to shift towards tools more suitable for developing parallel and distributed systems with the possibility to handle large populations. Looking for scalable approach, we have opted for the actor model [12,13] that features a high-level abstraction of agents. By definition, an actor is a concurrent process that communicates with other actors using asynchronous messaging. This has been proven to be a scalable and efficient model in multi-core and multi-node environments [14]. There are also numerous applications of the actor model (e.g., simulation of social networks dynamics [15] or workflows [16]).

In this paper we aim to analyze the results of the optimization of the IPD strategies (e.g. cooperativity, average number of states in strategies, average payoffs) obtained in the highly scalable framework. We have already conducted a thorough analysis of features of the framework for large-scale simulation of IPD [17]. It is to note that such experiments are practically inexistent nowadays, as researchers usually constrain themselves to several hundreds or thousands of agents in an IPD simulation. At the same time we have achieved appropriate scalability for reaching over 1.5 million agents. Therefore we try to do basic research in the IPD simulation for agents distributed according to several spatial structures in a large scale.

In this paper the basics of IPD simulations are recalled, then an asynchronous actor model is presented (that was used during the construction of the aforementioned framework). We also recall selected scalability-related results and present the optimization-related ones. Next we discuss several features observed regarding the scale of the simulation as well as show several obtained strategies in a form of finite state machines. Finally the paper is concluded and future work is sketched-out. Substantial preliminary results presented in this paper will be further extended in a HPC-grade simulation of IPD.

2   IPD Simulation: Reasons and Means

The prisoner's dilemma (PD) is a nonzero-sum game involving two players, traditionally named "prisoners". Each player individually selects one of the two possible actions - cooperation or defection. The game is resolved based on the players' actions with payoffs presented in Table 1.

Table 1. Prisoner's dilemma payoffs

	Cooperate B	Defect B
Cooperate A	A: Reward; B: Reward	A: Sucker; B: Temptation
Defect A	A: Temptation; B: Sucker	A: Punishment; B: Punishment

The common assumption in many works related to the prisoner's dilemma is that the payoffs must satisfy the following condition: $Temptation > Reward > Punishment > Sucker$[1]. Self-interested individuals acting rationally would decide to defect with this condition applied. Formally, mutual defection is the unique Nash equilibrium for this game [3]. As a result, we have the *dilemma*, i.e., participants find themselves in a worse state than if they had cooperated with each other.

The prisoner's dilemma game is often extended to the iterated version known as the iterated prisoner's dilemma (IPD) [4], where participants play against each other more than once. This modification introduces an opportunity for the prisoners to reason about the behavioral tendencies of their opponents. Based on this knowledge the players can develop more sophisticated strategies for playing successive games. In the iterated prisoner's dilemma there is another common payoffs condition ($2 * Reward > Temptation + Sucker$), which favors mutual cooperation against obtaining temptation and sucker payoffs successively.

The IPD players should not be aware of the number of game repetitions, otherwise the best strategy for both of them is always to defect. If the rational player knows that there is only one game left, he no longer cares about effects of his action and treats the last game as a standard prisoner's dilemma. As a result, they both will defect. The deduction for the penultimate game will be similar. As the result of the last game is known, we can ignore it and treat this game as the last one. This can be inductively applied to previous games, one by one, up to the first one, so the best strategy for the whole iterated game is always to defect.

Nevertheless, when the number of game is not defined in advance (or at least is not known to the opponents), always defecting is no longer a dominant strategy [1]. With this condition applied, the players should cooperate in order to maximize their payoffs, because they cannot defect without worrying about consequences. In fact, cooperative strategies would maximize the payoff received by the players [1].

Numerous studies regarding to prisoner's dilemma (PD) and iterated prisoner's dilemma (IPD) since 1950's [5], aim to find relation between game conditions and cooperation level between players. The common game properties

---

[1] Classic values for the payoff matrix are $Temptation = 5$, $Reward = 3$, $Punishment = 1$ and $Sucker = 0$.

are: a number of players, payoffs, mutations of strategies, matching prisoners in pairs for games, etc. Usually the goal is to enhance cooperation in the whole population. Here are some examples of the population behaviors:

- Direct reciprocity - prisoners gratify the opponent for cooperative behavior when playing multiple games [6].
- Indirect reciprocity - the results of the previous games can be analyzed by the other players and it can be interpreted in two ways: upstream and downstream reciprocity. When a prisoner, whose past opponents have cooperated with him, becomes eager to cooperate with new players - it is upstream reciprocity. Downstream reciprocity can be interpreted as a sort of a player's reputation in the population. If the player is known to be cooperative, the opponents become also more open to cooperating with him [7, 18].
- Coalitions - the players can coalesce and work together when playing games. For example: players in a coalition can decide about the next move of the member in his game by voting [19].
- Partner switching or rewiring is a mechanism to change the social links between the prisoners, affecting the set of prisoners that play against each other [20], i.e., changing their neighborhoods.

The majority of research use simulations implemented in a sequential way. These also involve a relatively low number of prisoners. Nowadays the easy access to multi-core processors and multi-node clusters allows us to focus on asynchronous models, introducing time-delays within the simulation and big populations of players. There is research arguing that the results of asynchronous simulation are sensitive to the updating strategy and the delays [21]. New strategies of IPD are sought and advocated in the asynchronous simulations by Grilo and Correia [22, 23] and Newth [24, 25]. However, the important property of these implementations is that simultaneousness of games was simulated by introducing random time delays to the actions of prisoners.

To sum up, lack of flexibility and relatively low-level realizations of the simulation frameworks that may be used for IPD and similar simulations encourage seeking for high-level, reliable and flexible techniques, making possible easy implementation, testing and debugging, finally reconfiguring of such systems, especially in today's presence of widely developing modern technological solutions.

Therefore, in order to make concurrent simulations and to enable the modeling of large populations, we need a scalable framework. Nowadays, there are many simulation frameworks supporting simulations like IPD, especially those agent-based [26], but only some of them are actually suited for large scale execution in parallel and distributed infrastructures. Good examples are REPAST HPC [27], FLAME [28], PDES-MAS [29] or Pandora framework [30]. All the mentioned platforms use the standard message passing (MPI) protocol to create processes for parallel and distributed execution, as well as for communication and synchronization mechanisms – a well-established standard used in simulation for many years. The standard approaches employing MPI are implemented in C++, which can offer good performance but is inefficient in terms of rapid experiments development and rather inflexible as a general implementation technique. This situation creates an opportunity to develop novel, dedicated solutions leveraging contemporary, high-level languages and technologies that would ease the development, debugging, deploying and modification process.

Taking all these into account, We have decided to use the actor model [12,13]. This is a concurrent programming model that is based on an abstraction of actors, that are defined as concurrent processes that use asynchronous messages as a communication mechanism among them. As a result of receiving a message, an actor can create new actors, send messages or change its behavior. This model has been proven to be efficient and scalable, including multi-core scenarios [14]. It has also been used in numerous applications, like actor-based work-flows [16] and social networks dynamics simulation [15].

Thus, in this paper, we propose to use an asynchronous communication model provided by means of the modern Akka actors platform [31] that supports concurrent, distributed and resilient message-driven applications. The basic Akka features to manage distributed execution include: dynamic creation of lightweight actors, programming of actor's behavior changes (i.e., states), and support for asynchronous communication in concurrent environments. Additionally, Akka provides scalability and fault-tolerance together with persistence and supervision mechanisms.

3   An Asynchronous Actor Model for IPD Simulations

We have implemented a scalable system for simulating iterated prisoner's dilemma games considering big populations of players. The system is designed with focus on scalability. We take some assumptions that differ from the classical approaches to simulate the IPD. We removed the sequential loop of games, crossovers and mutations from the simulation. It is replaced with asynchronous and independent agents representing prisoners and managing game processes. As a result, each player can take part in multiple games simultaneously, or continue to play games even during the process of mutation.

The agents in the system are implemented by means of the actor model. Each player is an actor. Furthermore all entities managing the processes of games, crossover, and mutations are also represented as actors. Excessive communication among remote actors can easily become a bottleneck when scaling to multiple nodes, hence the design puts a strong emphasis on limiting it.

Actor model is a mathematical description of concurrent computation with entities called actors as the universal primitives of concurrent computation [12,20]. Actors communicate with asynchronous messages: after receiving a message they perform actions which can include creating more actors, sending more messages, making local decisions, and answering to the next message. The aforementioned actor model is used both for a theoretical understanding of computation and also as a basis for practical implementations of concurrent systems like Akka [31].

A Prisoner takes part in games against other Prisoners and can be subjected to the process of mutation. Each player has a strategy and he follows while playing games during the simulation. Moreover, he accumulates the payoffs during consecutive games as the energy, starting from a positive initial value. If the payoff is positive, the value of energy increases, and if it's negative, the energy decreases. When the energy reaches 0, the Prisoner dies and the simulation system replaces it with the new one.

In other iterated prisoner's dilemma implementations [6,32], the strategy of a player is represented as a finite state machine. We have adapted this approach in our simulation. Each state implies which action the Prisoner chooses during the next game, and transitions between states are based on the opponents actions.

The whole simulation works asynchronously, so each player can be involved in multiple games at the same time. In order to eliminate race-conditions in traversing the strategy during the multiple simultaneous games, the player keeps a separate copy of the strategy for each opponent.

When the simulation is deployed on a cluster, the system has to handle games between players running on different nodes. The simplest way is to allow remote communication between the Game Manager and the remote Prisoner. Unfortunately, this solution does not scale with dense population structures. Therefore, in order to prevent this, a concept of Prisoner's Stub was introduced.

A Prisoner's Stub is representing the origin remote Prisoner locally on the node. In case of game involving a remote actor, the Game Manager communicates with a proper Stub deployed locally, instead of asking the remote opponent for

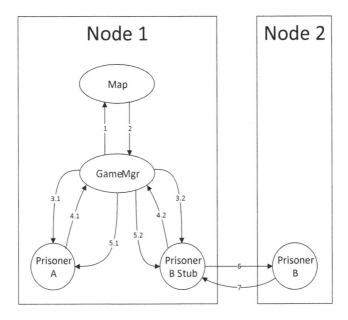

Fig. 1. Game process using stubs

the next action and sending him the results afterwards. This solution keeps the communication within the same node, when the standard approach requires communication through the network between the two nodes. Figure 1 presents how a remote game can be handled as a local game using the stub.

The Game Manager selects one of the Prisoners and asks the Map for a neighbor (messages 1 and 2 on Fig. 1). Next, the Manager asks the Prisoners (or their Stubs) for next moves (3.1 and 3.2), resolves payoffs based on received decisions (4.1 and 4.2) and sends the payoffs to the playing entities (5.1 and 5.2). If one of the Prisoners was represented by its Stub, the Stub synchronizes the payoffs (6) and the strategy (7) with the original Prisoner.

The game with a Stub looks exactly the same as the game with the original Prisoner from the perspective of the opponent or the Game Manager. This optimization is also supposed not to influence the simulation results. That is why it is necessary to synchronize the state between the Prisoner and the Stub, which is also presented in Fig. 1.

The synchronization process is triggered by one of two factors: the number of games played by the Stub or the time since the last synchronization. The former occurs when the Stub plays a lot of games – his results should be passed to the original Prisoner in order to accumulate payoffs. The latter takes place even if the Stub did not play a required number of games, it checks if the Prisoner's strategy has changed and updates the Stub's strategy if necessary.

When one of these conditions is satisfied, the Stub sends the information about the played games to the remote Prisoner. If the Prisoner's strategy did not change since last Stub synchronization, the Prisoner knows that the Stub's strategy was up-to-date, and it collects the Stub's information. Otherwise, the results sent by the Stub are ignored, and the Prisoner sends his current strategy to update the Stub's.

Besides the Prisoner and its stub, there are also Game Manager and Map actors. Each Game Manager has a group of local Prisoners assigned to itself. Repeatedly, it chooses a random subordinate and initiates the game process. It asks the Map for the prisoner's neighbors and randomly chooses one of them as an opponent. Then, the Game Manager asks the selected Prisoners to choose their actions in the upcoming game, and based on that it sends them the obtained results: the payoff and the action that the opponent chose. Then another game process is initiated, but based on a configurable game continuation probability P_{gc}; the opponents selection process is skipped, and the same two Prisoners may take part in the next game. This models IPD, so cooperation may emerge.

4   Scalability and Performance

The described system is supposed to manage experiments with large Prisoners populations and high games count. In this section we inspected the ability to efficiently scale up to multiple nodes by conducting experiments using four population structures with and without Stubs. The scalability-related results are recalled here after [17] for sake of clarity, the optimization-related results belong to main contributions of this paper.

All experiments were executed on the Prometheus[2] cluster. Each node in such cluster has two *Intel Xeon E5-2680v3* processors, 24 cores per node and 128 GB RAM. The platform runs under *CentOS 7* operation system with the *SLURM*[3] workload manager. We were using up to 10 nodes in our simulations.

Each population consisted of fifty thousand Prisoners. Every prisoner was initialized with random strategy and energy of 10. All payoffs were positive, and mutations were disabled. Game continuation probability was set to 0.5 and game timeout was 500 ms. Stubs, if enabled, were synchronizing every 1 s or 100 games. Simulation lasted 180 s and was preceded with 30 s of warmup.

The simplest population structures that we used was arranging the Prisoners population in a row (one-dimensional array) or a grid (two-dimensional array). In such cases, most Prisoners have two or four neighbors, respectively, assuming a neighborhood composed by the closer individuals. Another structure that was taken into account was a complete graph (a panmictic population), in which each Prisoner is a neighbor of any other Prisoner. In the real world, social networks are very often modeled with the so called scale-free topologies [33]. In such network vertices degrees distribution follows a power law, at least asymptotically. That is the last type of the structures presented in this paper.

The performance was measured as the number of games played in a fixed period of time. The system's speedup was calculated according to Formula 1, where $Games_N$ is the number of games played during a simulation running on N nodes. Each experiment was repeated 5 times and the results are averaged.

$$Speedup_N = \frac{Games_N}{Games_1} \qquad (1)$$

The results of the experiments with one-dimensional and two-dimensional structures are presented on Fig. 2. The figures show that this configuration scales well in both cases. For one-dimensional network, the efficiency is even slightly better when no Stubs are used. This is a result of the fact that using this structure with a reasonable distribution of the Prisoners across nodes strongly limits the remote communication, i.e., no more than two Prisoners on each node might require remote communication for game process and each of them may have at most one remote neighbor. As a result, the Stubs mechanism creates an unnecessary overhead. However in the case of the two-dimensional structure, we can already see a little profit from using Stubs instead of a direct remote communication, as both the number of played games and the efficiency is slightly higher when using Stubs.

The complete graph population structure is the hardest example to scale up, as it requires a lot of remote communication. The results of these experiments are presented on Fig. 3a. The performance when running on multiple nodes without Stubs was very poor - even when using 10 nodes, the system was performing worse than on a single node. However, introducing Stubs strongly improved the performance. The speedup was even further enhanced by increasing the

---

[2] http://www.cyfronet.krakow.pl/computers/15226,artykul,prometheus.html.
[3] https://slurm.schedmd.com/.

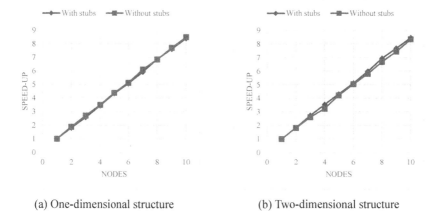

(a) One-dimensional structure   (b) Two-dimensional structure

Fig. 2. Simple structures efficiency

synchronization interval between the Stubs (to 3 s) and the Prisoners which resulted in a decreased amount of remote communication.

The speedup of experiments using scale-free network is presented on Fig. 3b. It does not scale up well without Stubs, because the number of remote neighbors is still quite high. However it is significantly lower than in case of a complete graph, so the performance is a little better. The system scalability was very good when using Stubs.

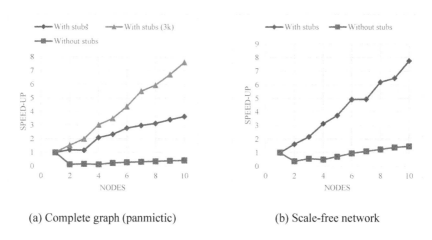

(a) Complete graph (panmictic)   (b) Scale-free network

Fig. 3. Graph structures efficiency

Summing up, we have shown that the system scales well thus being able to manage large populations better than sequential implementation. The Stubs mechanism reduced remote communication which improved performance on complex structures, but there was an unnecessary overhead in the case of trivial structures like one-dimensional grid.

5   Optimization Results

In this section we will focus on the best strategies found in different configurations. Each strategy used by the prisoners is evaluated based on the payoff points collected since its last mutation. The strategies that collect the higher payoffs are considered the best.

In this set of experiments we used four population structures described in the previous section with a population size of 10^5 prisoners. The game continuation probability $P_{gc} \in [0, 0.99]$. The matrix payoff values are $Temptation = 2$, $Reward = 1$, $Punishment = -1$, $Sucker = -2$. and the prisoners had 10 points of initial energy. The initial strategy can be one of the following: All-Cooperate, All-Defect, Tit-for-Tat and random strategy for each prisoner. Fights to mutations ratio was 200 and Stubs, if enabled, were synchronizing every 100 ms or 100 games for one-dimensional and two-dimensional structures; and every 15 s or 250 games for the complete graph (panmictic) and the scale-free network. All configurations were repeated 10 times, and in each run we collected the top 10 strategies.

Table 2 presents the highest and average payoffs collected by strategies from the given configuration. We can observe the relationship between the results and the continuation probability: the higher the continuation probability, the higher the payoff collected by the best strategies. On the other hand we can also notice that increasing the neighborhood reduces the cumulated payoff. Both remarks correspond to the results contained in the paper under review, where similar observations related to the cooperation level in population were presented.

Table 2. Maximum and average payoffs collected by the top 10 strategies depending on the continuation probability P_{gc} and the topology: line, grid, panmictic and scale-free.

		One-dim	Two-dim	Panmictic	Scale-free
Cont. prob.	0	1070/246.6	1155/141.2	248/12.4	6489/377.5
	0.25	1302/356.4	1091/166.7	250/25.9	8721/415.4
	0.5	1427/356.5	1066/173.1	220/50.4	4238/380.3
	0.75	1658/558.1	1276/316.6	248/96.2	5105/603.9
	0.99	16686/3111.6	13199/2383	3134/1507.5	25648/2468

The results contained in the paper under review show that a high continuation probability brings a higher cooperation level in the population. The above results also show that the most efficient strategies collected higher payoffs when the continuation probability was high, as most of these strategies always defect and take advantage of cooperating opponents.

Taking all these into account, in the next experiments we decided to investigate strategies developed in the Scale-free Network topology with $CP = 0.99$, focusing on the strategies from vertices with various degrees.

Table 3 presents average payoffs collected by all strategies depending on the degree, and Table 4 shows the average size of strategies on different vertices. First of all we noticed that the average payoffs are bigger on vertices with a smaller degree. This observation corresponds with a thesis that it is easier to develop efficient strategies playing in smaller neighborhoods. Furthermore the size of the strategies played on vertices with a higher degree are smaller in average than the ones played in lower degree vertices. Besides, in both cases, vertices with the highest degree have also the highest standard deviation. This means that more complex strategies usually appear in vertices having smaller neighborhoods.

Table 3. Average payoffs collected and standard deviation, depending on the vertice degree.

Degree	Avg. payoffs
1	0.88 ± 0.11
2	0.83 ± 0.12
3	0.81 ± 0.12
4	0.79 ± 0.11
5	0.75 ± 0.13
6–10	0.7 ± 0.14
11–20	0.62 ± 0.16
21–50	0.54 ± 0.27
51–100	0.45 ± 0.4
101–1057	0.34 ± 0.4

Table 4. Average strategy size and standard deviation, depending on the vertice degree.

Degree	Avg. strategy size
1	1.54 ± 0.86
2	1.51 ± 0.88
3	1.48 ± 0.9
4	1.47 ± 0.91
5	1.46 ± 0.93
6–10	1.42 ± 0.97
11–20	1.41 ± 0.99
21–50	1.39 ± 1.17
51–100	1.36 ± 1.38
101–1057	1.31 ± 1.68

In the next part of this section we present a case study considering some strategy examples. Figure 8 presents a strategy used by a prisoner playing on a vertex with 149 neighbors, which collected average 0.12 points of payoff. Strategies presented on Figs. 9 and 10 are two of its opponents, which collected respectively 1.5 and 1.48 average payoffs. Two main strategies were compared with the following well-known strategies: Tit-for-Tat (Fig. 4) [34], Suspicious Tit-for-Tat (Fig. 5) [35], Grim (Fig. 6) [36], All Cooperate and All Defect (Fig. 7).

First of all, this strategy does not exploit the All-Cooperate strategy, but also it cannot get exploited by the All-Defect strategy. When playing against the Tit-for-Tat strategy, both opponents will finally loop using Cooperation and Defection alternatively, and it will get a payoff equal to 1 if moves count is odd and 3 otherwise. In the case of a Suspicious Tit-for-Tat opponent, the situation is almost identical to the standard Tit-for-Tat except in the first four moves.

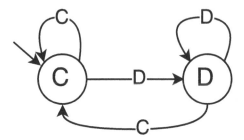

Fig. 4. Tit-for-Tat strategy

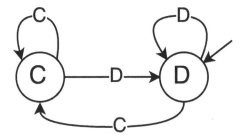

Fig. 5. Suspicious Tit-for-Tat strategy

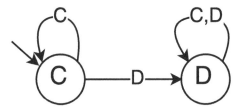

Fig. 6. Grim strategy

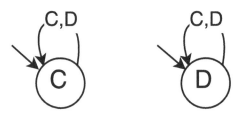

Fig. 7. All Cooperate and All Defect strategies

The cumulated payoff after the first four plays is as follows: −2, −1, 0, 1. If the game is longer than four plays, then payoff equals 1 if plays count is even, and 3 otherwise. A game against Grim strategy ends up as a loop of mutual defection. Both neighbor strategies, presented next, start from defection and then alternate

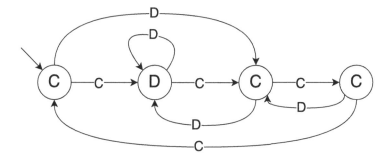

Fig. 8. Sample strategy played by a vertex with 149 neighbors (avg. payoff: 0.12).

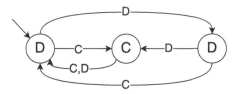

Fig. 9. Sample strategy played by a vertex with only 1 neighbor (avg. payoff: 1.5).

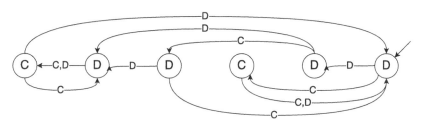

Fig. 10. Sample strategy played by a vertex with 2 neighbors (avg. payoff: 1.48).

between Cooperation and Defection therefore this keeps the strategy in Fig. 8 in Cooperation states and grants 3 points every two moves. The strategy presented in Fig. 8 is good enough to keep alive playing with a variety of strategies. We also noticed that vertices with the lower degree can develop strategies fitting the only neighbor they have.

Another strategy is presented on Fig. 11, has 23 neighbors and reached 1.53 points of average payoff. Graphs presented on Figs. 12 and 13 are two neighbors' strategies. Unlike the previous example, this strategy exploits the All-Cooperate strategy, but cannot be exploited by the All-Defect one. When confronted with Tit-for-Tat, the strategies repeat three states losing 1 point every full cycle. Anyway this strategy achieves a better result than the opponent when the game ends inside the cycle. Playing against Suspicious Tit-for-Tat becomes a loop of defection from both sides. The presented strategy is non-effective against Grim, as it loses 3 points every two moves (except first) trying to cooperate and defect by turns. The first neighbor (Fig. 12) did not develop an effective strategy against

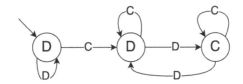

Fig. 11. Strategy with 23 neighbors. Avg. payoff: 1.53

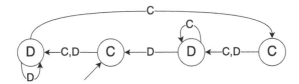

Fig. 12. Strategy with 1 neighbor. Avg. payoff: −0.06

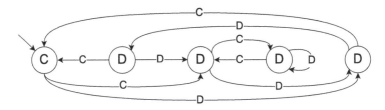

Fig. 13. Strategy with 39 neighbor. Avg. payoff: −0.07

the only opponent. After two first moves it ends up with a balance of −3 points (while the discussed strategy cumulates 1 point), and both strategies repeat the following actions: (C, D), (D, C), (D, D), (C, C). Confrontation with the second neighbor strategy, presented in Fig. 13, repeats the next cycle: (D, C), (D, D), (C, D); and both strategies lose 1 point along the whole cycle.

To sum up, first of all we discussed the relation among the continuation probability (P_{gc}), the topology and the payoffs collected by the top ten strategies in the population. The higher the continuation probability, the higher were the payoffs collected by the best strategies. We also noticed that bigger neighborhood reduces the cumulated payoffs. Then we focus on scale-free topologies using high continuation probability. We have shown that it is hard to develop one effective strategy against a high variety of opponents, and that the easiest way to cumulate high payoffs is by defecting a few cooperating neighbors. On high degree vertices, cooperation is much more efficient. We also discussed two example strategies against two of their neighbors, and also against some well known strategies. The first example shows a strategy from the vertex with high degree and its two exploiting neighbors. On the other hand the second set of strategies shows a strategy from vertex with low degree and its two opponents could not fit to this strategy. Basing on the asynchronous framework for IPD simulations we are able to analyze behavior of big populations and we are going to extend these results in the future.

6   Conclusions

In this paper a preliminary results concerning large-scale simulation of the Iterated Prisoner's Dilemma (IPD) game has been presented. The simulation framework is based on a high-level language and technology, which allows the rapid verification of different variants and strategies. It can be deployed in a distributed HPC environment providing good scalability, and it has been used to conduct experiments with about 1.5 millions of agents, thanks to the asynchrony introduced at the algorithm level.

The comparison of the asynchronous game version with the one based on stubs yielded very similar results, showing that simulations can be performed in parallel or in distributed environments without any substantial loss with respect to the non-parallel scenarios.

Moreover, the conducted experiments yielded several interesting results. A discussion on the relation among the continuation probability, the population topology and the payoffs collected by the top ten strategies was performed for different games. Then experiments were focused on Scale-free networks, using a high continuation probability. A quite interesting outcome was that it is hard to develop a unique strategy effective against the rest of the opponents' strategies, and that the easiest way to cumulate high payoffs is defecting a few cooperating neighbors. On vertices with high degree, however, cooperation becomes more efficient. Last but not least, the behavior of two example strategies against two of their respective neighbors, and some classical strategies was also presented.

In the future we plan to evaluate the system on a more sophisticated HPC dedicated hardware (i.e., a supercomputer), aiming at testing the scalability over a high number of computing nodes. Moreover, the influence of the introduced asynchrony on the simulation results will be evaluated in detail. Another possible extension would involve introducing new mechanisms into the actor-based IPD framework, for instance, designing and implementing a coalitions model to support player groups deciding how to play using a common policy. Finally, we will focus in more practical scenarios related with economics like financial markets.

Acknowledgment. This research was supported by AGH University of Science and Technology Statutory Project.

References

1. Axelrod, R.: The Evolution of Cooperation. Basic Books, New York (2006)
2. Rapoport, A., Chammah, A.M.: Prisoner's Dilemma: A Study in Conflict and Cooperation. University of Michigan Press (1965)
3. Roth, A., Murnighan, J.: Equilibrium behavior and repeated play of the prisoner's dilemma. J. Math. Psychol. **17**(2), 189–198 (1978)

4. Fogel, D.: Evolving behaviors in the iterated prisoner's dilemma. Evol. Comput. **1**, 77–97 (1993)
5. Kendall, G., Yao, X., Chong, S.: The Iterated Prisoners' Dilemma: 20 Years on. World Scientific, Singapore (2006)
6. Van Veelen, M., Garcia, J., Rand, D., Nowak, M.: Direct reciprocity in structured populations. Proc. Natl. Acad. Sci. **109**(25), 9929–9934 (2012)
7. Peleteiro, A., Burguillo, J.C., Chong, S.Y.: Exploring indirect reciprocity in complex networks using coalitions and rewiring. In: Proceedings of the 2014 International Conference on Autonomous Agents and Multi-agent Systems, AAMAS 2014, Richland, SC, pp. 669–676. International Foundation for Autonomous Agents and Multiagent Systems (2014)
8. Wellman, M.: Putting the agent in agent-based modeling. Auton. Agent. Multi-Agent Syst. **30**, 1175–1189 (2016)
9. Wiedenbeck, B., Wellman, M.: Scaling simulation-based game analysis through deviation- preserving reduction. In: Proceedings of 11th International Conference on Autonomous Agents and Multi-Agent Systems. ACM (2012)
10. Faber, L., Pietak, K., Byrski, A., Kisiel-Dorohinicki, M.: Agent-based simulation in AgE framework. In: Byrski, A., Oplatková, Z., Carvalho, M., Kisiel-Dorohinicki, M. (eds.) Advances in Intelligent Modelling and Simulation: Simulation Tools and Applications, vol. 416, pp. 55–83. Springer, Heidelberg (2012). https://doi.org/10.1007/978-3-642-28888-3_3
11. Kisiel-Dorohinicki, M.: Agent-based models and platforms for parallel evolutionary algorithms. In: Bubak, M., van Albada, G.D., Sloot, P.M.A., Dongarra, J. (eds.) ICCS 2004. LNCS, vol. 3038, pp. 646–653. Springer, Heidelberg (2004). https://doi.org/10.1007/978-3-540-24688-6_84
12. Hewitt, C., Bishop, P., Steiger, R.: A universal modular actor formalism for artificial intelligence. In: Proceedings of the 3rd International Joint Conference on Artificial Intelligence. IJCAI 1973, San Francisco, CA, USA, pp. 235–245. Morgan Kaufmann Publishers Inc. (1973)
13. Agha, G.: Actors: A Model of Concurrent Computation in Distributed Systems. MIT Press, Cambridge (1986)
14. Haller, P., Odersky, M.: Scala actors: unifying thread-based and event-based programming. Theoret. Comput. Sci. **410**(2), 202–220 (2009)
15. Snijders, T.A., van de Bunt, G.G., Steglich, C.E.: Introduction to stochastic actor-based models for network dynamics. Soc. Netw. **32**(1), 44–60 (2010). Dynamics of Social Networks
16. Esposito, A., Loia, V.: Integrating concurrency control and distributed data into workflow frameworks: an actor model perspective. In: 2000 IEEE International Conference on Systems, Man, and Cybernetics, vol. 3, pp. 2110–2114 (2000)
17. Skiba, G., et al.: Flexible asynchronous simulation of iterated prisoner's dilemma based on actor model. Simul. Model. Pract. Theory **83**, 75–92 (2018)
18. Peleteiro, A., Burguillo, J.C., Luck, M., Arcos, J.L., Rodígruez-Aguilar, J.A.: Using reputation and adaptive coalitions to support collaboration in competitive environments. Eng. Appl. Artif. Intell. **45**, 325–338 (2015)
19. Peleteiro, A., Burguillo, J.C., Bazzan, A.L.C.: How coalitions enhance cooperation in the IPD over complex networks. In: 2012 Third Brazilian Workshop on Social Simulation, pp. 68–74, October 2012
20. Peleteiro, A., Burguillo, J.C., Arcos, J.L., Rodriguez-Aguilar, J.A.: Fostering cooperation through dynamic coalition formation and partner switching. ACM Trans. Auton. Adapt. Syst. **9**(1), 1:1–1:31 (2014)

21. Huberman, B., Glance, N.: Evolutionary games and computer simulations. Proc. Natl. Acad. Sci. USA **90**, 7716–7718 (1993)
22. Grilo, C., Correia, L.: What makes spatial prisoner's dilemma game sensitive to asynchronism? In: Proceedings of 11th International Conference on the Simulation and Synthesis of Living Systems, Alife XI. MIT (2008)
23. Grilo, C., Correia, L.: The influence of asynchronous dynamics in the spatial prisoner's dilemma game. In: Asada, M., Hallam, J.C.T., Meyer, J.-A., Tani, J. (eds.) SAB 2008. LNCS (LNAI), vol. 5040, pp. 362–371. Springer, Heidelberg (2008). https://doi.org/10.1007/978-3-540-69134-1_36
24. Newth, D.: Asynchronous iterated prisoner's dilemma. Adapt. Behav. **17**(2), 175–183 (2009)
25. Newth, D., Cornforth, D.: Asynchronous spatial evolutionary games. Biosystems **95**(2), 120–129 (2009)
26. Abar, S., Theodoropoulos, G.K., Lemarinier, P., O'Hare, G.M.: Agent based modelling and simulation tools: a review of the state-of-art software. Comput. Sci. Rev. **24**, 13–33 (2017)
27. Collier, N., North, M.: Parallel agent-based simulation with repast for high performance computing. Simulation **89**(10), 1215–1235 (2013)
28. Coakley, S., Gheorghe, M., Holcombe, M., Chin, S., Worth, D., Greenough, C.: Exploitation of high performance computing in the flame agent-based simulation framework. In: 2012 IEEE 14th International Conference on High Performance Computing and Communication and 2012 IEEE 9th International Conference on Embedded Software and Systems, pp. 538–545, June 2012
29. Suryanarayanan, V., Theodoropoulos, G., Lees, M.: PDES-MAS: distributed simulation of multi-agent systems. Procedia Comput. Sci. **18**, 671–681 (2013)
30. Wittek, P., Rubio-Campillo, X.: Scalable agent-based modelling with cloud HPC resources for social simulations. In: 4th IEEE International Conference on Cloud Computing Technology and Science Proceedings, pp. 355–362, December 2012
31. Allen, J.: Effective Akka. O'Reilly Media, Sebastopol (2013)
32. Piccolo, E., Squillero, G.: Adaptive opponent modelling for the iterated prisoner's dilemma. In: 2011 IEEE Congress of Evolutionary Computation (CEC), pp. 836–841, June 2011
33. Hein, O., Schwind, M., König, W.: Scale-free networks. Wirtschaftsinformatik **48**(4), 267–275 (2006)
34. Axelrod, R., Axelrod, R.M.: The Evolution of Cooperation, vol. 5145. Basic Books, New York (1984)
35. Boyd, R., Lorberbaum, J.P.: No pure strategy is evolutionarily stable in the repeated prisoner's dilemma game. Nature **327**(6117), 58–59 (1987)
36. Friedman, J.W.: A non-cooperative equilibrium for supergames. Rev. Econ. Stud. **38**(1), 1–12 (1971)

GuruWS: A Hybrid Platform
for Detecting Malicious Web Shells
and Web Application Vulnerabilities

Van-Giap Le, Huu-Tung Nguyen, Duy-Phuc Pham, Van-On Phung,
and Ngoc-Hoa Nguyen$^{(\boxtimes)}$

VNU University of Engineering and Technology, Hanoi, Vietnam
{giaplv_57,tungnh_57,duyphuc,onphungvan,hoa.nguyen}@vnu.edu.vn

Abstract. Web application/service is now omnipresent but its security
risks, such as malware and vulnerabilities, are indeed underestimated.
In this paper, we propose a protective, extensible and hybrid platform,
named GuruWS, for automatically detecting both web application vulnerabilities and malicious web shells. Based on the original PHP vulnerability scanner THAPS, we propose E-THAPS which implements a novel
detection mechanism, an improved SQL injection, Cross-site Scripting
and vulnerability detection capabilities. For malicious web shell detection, taint analysis and pattern matching methods are chosen to be implemented in GuruWS. A number of extensive experiments are carried out
to prove the outstanding performance of our proposed platform in comparison with several existing solutions in detecting either web application
vulnerabilities or malicious web shells.

Keywords: White-box penetration testing
Web application vulnerability · Web shell · Taint analysis
Pattern matching · SQLi detection · XSS detection · YARA rules

1 Introduction

According to Internet Live Stats up to May 2017 [1], there is an enormous
amount of websites being attacked everyday, causing both direct and significant
impact on nearly 3.64 billion Internet users. Even with support from security
specialists, they continue having troubles due to the complexity of penetration
procedures and the vast amount of testing cases in both penetration testing and
code reviewing. As a result, the number of hacked websites per day is increasing:
from 25.000 hacked websites per day on April 2015 to 56.470 hacked websites
per day on May 2017.

Several popular approaches for securing web applications [4] have been investigated, for example safe web development [3], implementing intrusion detection
and protection systems, code reviewing, and web application firewalls. Petukhov
et al. [10] presented an efficient way for securing web applications by searching
and eliminating vulnerabilities therein. In fact, an attack campaign is temporary.

© Springer-Verlag GmbH Germany, part of Springer Nature 2019
N. T. Nguyen et al. (Eds.): TCCI XXXII, LNCS 11370, pp. 184–208, 2019.
https://doi.org/10.1007/978-3-662-58611-2_5

However, attackers might upload their backdoors to that system for persistence, as they can come back to interact and steal information anytime without exploiting any vulnerability. This situation leads to serious consequences [5] since these backdoors are *Web shells*, and they allow to remotely control files, databases and execute commands. They are not only flexible but also countless.

Indeed, lacking of secure programming awareness and of ability to discover both malicious web shells and web vulnerabilities from web developers are main root causes. These current issues in web application security raise a demand for one solution which allows web developers and security penetration testers to detect security-related problems in the easiest way. In this research, we propose **GuruWS**: a hybrid platform for automatically detecting both web application vulnerabilities and malicious web shells using white-box testing approach. Moreover, we focus on web applications written in the PHP language because the popular usage of PHP in server-side programming languages – about 82.6% of all the websites [16].

This paper is an extended version from our previous work [2] in which we improve and clarify more details about our platform and related works. Additional experiments and functional improvements to **GuruWS** have been made at the time writing this paper as well.

The rest of this paper is organized as follows: In Sect. 2, we revise some basic principles, literature research and related work in vulnerabilities scanning and taint analysis. In Sect. 3, we describe our hybrid and extensible platform for automatically detecting both web application vulnerabilities (based on E-THAPS) and malicious web shells (using taint-analysis, pattern matching and YARA rules). In Sect. 4, we present our experiment results, evaluate our work and provide benchmarks. The last section is dedicated to some conclusions and future work.

2   Background and Related Work

In this section, we first describe the concept of detecting web application security risks (resulting from either malicious files or vulnerabilities). Then, two main techniques used in our platform are presented before summarizing some related works.

2.1   Detection of Web Application Security Risks

In general, the security risks of web applications are typically composed of threats that exploit the vulnerabilities and malicious codes inside those applications. Actually, there are two main approaches to hunt for malicious web shells and vulnerabilities in PHP applications [6]:

- White-box testing: An attempt to track down defective and vulnerable chunks of code by analysing application source code. This operation is often integrated into the development process by creating add-on tools for common development environments.

– Black-box testing: The source code is not directly examined. Instead, special input test cases are generated and sent to the application. Then, the results returned by the application are analysed for unexpected behaviour that indicates errors and potential vulnerabilities.

In general, security researchers prefer using black-box vulnerability and malware scanners to find threats in Web applications. These tools are operated by launching attacks against an application using the fuzzing technique [15]. Although often being valuable components when testing the security of a website, they are both time and resource consuming because of fuzzing limitations.

So far, white-box testing has not broadly used for finding security threats in web applications. The main reason is detection capability limitations of white-box analysis tools, in particular due to heterogeneous programming environments and the complexity of applications involving database operations, business logic, and user interface components [6].

However, white-box testing provides an overall picture and better code coverage than black-box analysis does. In some cases, security risks arise when a specific piece of code is mistakenly accessible because the developer failed to follow the expected path flows. Furthermore, applications can be vulnerable if being accessed in an unexpected way that developers does not intend [7].

To better understand the detection of vulnerabilities and malicious codes in web applications, we will discuss two basic techniques, i.e. symbolic execution and taint analysis, in next section.

2.2   Symbolic Execution and Taint Analysis

It is irrefutable that symbolic execution has a significant potential for programmatically detecting wide-ranging classes of security flaws in modern software due to its efficiency. In the past decade, the topic of symbolic execution attracted many security researchers and had been the backbone of almost every security conference around the world. In general, symbolic execution denotes the process of analyzing what inputs cause each part of a program to execute.

In symbolic execution, an interpreter follows the code flow, assigning symbolic values to input rather than obtaining actual input which is generated during normal execution of the program [14]. In an ideal situation, it can simulate all possible outcomes of the application. Consider a piece of code written in PHP as below, which receives user input and trigger the `fail` function if the input value is equal to `"not good!"`:

```
1  <?php
     $x = $_GET['input']; $y = $x . " good!";
3    if ($y == "not good!") {   fail();   }
     else {   echo "good news!";   }
5  ?>
```

During normal execution, this program will retrieve user input (e.g., `"oh"`) and assign it to the $x variable. Execution would then proceed with the string concatenation ($y = "oh good!") and routes to the false branch, which print "good news!".

During symbolic execution, the aforementioned program processes a symbolic value (for example: λ) and assigns it to the variable $x. The program would then proceed with the concatenation and assign λ . "good!" to $y. When reaching the if statement, it will check λ. "good!" with "not good!". λ could take any value at this point of the program; therefore, symbolic execution can proceed along both branches, by "forking" two different paths. Each path assigns a copy of the program state at the branch instruction as well as a path constraint. In this example, the path constraint is λ. "good!" is equal to "not good!" for the True branch and λ. "good!" is not equal to "not good!" for the False branch. Both paths can be symbolically executed independently.

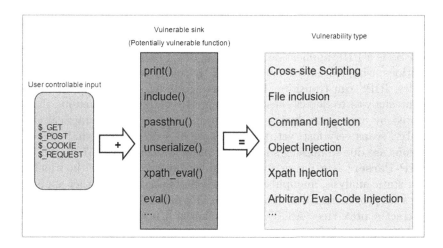

Fig. 1. Concept of taint-style vulnerabilities in PHP

To identify vulnerabilities, a taint analysis is performed after the symbolic execution process. Taint analysis attempts to identify which variables have been "tainted" with user controllable input and how they are propagated through the application. If user input reaches a critical point of the application such as a vulnerable sink, where it is able to alter the outcome of the application, without being properly sanitised, thereafter it will be flagged as a potential vulnerability [7,19]. Specifically, a web application security vulnerability can be denoted when user input data (tainted data) is not appropriately sanitised before being used in the critical operations of the dynamic execution. These kinds of flaws is defined as taint-style vulnerabilities. It is important to notice that any user controllable data must be considered as tainted one. For every vulnerability type, there exists different sanitization routines as well as vulnerable sinks which are potentially vulnerable functions (PVF) that execute critical operations and should only be called within trusted data [8]. Figure 1 is an illustration of taint-style vulnerabilities in the PHP programming language:

2.3 Related Work

Web application penetration testing has been extensively studied in literature however the existing industrial solutions are still struggling with web shell detection and white-box penetration testing. In this section, we briefly introduce some related solutions that we did research on and have been evaluated in the **GuruWS** implementation process:

Web Shell Detector [12] is a Python tool which can detect web shells. It is a good solution for easily using, developing and customizing. However, the web shell pattern set in web Shell Detector's database is outdated and very limited. Moreover, it is not able to detect simple and tiny web shells as well as self-written web shells, due to the lack of a taint analysis mechanism.

NeoPI is a Python script which uses statistical techniques to detect obfuscated and encrypted content within source code. Its approach is based on the recursive scanning and ranking of all files in the base directory [9]. This solution requires manual investigation to validate whether it is a web shell or not.

RIPS[1] is a PHP application with the ability to find vulnerabilities in PHP applications using statistical analysis [11]. By tokenizing and parsing all source code files, RIPS can transform PHP source code into a program model, then use taint analysis to detect sensitive potentially vulnerable functions that can be tainted by user input during the program flow. As in our practical evaluation, RIPS scans very fast, yet, the false positive rate is still high. Some of the limitations are due to missing support for object-oriented code [7,8].

PHP-Parser[2] is a parser for PHP programming language, in which it is used for static analysis, manipulation of code and basically any other application dealing with programmatically coding [18]. This parser has the ability to produce an abstract syntax tree (AST)[3], also known as a node tree, from PHP code. From the acquired AST, it is possible to traverse the syntax tree, manipulate it, and perform necessarily analysis for each node. Additionally, PHP-Parser supports in converting a syntax tree back to PHP code, which can be used in code preprocessing.

sqlmap is an open source penetration testing tool that automates the processes of detecting and exploiting SQL injection flaws and taking over database servers [24]. This tool uses black-box testing techniques and supports various database management systems (DBMS) including MySQL, Oracle, PostgreSQL, Microsoft SQL Server, etc.

THAPS [7] is a vulnerability scanner for web applications written in PHP. It uses symbolic execution as its static analysis approach on which it performs a taint analysis in generated AST to detect web application vulnerabilities. Based on our experiment, THAPS shows lower false positive rate compared to RIPS. However, it is only able to detect SQL injection and XSS vulnerabilities. That motivates us to extend this scanner in order to improve the performance of web application vulnerabilities detection.

---

[1] http://sourceforge.net/projects/rips-scanner/.

[2] https://github.com/nikic/PHP-Parser.

[3] https://en.wikipedia.org/wiki/Abstract_syntax_tree.

THAPS uses the PHP-Parser library, a parser for the PHP programming language, to generate an AST. Then it performs a taint analysis in the created AST by using the provided functionality of PHP-Parser to traverse the syntax tree, manipulate it, and perform the predefined analysis for each node. A node of the tree represents a part of the source code and describes some certain functionality.

Basic workflow of THAPS is presented in the following diagram (Fig. 2):

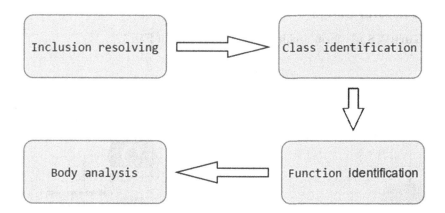

Fig. 2. Basic THAPS workflow

- **Inclusion resolving** is a module in which the inclusion nodes are replaced by the AST generated from the included file.
- **Class identification** module is responsible for identifying all user-defined classes. Moreover, all class members and methods will be also identified and used for further processing.
- **Function identification** is where all user-defined functions are being identified and analysed.
- **Body analysis** is a module in which the global scope, the body of methods and functions are analysed for potential vulnerabilities.

3   Hybrid Platform of GuruWS

In this section, we first propose the motivation of GuruWS, then we will detail our approach to design our proposed platform. Finally, we describe our contributions related to the detection of both malicious web shells and vulnerabilities.

3.1   Motivation

As mentioned in previous sections, web application vulnerability and malicious web code scanners operate independently and do not work together on the same platform. Moreover, existing solutions on scanning vulnerabilities and web shells in web application still have some limitation as described in Sect. 2.3. These reasons motivate us to propose a platform that allows both vulnerabilities and malicious code detection to avoid security risks in web applications.

In order to analyse PHP based web applications to identify the security risks, we propose a hybrid platform named **GuruWS**. It aims to detect both vulnerabilities and malwares in PHP applications by using the white-box testing techniques. And that is why GuruWS is called the hybrid platform.

3.2   Platform Design

The **GuruWS** platform architecture is described in Fig. 3.

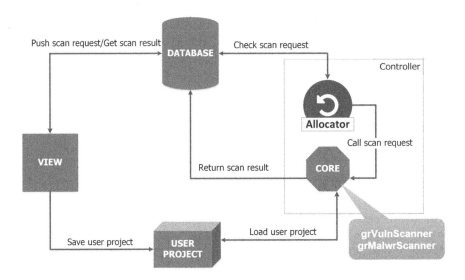

Fig. 3. GuruWS platform architecture

In this platform design:

- **View** is a web front-end service which receives compressed web application source code from the user; then validates, extracts the compressed source to *UserProject* and pushes scanning requests to the *Database*. After final scan results are available in the *Database*, the web service will also retrieves and displays them to the user
- **Database** assumes the role to store scanning requests and scanning reports
- **UserProject** module keeps user projects which are the input resource for *Core* module
- **Allocator** works as a background service, continuously retrieving scanning requests from the *Database*. If there is any available scanning request, it will be sent to the *Core* module to start scanning; the results will be pushed to the *Database* after the scanning processes are done
- **Core** consists of *grVulnScanner* and *grMalwrScanner* modules. Each module executes simultaneously as independent services:

- **grMalwrScanner** is an extensible scanner, in which its main objective is malicious PHP scripts detection. More details of this module are clarified in Sect. 3.3
- **grVulnScanner** is an extensible scanner for white-box web application vulnerability detection. More details of this module are clarified in Sect. 3.4.

The basic work-flow of can be described as following:

1. First, a user uploads his compressed web application project to **GuruWS**'s web UI. After being safely sanitised and extracted to the specified location, a scanning request will be pushed into scanning queue in the *Database*. This queue contains a list of projects which must be scanned by the *Core* module
2. The *Allocator* gets scanning requests from the scanning queue in the *Database* and then calls the *Core* module for scanning on demand of the request
3. After taking user extracted project as an input, the *Core* module scans this data and pushes final results to the *Database*
4. **GuruWS**'s web UI, which regularly checks for the scan progress, then will display scan results immediately after they are stored in the database.

Our platform has the ability to scan several projects at the same time. To achieve this feature, using multi-threading techniques while carefully avoiding race conditions is needed. By distributing the server resources into multiple threads with one separated SQL connection per thread, the race condition is automatically handled by the DBMS. The number of multi-thread projects at the same time can be customized, otherwise we set a default value of 10 scanning processes simultaneous projects due to our computing resources.

The reason that we have to implement the *Allocator* module and wait for the results instead of showing them immediately is because **grVulnScanner** and **grMalwrScanner** take a small amount of time to scan the whole project.

In the next section, we will describe in more detailed methods used in the *Core* module in order to detect the malicious web application files and vulnerabilities.

3.3   grMalwrScanner: Malicious Web Application File Detection

The goal of the **grMalwrScanner** module is to support developers, webmasters and security specialists in order to detect malicious files in their web application project. In their perspective, they will proactively disclose the source codes for answering two questions: (i) *Does their application contain malicious files?* and (ii) *If malicious files exist, where do these files locate in their application?*

To answer those questions, our first step is to detect web shells. Because of their flexibility, we decided to use taint analysis method [19]. Additionally, for other complex scripts, there are many common web shells which were protected by encoding themselves and challenge the taint analysis methods. There is a limited amount of popular web shells, thus we propose another method using pattern matching consisting of a set of strings and a boolean expression which determines its logic.

One key idea in our work is to improve and support all available approaches which are relevant to the corresponding type of web shells. Besides, a common post-exploitation technique, which intruders usually use, is to embed fraud advertisement scripts or malicious HTML frames. Fortunately, **grMalwrScanner** has special modus operandi to detect adware and its variants.

3.3.1   Taint Analysis for Detecting Web Shells

Taint analysis method is performed as following: The code is divided into tokens using a lexical analysis process to make it easier to manipulate and perform post analysis. Thereafter, **grMalwrScanner** analyses the token list of each file once in which it passes through the token list and identifies important tokens by name. Thus, potential dangerous functions (PDFs) are determined, then all significant arguments of these functions will be traced back to their 'source', that includes:

– *Environmental input:* get_headers(), get_browser(), etc.
– *User input:* $_GET, $_POST, $_COOKIE and $_FILES as well as other $_SERVER and $_ENV variables.
– *Server arguments:* HTTP_ACCEPT, HTTP_KEEP_ALIVE, etc.
– *File operations:* fgets(), dlob(), readdir() and so on.
– *Database handlers:* mysql_fetch_array(), mysql_fetch_object(), etc.

In the taint analysis method, we proposed some principles in **grMalwrScanner**'s as follow:

– The source is always marked as tainted.
– The string created from tainted variables is also marked as tainted.
– With a function (not belonging to secure functions or PDFs), if it has any tainted input arguments, its return value will be marked as tainted.
– With every function in the PDF list, there will be a set of corresponding securing functions. Hence, when significant arguments of the PDF are traced back, any argument passed through a securing function will make an untainted return value even though this is a tainted variable.

3.3.2   Pattern Matching for Detecting Web Shells

Regarding the taint analysis approach, **grMalwrScanner** only focuses on PHP web shells detection. We assume a certain file could be a relevant malicious sample only if the two following conditions are met. First, the sample must be written in PHP. Second, it has to be observed that it is working properly and shows some apparent PHP backdoor behavior.

The pattern set is based on powerful YARA rules [17] because of their flexibility and simplicity. Consisting both sub-parts of web shells and particular tricky patterns, our pattern set is very efficient in detecting in-the-wild web shells; this will be evaluated in the experiment section of this paper.

grMalwrScanner is developed to be a collaborative platform which combines the power of not only analysis tools but also social interactions between security analysts. Therefore, a novel feature, which allows analysts to write their own ruleset or refer to a social ruleset, will be helpful.

Consider a common lightweight PHP backdoor as below:

```
<?php   eval($_GET['c']);  ?>
```

This is a very simple and effective backdoor regardless of its small size, which receives and executes an attacker's commands through the HTTP GET c parameter, and allows attackers to perform remote code execution. Furthermore, consider another tiny backdoor which receives remote commands through HTTP headers:

```
<?php system($_SERVER['HTTP_USER_AGENT'])?>
```

Fortunately, all of these samples above can be detected using our YARA rules as demonstrated below:

```
1   rule GuruWS_LightWeightBackdoor
    {
3     strings:
        $ = /\<\?(php)?(.*|\n)system\(\$(.*)\]\)/
5       $ = /\<\?(php)?(.*|\n)eval\(\$(.*)\]\)/
        $ = /\<\?(php)?(.*|\n)passthru\(\$(.*)\]\)/
7       $ = /\<\?(php)?(.*|\n)shell_exec\(\$(.*)\]\)/
        $ = /\<\?(php)?(.*|\n)exec\(\$(.*)\]\)/
9       $ = /\<\?(php)?(.*|\n)fread\(popen\(\$\_(.*)\]\, \'r
    \'\)\,\$\_(.*)\]\)/
        $ = /\<\?(php)?(.*|\n)pcntl_exec\(\'(.*)'\,array\(\'\-
    c\'\,\$\_(.*)\]\)\)/
11      $ = /\<\?(php)?(.*|\n)preg_replace\(\'(.*)\'\,\$\_(.*)
    \],(.*)/
        $ = /\<\?(php)?(.*|\n)call_user_func_array\(\$\_(.*)
    \]\, array\(\$\_(.*)\]\)\)/
13      $ = /\<\?(php)?(.*|\n)assert\(\$\_(.*)\]\)/
        $ = /\<\?\=\@\$(.*)\(\$(.*)/
15      $ = /\<\?(php)?\$(.*)\=str_replace\((.*)\)\)\;\@\$(.*)
    \(\$\_(.*)\]\)/
        $ = /\<\?(php)?\$(.*)\;\@\$(.*)\(\$\_(.*)\]\)/
17      $ = /\<\?(php)?\$x\=strrev\(\"(.*)\"\)\;echo \@\$(.*)
    \(\$\_(.*)\]\)/

19    condition:
        any of them
21  }
```

For instance, adware and its variants can be observed, based on the unique pattern of their obfuscated code.

```
<?php
  echo('<html></html><script>var _0x5264 = ["\x3c\x73\x63\x72
    \x69\x70\x74\x20\x74\x79\x70\x65\x3d\x22\x74\x65\x78\x74\
    x2f\x6a\x61\x76\x61\x73\x63\x72\x69\x70\x74\x22\x20\x73\
    x72\x63\x3d\x22\x2f\x2f\x61\x64\x77\x61\x72\x65\x2e\x63\
    x6f\x6d\x22\x3e\x3c\x2f\x73\x63\x72\x69\x70\x74\x3e", "\
    x77\x72\x69\x74\x65", "\x3c\x73\x63\x72\x69\x70\x74\x20\
    x73\x72\x63\x3d\x22\x2f\x2f\x61\x64\x77\x61\x72\x65\x2e\
    x63\x6f\x6d\x22\x3e\x3c\x2f\x73\x63\x72\x69\x70\x74\x3e
    "];
  document[_0x5264[1]](_0x5264[0]);
  document[_0x5264[1]](_0x5264[2]);</script>');
?>
```

Basically the PHP above is to fetch obfuscated JavaScript in hex format from external host *adware.com*, to confuse and complicate the analysis process. Analysts can customize their default ruleset for their own purpose as simple as the YARA rule below:

```
1  rule adware001
   {
3    strings:
       $a = /var [\_0x\d(a-f)(A-F)]* = \[["'](\[\\\x\d(A-F)(a-f)]*)
       ["']/i
5      $a = /document\[[\_0x\d(a-f)(A-F)\[\]]*\]\(\[\_0x\d(a-f)(A-F)
       \[\]]*\)/i
     condition:
7      any of them
   }
```

For analyst customization, we provide a set of information such as lists of malicious Web application hashes, blacklisted patterns, common YARA rules etc. Moreover, analysts are able to interact and contribute to the social rulesets using the explicit API calls.

Besides, we analyzed and created another web shell statistical analysis module for **GuruWS** in PHP. Our module processes source code and returns a ranking table which is based on the probability of being a web shell.

The calculation is performed on these factors: Entropy, Language IC, Longest Word Test, Signature Potential Test and Signature Malicious Test. In detail, in the Entropy calculation, grMalwrScanner removes spaces then calculates a percentage (p) of each character, then the result will be $-p * \log_2 p$. Result from Language IC calculation will be $s/(t * (t + 1))$, s is the sum of pairs of the number of appearances of two adjacent character in ASCII map, t is the total of the appearance of all character. To calculate the Longest Word, grMalwrScanner ranks these files based on the length of its longest word. To calculate the

Signature Potential Test, grMalwrScanner counts the number of appearances of following malicious strings in the input file.

```
('/(eval(|fileput_contents|base64_decode|python_eval|exec(|
    passthru|popen|proc_open|pcntl|assert(|system(|shell)/i')
```

grMalwrScanner do the same with the following string to calculate Signature Mailicous Test.

```
1   '/(@\$[]=|\$=@\$_GET|\$[+""]=)/i'
```

We built this module as an optional feature for security experts.

3.4 grVulnScanner: Web Application Vulnerabilities Detection

The **grVulnScanner** module takes the role of web application vulnerabilities detection. For that purpose, we extended and improved the latest version of THAPS engine as described in the Sect. 2.3. The reason we chose THAPS to extend comes from the fact that it has lower false positive rate compared to RIPS and capability to detect SQL injection as well as XSS vulnerabilities. Our extended version of THAPS is named as **E-THAPS** (Enhanced THAPS). E-THAPS is totally superior to the original one, in which it is implemented with new vulnerability detection mechanisms and various improvements:

- Having abilities to detect further web application security flaws namely: Command Injection [20], Object Injection [21], File Inclusion [22], Arbitrary Eval Code Injection [23]. Details are denoted in Sect. 3.4.1
- Being equipped with an improved SQL injection vulnerability detection mechanism. Details are denoted in Sect. 3.4.2
- Being equipped with an improved Cross-Site Scripting vulnerability detection mechanism. Details are denoted in Sect. 3.4.3
- Other improvement to achieve better performance. Details are denoted in Sect. 3.4.4.

3.4.1 New Detection Mechanism

The intended purpose of THAPS is only XSS and SQL injection vulnerabilities detection, hence indeed it is not trivial to improve its vulnerabilities detection capability. Our contributed detection improvement is briefly illustrated in Fig. 4. Additionally, we implemented this new mechanism supporting object-oriented programming flaws detection.

Our contributed detection mechanism particularly consists of the following features:

- PHPParser_Node_Expr_FuncCall handles built-in function nodes which defines how a vulnerability should be detected with new vulnerable sinks and corresponding securing functions.

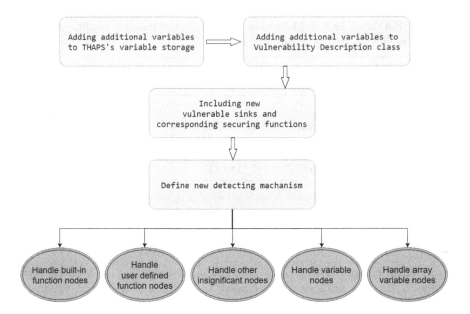

Fig. 4. Process of adding new detecting mechanism

- PHPParser_Node_Expr_MethodCall handles user-defined function nodes, including new variables in the variable storage and all user defined function types.
- PHPParser_Node_Expr_Variable handles variable nodes, considering whether variable comes from user input (e.g: GET, POST, etc.), and marks it as tainted for all new variables in the variable storage.
- PHPParser_Node_Expr_ArrayDimFetch handles array variable nodes, considering whether an array variable comes from user input, and marks every element inside as tainted for new variables in the variable storage.
- Other modifications to other nodes:
  - Conditional nodes (PHPParser_Node_Stmt:If—Elseif—Else)
  - Looping nodes (PHPParser_Node_Stmt:For—While—Foreach)
  - Logical nodes (PHPParser_Node_Expr_Logical:Or—And—Xor)
  - Casting nodes (PHPParser_Node_Expr_Cast:Bool—Int—Double)
  - Concat nodes (PHPParser_Node_Expr_Concat)
  - Assigning concat nodes (PHPParser_Node_Expr_AssignConcat)
  - Scalar Encapsed nodes (PHPParser_Node_Scalar_Encapsed)
  - Assigning plus node (PHPParser_Node_Expr_AssignPlus)
  - Static function (in class) nodes (PHPParser_Node_Expr_StaticCall)
  - Return nodes (PHPParser_Node_Stmt_Return)

The newly contributed vulnerable sinks and corresponding secure functions are listed below:

- **Command Injection**

```
$SINKS = array('exec', 'expect_popen', 'passthru',
    'popen', 'proc_open', 'shell_exec', 'system');
$SEC_FUNC = array('escapeshellarg', 'escapeshellcmd');
```

- **File Inclusion**

```
$SINKS = array('include', 'include_once',
'parsekit_compile_file', 'require', 'require_once',
    'set_include_path', 'virtual');
$SEC_FUNC = array('basename', 'dirname', 'pathinfo');
```

- **Object Injection**

```
$SINKS = array('unserialize', 'yaml_parse');
$SEC_FUNC = array();
```

- **XPATH injection**

```
$SINKS = array('xpath_eval, 'xpath_eval_expression',
    'xptr_eval');
$SEC_FUNC = array('addslashes');
```

- **Arbitrary Eval Code Injection**

```
$SINKS = array('assert', 'eval');
$SEC_FUNC = array();
```

3.4.2 Improved SQLi Detection Mechanism

In the wild, THAPS has some limitations in analyzing projects using modern built-in SQL functions such as prepared statement. Therefore, MySQL-Improved (**MySQLi**) potential vulnerable function were added to the SQLi detection mechanism. There are some further functions which were contributed in the securing functions set for SQL injection:

- **mysqli_real_escape_string(mysqli $link, string $escapestr):** escapes special characters in a string for use in an SQL statement.
- **mysqli_escape_string(mysqli $link, string $escapestr):** alias of the mysqli_real_escape_string() function.

Additionally, **mysqli_query()** function was added to SQL sink because along with tainted arguments, it can lead to SQL injection vulnerabilities.

These simple, yet efficient implementations significantly improved the ability to detect SQL injection vulnerabilities of THAPS. This statement will be proved in the Experiment section.

3.4.3   Improved XSS Detection Mechanism

THAPS' XSS sinks are defined via PHP-Parser nodes:

– PHPParser_Node_Stmt_Echo: represents the **echo()** function.
– PHPParser_Node_Expr_Print: represents the **print()** function.
– PHPParser_Node_Expr_Exit: represents the **exit()** function.

Besides, there are other different functions that can likely be XSS sinks such as **print_r()**, **die()**, **printf()**, **vprintf()**, **trigger_error()** and **user_error()**.

By adding these functions to THAPS's XSS sinks, the XSS detecting capacity of THAPS significantly improved. There were some difficulties when making this inclusion since the arguments' positions in each function is not the same. In the next release version, E-THAPS should be more flexible on adding functions to sinks without considering the variable arguments position.

Furthermore, the **highlight_string()** function was added to the securing functions set for XSS. This implementation reduces the false positive rate of THAPS while scanning for XSS vulnerabilities.

3.4.4   Other Improvements

– **Update secure functions in conditional statements:** This secure function set contains a list of functions used in conditional statements (if/elseif/else) to ensure that passed argument is safe for all sinks.
There were some further functions added to this set: is_bool(), is_null(), is_finite() and is_infinite().
– **Update secure functions for every vulnerability:** This secure function set contains a list of function names which return untainted values with all passed tainted/untainted arguments. These untainted values are safe with all vulnerable sinks. 39 further functions are included in this set, e.g. *strftime()*, *md5_file()*, *sha1_file()*, etc.
– **Update functions for insecure strings:** This function set contains a list of functions that return tainted value with all passing tainted/untainted arguments. These tainted values are presumably unsafe with all vulnerable sinks. 23 further functions included to this set in total, including: *gzdecode*, *hex2bin()*, *recode()*, *gzinflate()*, etc.

This implementation allows the detection capabilities of **E-THAPS** to become more efficient than THAPS as explained in Sect. 4.

4   Experiment and Evaluation

4.1   Environment Setup and Results

The experiment with **GuruWS** platform was taken on our computing system–Intel Xeon E5-2630L with 2 GB memory. This server runs CentOS 6.7 (2.6.32-642.15.1.el6.x86_64), Python 2.7.10, YARA 3.4.0 [4], PHP 5.6.12, Apache 2.2.15 and MySQL 5.6.35.

---

[4] https://github.com/plusvic/yara/releases/latest.

GuruWS platform is now published for public use[5]. The source codes and datasets of **GuruWS** are freely accessible[6]. In order to validate **GuruWS**'s competency, we separately evaluated its two core modules **grMalwrScanner** and **grVulnScanner**.

4.2   Evaluation of grMalwrScanner

4.2.1   Evaluation Method

To evaluate our method of malicious Web application files detection to other prevalent anti-virus products, we use the online service of VirusTotal[7] reports via its public API. In this service, it allows to interact with a lot of popular anti-virus engines for analysing and detecting malicious files, including viruses, worms, ... Thus, we built an evaluation system which is illustrated in Fig. 5.

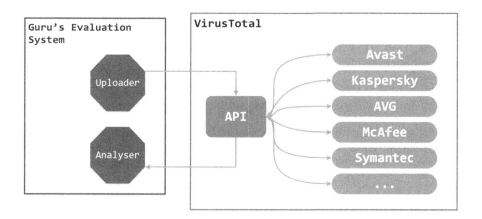

Fig. 5. grMalwrScanner's evaluation system model

In this system, **Uploader** is a script module which gathers web shells from web shell test set, then sends every web shell to the VirusTotal system. Each web shell will have a *scan_id* belonging to VirusTotal's response. **Uploader** keeps these *scan_id* and waits for the scanning progresses of VirusTotal. After the scanning progress is finished, **Analyser** uses the *scan_id* to retrieve the corresponding result containing a list of anti-viruses and their answer when scanning these web shells in JSON format.

To evaluate the ability of **grMalwrScanner**, we will use two different test sets: one contains malicious PHP web shells and one is a collection of clean, benign PHP codes. We will observe the true positive (TP), false negative (FN)

---

[5] http://112.137.130.56/guruws/.

[6] https://github.com/giaplv57/GuruWebScanner/.

[7] https://virustotal.com/.

and False Positive (FP) scores, then compute the Recall (sensitivity, or true positive rate - TPR), Fall-out (or Fall Positive Rate - FPR), F1-score and Precision with the following formulas [13]:

$$Recall = TPR = \frac{TP}{TP + FN} \quad Fall\text{-}out = FPR = \frac{FN}{FN + TP}$$

$$F1\text{-}score = \frac{2TP}{2TP + FP + FN} \quad Precision = \frac{TP}{TP + FP}$$

4.2.2 Datasets

For web shells detection, from reliable sources[8], we collected a wide range of web shells in various types and programming language such as ASP, PHP, Perl, Python etc. Then, we only select PHP web shells and divide this dataset into two parts with the ratio of 7:3 as the rule of thumb [25]. The larger part will be used to construct the training dataset, and the rest, named the testing dataset, will be used to measure the efficiency of both **grMalwrScanner** and other similar scanners. After removing all the irrelevant files in both datasets, the web shells are distributed as follow:

- Number of web shells in training dataset: 1507 (71%)
- Number of web shells in testing dataset: 616 (29%)

In addition, to evaluate the accuracy of **grMalwrScanner** for the benign web applications, we collected 150 clean PHP codes from the official site of WordPress plugins[9]. This clean dataset contains 3,843 benign PHP scripts in total.

4.2.3 Evaluation Results

By using the malicious testing dataset of 616 web shells, Table 1 shows the final results we obtained from **grMalwrScanner** and 58 others scanners:

Note that, in this table, to save the space, we do not show the FP due of its value 0. Apparently the differences of both Recall and F1-score rate from **grMalwrScanner** compared to other scanners although they were tested on the same test set. **grMalwrScanner** achieved an outstanding precision rate (85.56%) and F1-score (0.92), much higher than the rest.

In the case of benign dataset, there is zero FN in **grMalwrScanner**'s untainted files detection (that means its FPR is 0%). This result is the same for the other scanners, except BKAV scanner. The latter produced 18 FN cases for the benign dataset. Thus, the BKAV scanner has its FPR rate 0.47%.

---

[8] https://sourceforge.net/p/laudanum/code/25/tree/, Github: /tennc/webshell, /shiqiaomu/webshell-collector, /tdifg/WebShell, /BlackArch/webshells, /John-Troony/other-webshells, /lhlsec/webshell, /fuzzdb-project/fuzzdb, /JohnTroony/php-webshells.

[9] https://wordpress.org/plugins/browse/popular/.

Table 1. Number of detected web shells, F1-score and precision

Scanner	TP	FN	Recall	F1-score	Precision
grMalwrScanner	**527**	**89**	**85.56%**	**0.92**	**85.55%**
Web Shell Detector	407	209	66.07%	0.8	66.07%
AhnLab-V3	320	296	51.95%	0.68	51.95%
Ikarus	284	332	46.10%	0.63	46.10%
AegisLab	278	338	45.13%	0.62	45.13%
GData	273	343	44.32%	0.61	44.32%
Qihoo-360	269	347	43.67%	0.61	43.67%
Avast	266	350	43.18%	0.6	43.18%
Symantec	246	370	39.94%	0.57	39.94%
ALYac	242	374	39.29%	0.56	39.29%
Tencent	239	377	38.80%	0.56	38.80%
ESET-NOD32	235	381	38.15%	0.55	38.15%
Avira	234	382	37.99%	0.55	37.99%
TrendMicro-HouseCall	229	387	37.18%	0.54	37.18%
Baid	221	395	35.88%	0.53	35.88%
Arcabit	220	396	35.71%	0.53	35.71%
MicroWorld-eScan	219	397	35.55%	0.52	35.55%
BitDefender	219	397	35.55%	0.52	35.55%
NANO-Antivirus	218	398	35.39%	0.52	35.39%
Comodo	217	399	35.23%	0.52	35.23%
Ad-Aware	217	399	35.23%	0.52	35.23%
F-Secure	215	401	34.90%	0.52	34.90%
ZoneAlarm	213	403	34.58%	0.51	34.58%
Kaspersky	213	403	34.58%	0.51	34.58%
Emsisoft	213	403	34.58%	0.51	34.58%
TrendMicro	195	421	31.66%	0.48	31.66%
AVG	195	421	31.66%	0.48	31.66%
Sophos	172	444	27.92%	0.44	27.92%
Fortinet	169	447	27.44%	0.43	27.44%
ClamAV	166	450	26.95%	0.42	26.95%
VBA32	142	474	23.05%	0.37	23.05%
DrWeb	140	476	22.73%	0.37	22.73%
McAfee-GW-Edition	134	482	21.75%	0.36	21.75%
Cyren	127	489	20.62%	0.34	20.62%
Bkav	126	490	20.45%	0.33	20.45%
McAfee	125	491	20.29%	0.34	20.29%

(*continued*)

Table 1. (*continued*)

Scanner	TP	FN	Recall	F1-score	Precision
Microsoft	121	495	19.64%	0.33	19.64%
AVware	117	499	18.99%	0.32	18.99%
CAT-QuickHeal	115	501	18.67%	0.31	18.67%
CMC	97	519	15.75%	0.27	15.75%
Rising	96	520	15.58%	0.27	15.58%
ViRobot	95	521	15.42%	0.27	15.42%
F-Prot	95	521	15.42%	0.27	15.42%
VIPRE	74	542	12.01%	0.21	12.01%
Jiangmin	65	551	10.55%	0.19	10.55%
TotalDefense	54	562	8.77%	0.16	8.77%
Yandex	52	564	8.44%	0.16	8.44%
Panda	33	583	5.36%	0.1	5.36%
Antiy-AVL	27	589	4.38%	0.08	4.38%
K7GW	24	592	3.90%	0.08	3.90%
K7AntiVirus	24	592	3.90%	0.08	3.90%
TheHacker	18	598	2.92%	0.06	2.92%
Webroot	10	606	1.62%	0.03	1.62%
Zillya	8	608	1.30%	0.03	1.30%
Kingsoft	4	612	0.65%	0.01	0.65%
nProtect	1	615	0.16%	0	0.16%
Zoner	0	616	0.00%	-	0.00%
SUPERAntiSpyware	0	616	0.00%	-	0.00%
Malwarebytes	0	616	0.00%	-	0.00%

4.3   Evaluation of grVulnScanner

4.3.1   Evaluation Method

To justify the performance of **grVulnScanner** with the E-THAPS scanner, we created a test set including vulnerable code in PHP and do evaluate it with other similar scanner like original THAPS and RIPS v0.55.

For evaluation, we observed a number of TP and FP cases in every test case scanning process. A TP case is defined when the PVF leads to a vulnerability and the scanner reports a vulnerability. Meanwhile, when the PVF does not lead to a vulnerability and the scanner still reports a vulnerability, we consider it as an FP case. F1-score and Recall will be also used to measure the performance of scanners.

The total number of vulnerabilities (TNOV) of every test case is also depicted as well. TNOV is computed by the sum of TP and FN: $TNOV = TP + FN$. Besides, the execution time of these white-box scanners is not significant. Hence, we decided not to mention in the evaluation result.

4.3.2 Datasets

We construct a test set to compare the performance of 3 scanners, including 16 test cases that were built by us. All of them are vulnerable PHP scripts and they cover classical cases of various vulnerability types: *Command Injection, Object Injection, File Inclusion, Arbitrary Eval Code Injection, XSS, SQL Injection.* Some of them also include object-oriented code. Additionally, the testing set contains a series of web application challenges which belong to the BKAV WhiteHat Contests[10] including:

- Web challenge in BKAV WhiteHat Contest 7, belongs to a monthly Whitehat contest of Bkav
- Web challenge in BKAV WhiteHat Contest 8, belongs to a monthly Whitehat contest of Bkav
- Web challenge in BKAV WhiteHat Contest 10, belongs to a monthly Whitehat contest of Bkav
- WhiteHat Grand Prix 2014 scanning result, belongs to an annual Whitehat contest organised by Bkav

These web challenges trustworthy simulate real vulnerable web applications in the wild. All of our 20 test cases are available and freely accessible from GitHub (See footnote 6). Note that in these test cases, there are totally 52 vunerabilites.

To verify the FP rate of grVulnScanner, we collect 4 featured plugins of WordPress[11] (named Akismet Anti-Spam v4.01, WP Super Cache v1.5.8, Theme Check v.20160523.1 and bbPress v.2.5.14). Based on the WPVulnDB[12] and CVE Detail[13], these plugins are considered benign and have no vulnerability. Thus, these plugins constitute the clean/benign test set of 262 PHP files.

4.3.3 Evaluation Result

By using our 20 test cases, we performed also deep experiments to detect web application vulnerabilities by using 3 scanners: E-THAPS (our scanner), THAPS and RIPS. The results we obtained are summarized in Table 2 and listed in detail in Table 3. According to Table 2, E-THAPS has the highest TPR as well as F1-score: 0.893 compared with 0.377 (THAPS) and 0.804 (RIPS). Note that in Table 2, FN is calculated from TNOV subtracted by TP.

---

[10] https://ctftime.org/ctf/112.

[11] https://wordpress.org/plugins/browse/featured/.

[12] https://wpvulndb.com/plugins.

[13] https://www.cvedetails.com/vulnerability-list/vendor_id-2337/product_id-4096/.

Table 2. Overall results in comparison

Using scanner	TP	FP	FN	Recall/TPR	F1-score
RIPS	41	9	11	78.85%	0.804
THAPS	13	**4**	39	25.00%	0.377
E-THAPS	**46**	5	**6**	**88.46%**	**0.893**

Table 3. Detailed performance comparison of THAPS, E-THAPS and RIPS

Input		THAPS		E-THAPS		RIPS	
Test name	TNOV	TP	FP	TP	FP	TP	FP
Test case 1	2	0	0	2	0	2	0
Test case 2	1	0	1	1	1	1	1
Test case 3	2	0	0	2	0	2	0
Test case 4	1	0	0	1	0	1	0
Test case 5	2	0	0	2	0	2	0
Test case 6	1	0	0	0	0	0	1
Test case 7	2	1	0	2	0	1	0
Test case 8	1	0	1	0	1	0	1
Test case 9	2	0	0	2	0	2	0
Test case 10	1	1	0	1	0	1	1
Test case 11	2	2	0	2	0	0	0
Test case 12	1	0	0	1	0	1	0
Test case 13	2	0	0	2	0	2	0
Test case 14	2	2	0	2	0	2	0
Test case 15	2	0	0	2	0	2	0
Test case 16	2	2	0	2	0	1	0
White-hat 7	3	0	0	2	0	3	0
White-hat 8	4	1	2	4	3	4	3
White-hat 10	4	2	0	3	0	3	1
Grand Prix 2014	15	2	0	13	0	12	1
Total	52	13	**4**	**46**	5	41	9

Following are the detailed results and explanation after we examine 3 scanners to BKAV WhiteHat Contests web applications:

– **Web challenge in BKAV WhiteHat Contest 7**

Table 4. WhiteHat Contest 7 scanning result

Using scanner	Objection injection	File inclusion	Possible flow control
RIPS	1	1	1
THAPS	0	0	0
E-THAPS	1	1	0

THAPS demonstrated the lowest performance since it was unable to detect any vulnerability. RIPS showed the best performance with 3 detected flaws while E-THAPS detected Objection Injection flaw, File Inclusion flaw and unable to detect the Possible Flow Control flaw. The ability to detect Possible Flow Control has not been implemented in E-THAPS yet. Since this feature will be carefully considered since it can lead to FP rate rising in E-THAPS (Table 4).

– **BKAV WhiteHat Contest 8 Web challenge**

Table 5. WhiteHat Contest 8 scanning result

Using scanner	Cross site scripting		SQL injection		File inclusion	
	TP	FP	TP	FP	TP	FP
RIPS	1	2	2	1	1	0
THAPS	1	2	0	0	0	0
E-THAPS	1	2	2	1	1	0

In this test, it is evident that E-THAPS and RIPS are performing equally, however both are better than THAPS in detecting SQL injection and File Inclusion flaws. There also appeared some FP cases in these vulnerabilities as the table shows (Table 5).

– **Web challenge in BKAV WhiteHat Contest 10**

Table 6. WhiteHat Contest 10 scanning result

Using scanner	Cross site scripting		SQL injection	
	TP	FP	TP	FP
RIPS	2	0	1	1
THAPS	2	0	0	0
E-THAPS	2	0	1	0

This time, E-THAPS showed the best performance with 3 identified vulnerabilities: 2 XSS and 1 SQL injection. Additionally, in the detected SQL injection flaw, E-THAPS, unlike RIPS, did not make any False Positive case (Table 6).

– **WhiteHat Grand Prix 2014 web challenge**: This web challenge is based on the attack-defense category of this contest, and it is a practical web application (Table 7).

Table 7. WhiteHat Grand Prix 2014 scanning result

Using scanner	Cross site scripting		SQL injection	
	TP	FP	TP	FP
RIPS	1	1	11	0
THAPS	2	0	0	0
E-THAPS	2	0	11	0

E-THAPS, again showed the best performance with the highest TP and lowest FP rates in both XSS and SQL injection vulnerabilities. It is evident that E-THAPS can detect SQL injection flaws much more efficient than the others.

To validate deeply the FP rate of our E-THAPS engine, we perform the last experiment with the benign test set of 262 PHP collected from 4 featured Word-Press plugins (as mentioned above). As figures shown in Table 8, THAPS and E-THAPS result 0 flaw in all vulnerability types, while RIPS shows considerable number in every vulnerability types and all of them are False Positive cases. It is obvious to see that the FP rate of THAPS and E-THAPS in this test is 0%, RIPS got 100%.

Table 8. Scanning results with WordPress featured plugins

Scanner	File disclosure			Cross site scripting			File manipulation		
	Found	Confirmed	FP	Found	Confirmed	FP	Found	Confirmed	FP
RIPS	5	0	5	23	0	23	32	0	32
THAPS	0	0	0	0	0	0	0	0	0
E-THAPS	0	0	0	0	0	0	0	0	0

5   Conclusion and Future Work

In this paper, we presented an extensible and hybrid platform, **GuruWS**, which allows us to automatically detect both vulnerabilities and malicious web shells. **GuruWS** is composed of two core modules named **grMalwrScanner** and **grVulnScanner**.

For detecting malicious files in **grMalwrScanner**, our work is based on taint analysis and pattern matching techniques. By using the taint analysis, we first identify the PDFs, then all significant arguments of these functions will be traced back to their 'source'. We proposed also some principles in order to hunt the web shells during the taint analysis. For the pattern matching technique, we used the powerful Yara rules, added our new rules to detect both web shells and adware. For validating our method, we collected a wide range of 2123 web shells (1507 + 616) and used VirusTotal to evaluate **grMalwrScanner** with 58 others popular scanners. Our evaluation experiment shows that **grVulnScanner** is able to achieve an outstanding precision (85.55%) and F1-score (0.92), much higher than other similar scanners.

Regarding the detection of web application vulnerabilities, we proposed a number of significant improvements in E-THAPS to a state of the art in modern web static vulnerabilities analysis. It applies advanced detection improvements to original THAPS: accurate SQLi flaws, XSS sinks, securing functions in conditional statements, revised all vulnerable functions, and declared a set of functions that create insecure strings. E-THAPS showed the best performance with the highest found and confirmed result for security flaws, XSS and SQLi vulnerabilities.

Furthermore, we consider developing **grVulnScanner** to become a gray-box scanner and able to detect possible flow control. For the malicious web application file detection, improved and optimize web shell pattern sets, strong enough rules for detecting stealthy web shells will be considered to be implemented in **grMalwrScanner**. The combination of these two solutions outstandingly eases web penetration procedure, and the whole module is an open source. We believe that in the future, with our adopted social ruleset and web shell statistic analysis modules, **GuruWS** will be a step forward for both the academia and the industry.

Acknowledgments. The authors would like to thank the anonymous reviewers for their valuable comments and suggestions to improve this paper.

This work is partially supported by the national research project No. KC.01/16-20, granted by the Ministry of Science and Technology of Vietnam (MOST).

References

1. Internet Live Stats. http://www.internetlivestats.com/. Accessed 21 May 2017
2. Le, V.-G., Nguyen, H.-T., Lu, D.-N., Nguyen, N.-H.: A solution for automatically malicious web shell and web application vulnerability detection. In: Nguyen, N.-T., Manolopoulos, Y., Iliadis, L., Trawiński, B. (eds.) ICCCI 2016. LNCS (LNAI), vol. 9875, pp. 367–378. Springer, Cham (2016). https://doi.org/10.1007/978-3-319-45243-2_34
3. Mazumder, M., Braje, T.: Safe client/server web development with Haskell. In: 2016 IEEE Cybersecurity Development (SecDev), p. 150 (2016)
4. Bherde, G.P., Pund, M.A.: Recent attack prevention techniques in web service applications. In: International Conference on Automatic Control and Dynamic Optimization Techniques (ICACDOT), pp. 1174–1180 (2016)
5. Khari, M., Sangwan, P., Vaishali: Web-application attacks: a survey. In: 2016 3rd International Conference on Computing for Sustainable Global Development (INDIACom), New Delhi, pp. 2187–2191 (2016)
6. Kals, S., Kirda, E., Kruegel, C., Jovanovich, N.: SecuBat: a web vulnerability scanner. In: 15th International Conference on World Wide Web, pp. 247–256 (2006)

7. Jensen, T., Pedersen, H., Olesen, M.C., Hansen, R.R.: THAPS: automated vulnerability scanning of PHP applications. In: Jøsang, A., Carlsson, B. (eds.) NordSec 2012. LNCS, vol. 7617, pp. 31–46. Springer, Heidelberg (2012). https://doi.org/10.1007/978-3-642-34210-3_3
8. Dahse, J.: RIPS - a static source code analyser for vulnerabilities in PHP scripts. In: Seminar Work at Chair for Network and Data Security (2010)
9. Sasi, R.: Web backdoors - attack, evasion and detection. In: C0C0N Sec Conference (2011)
10. Petukhov, A., Dmitry, K.: Detecting security vulnerabilities in Web applications using dynamic analysis with penetration testing. In: OWASP Application Security Conference. Computing Systems Lab, Department of Computer Science, Moscow State University (2008)
11. Dahse, J., Holz, T.: Static detection of second-order vulnerabilities in web applications. In: 23rd USENIX Security Symposium (USENIX Security 2014), pp. 989–1003 (2014)
12. Starov, O., Dahse, J., Ahmad, S., Holz, T., Nikiforakis, N.: No honor among thieves: a large-scale analysis of malicious web shells. In: 25th International Conference on World Wide Web, pp. 1021–1032 (2016)
13. Le, H.H., Nguyen, N.H., Nguyen, T.T.: Exploiting GPU for large scale fingerprint identification. In: Nguyen, N.T., Trawiński, B., Fujita, H., Hong, T.-P. (eds.) ACIIDS 2016. LNCS (LNAI), vol. 9621, pp. 688–697. Springer, Heidelberg (2016). https://doi.org/10.1007/978-3-662-49381-6_66
14. Wang, H., Liu, T., Guan, X., Shen, C., Zheng, Q., Yang, Z.: Dependence guided symbolic execution. IEEE Trans. Softw. Eng. **43**(3), 252–271 (2017)
15. Bhme, M., Paul, S.: A probabilistic analysis of the efficiency of automated software testing. IEEE Trans. Softw. Eng. **42**(4), 345–360 (2016)
16. Web Technology Surveys. http://w3techs.com/technologies/overview/programming_language/all/. Accessed 21 May 2017
17. YARA - The pattern matching swiss knife for malware researchers. http://virustotal.github.io/yara/. Accessed 10 May 2017
18. Popov, N.: PHP-parser introduction. https://github.com/nikic/PHP-Parser/blob/master/doc/0_Introduction.markdown. Accessed 15 Apr 2016
19. The Open Web Application Security Project. Static Code Analysis. https://www.owasp.org/index.php/Static_Code_Analysis. Accessed 22 May 2017
20. The Open Web Application Security Project. Attack Category: Command Injection. https://www.owasp.org/index.php/Command_Injection. Accessed 18 May 2017
21. The Open Web Application Security Project. Attack Category: PHP Object Injection. https://www.owasp.org/index.php/PHP_Object_Injection. Accessed 18 May 2017
22. The Open Web Application Security Project. Testing for Local File Inclusion. https://www.owasp.org/index.php/Testing_for_Local_File_Inclusion. Accessed 18 May 2017
23. The Open Web Application Security Project. Attack Category: Direct Dynamic Code Evaluation ('Eval Injection'). https://www.owasp.org/index.php/Direct_Dynamic_Code_Evaluation_('Eval_Injection'). Accessed 18 May 2017
24. Bernardo Damele, A.G., Stampar, M.: SQLMap - automatic SQL injection and database takeover tool. http://www.sqlmap.org/. Accessed 12 May 2017
25. Deng, W., Liu, Q., Cheng, H., Qin, Z.: A malware detection framework based on Kolmogorov complexity. J. Comput. Inf. Syst. **7**, 2687–2694 (2011)

Author Index

Printed in the United States
By Bookmasters